INSIDE THE MACHINE LEARNING INTERVIEW

151 Real Questions from FAANG and How to Answer Them

PENG SHAO

INSIDE THE MACHINE LEARNING INTERVIEW

Dedicated to my training data.
Without you I'd have no clue.

Contents

1. Introduction

Machine Learning (ML) has gained immense popularity in recent years and has become a crucial component in the development of modern technology. As a result, the demand for talented ML practitioners has increased, and mastering the interview process is critical to success in this rapidly growing field. For many interview candidates, these interviews can be intimidating and challenging, requiring a different set of skills than traditional coding and design interviews.

Consider, for example, the following question: *"In solving classification problem X, how might one identify the most useful features?"*

To answer this question, candidates can tap into their academic or industry experience. Those with academic backgrounds may recommend statistical techniques such as chi-squared tests or information gain. Conversely, individuals with industry experience may suggest embedded approaches such as perturbing feature values or performing ablation studies. In addition, candidates may emphasize the importance of selecting features that are not only informative but also efficient to collect offline within the constraints of existing systems, as well as fast and reliable to hydrate for online inference in a production environment.

As an interviewee, transitioning from problem-solving in coding and design interviews to active recall in ML questions can feel jarring. It doesn't help that ML practitioners are often expected to meet the Software Engineering bar while also being proficient in ML knowledge. But don't worry! ML interviews don't have to be a grueling experience. In fact, they can be quite the opposite.

By identifying the most crucial ML topics and adopting a solid studying strategy, candidates can increase their confidence in tackling even the toughest ML interview questions. And that's where this guide comes in. We'll walk you through the ML interview process step-by-step, presenting questions that you're likely to encounter and providing solutions that cover all the essential elements of an answer.

The concepts presented in this guide are broadly applicable, so even if you face variations of the questions, you'll have the knowledge and skills to succeed in your next ML interview. So let's get started!

How to Use This Guide

In this guide, we will take you step-by-step through the ML interview process, identifying common interview questions you will encounter in each session, and walking you through strategies for formulating strong answers.

We understand that the vast amount of academic and applied ML material can be overwhelming, which is why our aim is to present condensed and easily understandable answers. Whether you're a seasoned ML professional or just starting, this guide is designed to provide valuable insights to help you navigate your next interview with confidence.

To best utilize this guide, first complete the Prerequisites, as a certain level of fluency in ML is assumed and the rest of the chapters won't make a lot of sense otherwise – and might even be frustrating to read.

If you are relatively new to ML interviewing, briefly skim over the practice interviews contained in each chapter to get a feel for the types of questions asked in ML interviews. Then, go back and review each interview session in the Interview Process, identifying your gaps and strengths. Use this information to determine which chapters of this guide will be most helpful in improving your interview performance.

More seasoned ML practitioners may treat this guide as a helpful study companion. With knowledge and experience under your belt, challenge yourself by taking the practice interviews included in each session. This may reveal areas to refresh your skills or uncover unexpected blind spots: for example, *"What are some ways to overcome label imbalance in a dataset?"*. Jump to ML Fundamentals for a solution.

Prerequisites

Interview candidates should have an academic background in ML and/or Natural Language Processing (NLP). A degree in a relevant field certainly helps, but is not strictly necessary. Having taken some courses, such as Andrew Ng's ML courses (Ng, n.d.), may be sufficient. Make sure you can explain terms like "overfitting", "gradient descent", and "hyperparameters" – they are used throughout this guide and ML interviews will assume you know them.

The prepared candidate will have also built several models from scratch, having gone through the ML practitioner workflow in full at least once prior to the interview. The ML practitioner workflow consists of the following steps:

1. Offline data exploration
2. Offline creation of features
3. Offline creation of dataset, or join features with existing dataset
4. Offline model training
5. Offline model evaluation
6. Offline model hyperparameter tuning
7. Online hydration of features
8. Online serving the model
9. Online periodic model refresh

Familiarity with the ML practitioner workflow is important to mastering the ML interview, since strong candidates can apply ML to real-world industry problems and demonstrate proficiency in the entire ML lifecycle. If you haven't completed the ML practitioner workflow before, hop over to the Tensorflow documentation and walk through some of their tutorials in full:

- TFX: Getting Started tutorials (*TFX Tutorials | TensorFlow*, 2021) walk through building an offline pipeline for data extraction, feature engineering, model training, model evaluation, and model export.

- Use the Tensorflow Serving tutorial (*Train and Serve a TensorFlow Model With TensorFlow Serving | TFX*, 2023) to deploy your trained model to a hosted environment, and try making some classification or regression requests.

- Play around with Tensorflow Serving Configuration (*Tensorflow Serving Configuration / TFX*, 2021) to monitor your model and enable periodic model refresh.

If you've never held an industry position in ML you likely won't be familiar with all the steps of the above workflow, particularly steps 7-9. Don't worry, as those steps are mainly evaluated in the ML Infrastructure interview session, which is more directed towards Senior+ candidates.

Interview Process

ML practitioners are assessed for proficiency in the following areas:

- **ML Fundamentals**, which refers to the foundational concepts and principles of machine learning, including supervised and unsupervised learning, model selection, regularization, and model evaluation.

- **Software Engineering** skills, such as proficiency in technical problem solving, coding, data structures and algorithms, testing, and potentially knowledge of distributed systems.

- **ML System Design**, which involves the integration of different system components such as data collection, model architecture, feature engineering, training, inference, and monitoring into a cohesive whole.

ML interviewers seek candidates who do not have any apparent weaknesses in these competencies, while the most successful candidates exhibit exceptional strength in one or more areas. In an ML interview, competencies are evaluated in individual interview sessions, which we outline below.

As you take in each interview session, ask yourself the following questions:

1. Do I have a weakness here? If so, attempt to pinpoint the specific areas of weakness. Navigate to the pertinent chapter of this guide and read the related practice questions. For instance, if you lack confidence in model serving at scale, refer to the ML Infrastructure Design – Online questions and review the solutions carefully. Follow references as needed to ensure you have built a firm grasp of its contents.

2. Can I highlight a strength for this session? For example, take a question like, *"Can you describe how logistic regression works?"*. If your strength is in ML fundamentals, provide a clear, textbook-like definition and demonstrate understanding of the mathematics. If your strength is more on the applied side, direct the discussion towards the use cases and tradeoffs of logistic regression compared to other approaches.

Here are the technical interview sessions comprising an ML interview:

Technical Phone Screen

Consists of: a ML coding or simple ML modeling problem.

Evaluates:
- What is the general ML knowledge of this candidate?
- Can they apply ML to a practical product problem?
- Can they convert basic ML algorithms into code?

Sample questions:
- How does k-means work? Can you implement it?
- What is overfitting?
- Describe a system, at a high-level, that recommends X.

Insider Tip

It's not recommended to prepare specifically for the Technical Phone Screen, since it typically involves a relatively easier question from one of the other interview sessions. Therefore, it is more beneficial to allocate your preparation time towards other interview sessions.

ML Fundamentals Interview

Consists of: one or two questions probing the breadth and depth of your ML knowledge.

Evaluates:
- How familiar are they with essential ML concepts?

- Can they describe approaches in literature and/or industry to common ML problems?
- Are they able to compare and contrast several ML algorithms?
- Can they detail ML algorithms and/or techniques step-by-step?
- Can they deep dive into feature or modeling issues?

Sample questions: see ML Fundamentals.

ML Coding Interview

Consists of: one or two coding questions. Questions may ask you to (a) implement a familiar ML algorithm, (b) write code solving a Probability or Statistics question, or (c) write code not related to ML, but with emphasis on data structures, algorithms, and/or distributed systems.

Evaluates:
- Can they reason about and use appropriate data structures and algorithms?
- Can they design proper APIs?
- Can they write clean code and pertinent tests?
- Can they assess the runtime complexity of their code?
- Can they adapt their solution - rewriting if necessary - as the problem evolves?
- How do they prove their results are correct?

ML algorithm questions evaluate:
- Can they translate algorithms into code form?
- Are they familiar with mathematical libraries (e.g, numpy)?
- Are they comfortable doing math with code?

Probability & Statistics questions evaluate:
- Can they solve basic probability problems?
- Can they translate algorithms into code form?

Senior+ candidates:
- Are they familiar with distributed systems?
- Can they solve the problem at scale with a distributed design?

Sample questions: see ML Coding.

ML Design Interview

Consists of: (a) designing an end-to-end solution for an ML problem, encompassing the entire ML lifecycle, and/or (b) practical questions about the training and productionisation of ML models at scale.

Evaluates:
- Can they apply ML to a practical industry problem?
- Can they navigate the entire lifecycle of ML systems – from data collection, to modeling, to productionisation?

Senior+ candidates:
- Can they identify the right technical strategy and articulate their approach to complex industry problems?
- Can they spot issues, reason about tradeoffs, and propose appropriate solutions in each step of the ML lifecycle?

Sample questions: see ML System Design (Parts 1 and 2) for questions related to the ML lifecycle, and ML Infrastructure Design for questions related to ML at scale.

Other Interview Sessions

Behavioral Interviews:

Most ML interviews also assess a candidate's soft skills and/or leadership qualities. Since company cultures vary significantly, review documentation from the company you are applying in order to identify the most important character traits to consider.

Probability and Statistics:

In contrast to Data Science interviews, ML interviews do not typically assess Probability and Statistics skills as a separate competency. Nevertheless, basic comprehension is assumed since discussing certain topics without it may prove challenging. It is therefore important to grasp the foundational principles, such as:

- What is a confidence interval?

- Describe p-values.
- What's a uniform distribution? Normal? Bernoulli?
- How to compute variance?
- What's an independent variable and a dependent variable?
- Describe the difference between likelihood and probability.

Elements of a Strong Answer

Interviewers seek candidates who not only possess theoretical knowledge but can also handle practical challenges in an industry environment. Excellent candidates are skilled problem-solvers, communicators, and pragmatists. How does this reflect in the ML interview? Here are some elements of a strong answer:

- **Communication:** You can explain ML techniques in a way that is easy to understand. You are comfortable explaining concepts in different levels of detail, and can delve into mathematical specifics or cite research when needed.

- **Detail oriented:** You pay careful attention to every aspect of the ML practitioner workflow, such as data collection, feature engineering, modeling, and evaluation. You are able to recognize and address potential issues throughout the process, and can prioritize the most important factors. Your answers reflect not only a solid theoretical understanding, but also include practical examples of how to implement your ideas..

- **Limitations:** You clearly outline the limitations of a given technical approach. You are able to address the issues and propose solutions to each limitation. You effectively communicate the associated costs of implementing each workaround.

- **Tradeoffs:** You possess the ability to articulate the tradeoffs between different approaches. You identify specific scenarios where certain solutions are more suitable than others. You acknowledge that a combination of approaches is the most appropriate solution in some cases.

- **Strategic**: You are able to think ahead and anticipate potential issues and limitations with the current approach. You have the ability to come up with a plan for ongoing improvements and determine the most effective technical strategy going forward. This includes brainstorming ideas, gathering requirements, and establishing criteria for success.

Let's now take a closer look at each ML interview session, starting with ML Fundamentals, then ML Coding, and finally, ML Design. To help you prepare, we've included practice interviews for each session that covers a range of frequently asked questions. You are encouraged to take the practice interview, in whole or in part, to gauge your relative strengths and weaknesses. Make an effort to provide the best answers you can, incorporating elements of a strong answer in your response.

2. ML Fundamentals

This interview session tests the candidate's ML knowledge in various areas, assessing both their breadth and depth. Breadth refers to their ability to produce multiple valid solutions to a common ML problem, while depth refers to their ability to explain the details of one such approach.

While it may seem daunting that, as a candidate, you may be asked literally anything about ML in general, in practice there are often only a handful of subjects that make for good interview discussions. Interviewers prefer to ask questions that nearly everyone has either studied in school, or has encountered – regardless of their industry – to maximize signal and enable interviewers to substitute for one another. We will leverage this fact to limit our study to a smaller set of questions.

You probably won't be tested on the most recent advancements in the field, as interviewers prefer to concentrate on – you guessed it – the fundamentals of ML. For example, the interviewer is more likely to ask about logistic regression and boosted trees than about transformers, BERT, or attention mechanisms.

In this chapter, we will present the commonly asked ML Fundamentals questions that you'll want to know for your upcoming interview. We provide broad yet concise answers to these questions that cover the essential talking points. It is recommended that you supplement these responses with your own academic knowledge and/or industry experience, diving deep where you feel comfortable. We also provide tips on additional resources for you to gain more in-depth knowledge through further reading.

We include images and mathematical formulas where we believe they will be illustrative. While we have provided them to aid in your comprehension, you will not be expected to reproduce them during an interview.

Practice Interview

We have compiled a list of commonly asked questions for the ML Fundamentals interview session. It covers the essential areas of ML knowledge that you should be familiar with prior to your interview.

Challenge yourself by choosing a sample of questions from below. Write your answer before consulting the Interview Solutions section!

Datasets

2.1: How does one collect data and prepare a dataset for training?

2.2: What are some common problems in collecting data for training a model?

2.3: How to determine whether collected data is suitable for modeling?

2.4: What are several ways to handle label imbalance in a dataset?

2.5: How to deal when labels are missing?

Features

2.6: Can you describe different types of input features and their intuitions?

2.7: What is feature selection / importance?

2.8: How to perform feature selection?

2.9: How would you deal with missing feature values?

Modeling

2.10: What are some common modeling algorithms? List 3 and compare them.

2.11: Deep dive into one. Explain how the algorithm works.

2.12: What's the loss function? How is it optimized?

2.13: Is there a faster way to optimize the algorithm? What are the tradeoffs?

2.14: What are some ways to optimize gradient descent?

2.15: What's a reasonable procedure for hyperparameter tuning?

2.16: What is overfitting? How can you tell if your model is overfitting?

2.17: How to deal with overfitting?

2.18: Regularization – what is it? List 2 approaches and compare them.

2.19: What's the difference between linear and logistic regression?

2.20: Compare several different activation functions in neural networks.

2.21: Can you explain the difference between a decision tree, a random forest, and GBDTs?

2.22: What's the difference between boosting and bagging?

2.23: What are some unsupervised learning techniques? How do they work?

2.24: Describe k-means. How to initialize? What's the stopping criterion?

2.25: What are some semi-supervised learning techniques? How do they work?

Evaluation

2.26: What are common loss functions? Compare and contrast.

2.27: How to determine whether a loss function is convex?

2.28: How to evaluate a classifier model? List 3 metrics and describe when to use them.

2.29: How to evaluate the quality of a regression model?

2.30: Why not optimize a model directly on evaluation metrics?

2.31: If your model is performing poorly, how to debug and improve performance?

Interview Solutions

Datasets

Solution 2.1: How does one collect data and prepare a dataset for training?

Constructing a dataset is a crucial step in developing ML systems. The following are the main steps to follow:

1. **Collect the data:** Gather data you need to train the model. The data can come from existing streams generated by your system, such as user behavior, or from new data collections through conducting user research. Make sure to employ appropriate **sampling techniques**– such as random or stratified sampling – based on the task you want to perform. Evaluate the significance of streaming data into the model versus batching.

2. **Clean the data:** Check for missing or duplicate data, identify outliers, remove irrelevant information and correct any errors. If feature values are missing, data points may be discarded or imputed using an approach like mean-value imputation, or more sophisticated techniques.

3. **Label the data:** Assign labels to the data if the task is supervised learning. This may involve collecting user interaction data, or possibly hiring human annotators.

4. **Split the data:** Divide the data into train, validation, and test sets. The training set is used to train the model, the validation set is used to evaluate the performance of the model during training (e.g., for early stopping, hyperparameter tuning), while the test set is used to evaluate model performance after training. Training and validation sets can be folded into a single dataset if employing techniques like cross-validation. The test set provides an unbiased estimate of model performance, which can also be used to compare different modeling approaches.

5. **Preprocess the data:** Apply necessary preprocessing steps to the data, such as normalization, scaling or transforming the data into a format suitable for the model.

6. **Check for balance:** Imbalanced data occurs when one class is represented by a disproportionately large number of samples relative to the other classes. This can lead to problems during training because the model is likely to focus on the majority class and ignore the minority class. When working with an imbalanced dataset, first try training on the true distribution. If the model is able to learn and generalize well on the true distribution, the problem is likely not severe and no further action may be required.

7. **Shuffle the data:** Shuffle the data to reduce bias and ensure the model is not learning any order-based information, unless that is the objective of your training.

While the process of constructing a dataset for machine learning typically follows a sequence of steps, it is not always a strict linear process. There may be situations where you need to revisit certain steps or make modifications as you progress through the process. For instance, you might split the data after you have labeled it. Similarly, you may not need to balance the dataset before labeling it.

Solution 2.2: What are some common problems in collecting data for training a model?

While we outlined the general steps for data collection in the previous answer, we will delve into problems you may encounter along the way.

1. **Collecting the data:** Be aware of the biases that your data collection technique introduces, such as serving bias, and apply appropriate countermeasures, such as bandit approaches. Improper sampling may result in the dataset becoming narrow or homogeneous, leading to poor generalization and limited diversity in predictions.

2. **Cleaning the data:** Techniques used to clean the data, such as outlier and duplicate detection, and missing value imputation, may affect the

relevance of the dataset – particularly if the data are not missing at random – and may negatively impact the training of the model.

3. **Labeling the data:** Beware of noise that this step introduces, such as ambiguous annotation instructions, or misalignment between annotators. Consider employing techniques like weighted voting or annotation validation, to reduce annotation error. Read (Callison-Burch, 2009) for more on this approach.

4. **Splitting the data:** Ensure proper separation of data to prevent contamination between the training, validation, and test sets. For instance, consider splitting the data by dates where the training data includes all data up to a date and the test data includes data from the following date. See also (*Data Split Example / Machine Learning*, 2022).

5. **Preprocessing the data:** Improper normalization may affect the utility of certain features. For instance, normalization of counting features where the vast majority of occurrences are zero may be detrimental to model training.

6. **Checking for balance:** The distribution of classes in the data can affect the model's performance. Models may converge slowly, or be biased towards the majority class and have difficulty recognizing minority classes. Techniques like oversampling and undersampling can be used to address this, but issues may remain, such as poorly calibrated probabilities from model outputs. One solution is to upweight the downsampled class to improve calibration.

Insider Tip

Read more about handling imbalanced datasets below under *"2.4: What are several ways to handle label imbalance in a dataset?"*.

Solution 2.3: How to determine whether collected data is suitable for modeling?

The first step in constructing a dataset for training is to gather the raw data that you will use to train and validate your model. This data can come from a variety of sources such as logs, databases, web scraping, or even user studies. When gathering the raw data, there are several important considerations:

- **Quantity** is important because it directly impacts the model's performance. Having a large dataset allows the model to learn more patterns and generalize better. In general, a dataset should have an order of magnitude more data than the number of parameters in the model. Simple models trained on large datasets often outperform complex models trained on small datasets. Google has had success training simple linear regression models on large datasets (*The Size and Quality of a Data Set | Machine Learning*, 2022).

- **Quality** is equally important because unreliable data can negatively impact the model's performance. There are several reasons why a dataset might be unreliable:

  - Missing values in either the features or labels. This can be due to a variety of factors, such as human error in data collection or corrupted data.

Insider Tip

Gain a better understanding of how to handle missing values by reviewing the solutions below for *"2.5: How to deal when labels are missing?"*.

  - Rows in the dataset may be duplicated, which can skew the results and lead to overfitting.

  - Feature values may be incorrect, which can occur if there is a disparity between the training feature distribution and the prediction feature distribution. Reuse code between the training pipeline and serving pipeline where possible (Zinkevich, 2023).

  - Labels may be incorrect, which can happen if there are mislabeled data or errors in the data collection process.

Insider Tip

Read more about handling mislabeled data in <u>ML System Design: Part 2 –</u> <u>Data Collection</u> under *"5.6: What are some challenges when it comes to collecting labels?"*.

- Choosing an appropriate **sampling strategy** may be important for constructing high-quality datasets. The sampling strategy that you choose should align with the specific goals and metrics of your model. For instance, if your objective is to build a ranking model, then random sampling may not be sufficient. Instead, you may need to sample data in a way that reflects the ranking metrics that you want to evaluate, such as at the query level.

  Similarly, if your dataset is extremely imbalanced, this may result in slow convergence or poor predictive performance.

Insider Tip

Learn more about addressing label imbalance by referring to the solution provided below for *"2.4: What are several ways to handle label imbalance in a dataset?"*.

Solution 2.4: What are several ways to handle label imbalance in a dataset?

Handling label imbalance in a dataset is important to prevent a machine learning model from being biased towards the majority class. This is especially important when some classes have very limited representation. Here are several methods to handle label imbalance in datasets:

1. **Resampling:**

    - Oversampling the minority class: Duplicating samples from the minority class until the classes are balanced.

    - Downsampling the majority class: Removing samples from the majority class until the classes are balanced, which can lead to faster model convergence and reduced storage requirements.

Additionally, it may be beneficial to upweight the majority class after downsampling, as this can help to maintain model calibration throughout training.

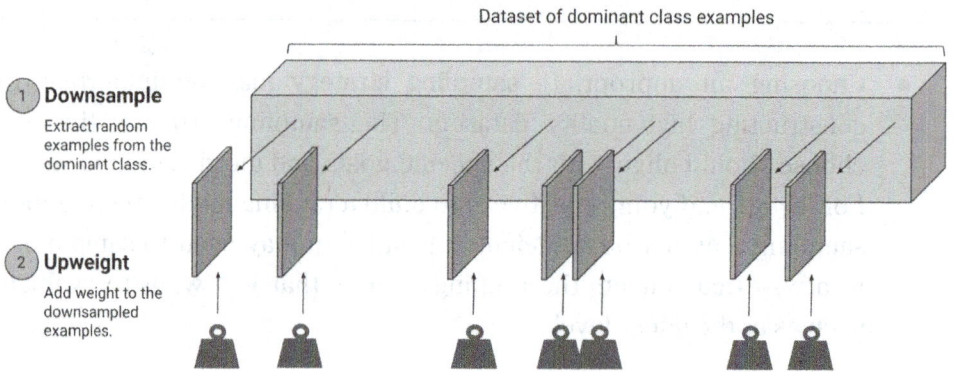

Note. Downsample and upweight technique. Source: (*Imbalanced Data | Machine Learning*, 2022).

2. **Synthetic data generation:** Creating new synthetic samples of the minority class to balance the dataset. This can be done using techniques like Synthetic Minority Over-sampling Technique (SMOTE).

3. **Cost-sensitive learning:** Assigning different weights to samples from different classes to account for the imbalance in the loss function used to train the model.

4. **Ensemble methods:** Using multiple models with different sampling strategies or using an ensemble of models trained on different subsets of the data with boosting or bagging.

5. **Precision-oriented modeling:** Some models are better suited for evaluation metrics sensitive to imbalanced datasets, such as precision or precision@k. For example, in decision trees and their variants – like random forest, boosted trees, etc. – one can prune paths with high entropy or with sparse samples. The trees can also be broken down into decision lists. In certain Natural Language Understanding (NLU) scenarios like domain-constrained intent classification, even rule-based models can perform effectively. Alternatively, models that generate probability-based outputs, such as logistic regression, can be thresholded to attain the desired performance outcomes.

The method chosen to handle label imbalance will depend on the specific problem and dataset, and that different methods can be combined to get the best results. It's important to keep in mind that sometimes the best approach is to do nothing, particularly with enough data and a model with sufficiently large capacity.

Insider Tip

An informative survey on this work is (López et al., 2013).

Solution 2.5: How to deal when labels are missing?

Handling missing labels in a dataset can be achieved in several ways:

1. **Annotate the data:** This is the most direct approach for providing accurate labels, however, can be expensive and time consuming.

2. **Remove missing labels:** This approach is suitable for datasets with small amounts of missing data, but it may result in loss of information.

3. **Impute missing labels:** Replace missing values with estimated values based on the available data, such as mean or mode. For example, in a highly unbalanced dataset (e.g., web clicks) the majority class may be imputed. However, the imputed values may also introduce bias into the dataset, leading to a decrease in performance.

4. Predict missing labels with modeling (aka. "**Induction**"): This involves training a model (self-training), or multiple models (co-training), on the available data and then using them to predict missing labels. The downside is that the trained models may reinforce poor predictions.

5. Predict missing labels with separation (aka. "**Transduction**"): Instead of building a model only on labeled data, consider both labeled and unlabeled data to predict missing labels. This can be achieved several ways: (a) clustering algorithms with partial supervision, (b) graph-based methods like label propagation algorithms (LPA), and (c) manifold learning which encourages neighboring points in a lower-dimensional space to have similar predictions.

6. When the data is missing at the instance level but aggregated labels are available at the group level, several techniques can be employed to leverage group labels to build an instance level classifier. Read more in Advanced ML Questions – Learning Without Labels.

Features

Solution 2.6: Can you describe different types of input features and their intuitions?

Broadly speaking, there are two fundamental types of features utilized in a ML model:

1. **Numerical features:** Features expressed by continuous or discrete numerical values, such as amounts, counts, rates, and durations.

   ○ Numeric features can be converted to categorical features. If the cardinality is small, numeric features may be treated as categorical features with identity values. Numeric features can also be bucketed (e.g., age) and discretized into categorical features.

2. **Categorical features:** Features expressed by categories, such keywords, device, demographic, language, location, IDs, etc. Categorical features can be represented as one-hot, multi-hot, or weighted (e.g., frequencies).

   ○ Categorical features can be converted to numerical vectors, for instance, via embeddings. This is useful if the input vocabulary is large and there are latent relationships between values, such as with natural language text.

   ○ Categorical features can also be compressed into a smaller space by using a hashing function (called the "hashing trick"). This is useful for features where there can be many out-of-vocabulary values at inference time, such as IDs, as the model can incrementally fit new samples without retraining from scratch.

Many kinds of features can be reduced to one of the fundamental types above. Here are some examples:

1. Binary features: Features expressed by yes/no or true/false values, such as membership ("is-a"), traits ("has-a"), and thresholds ("greater-than", "less-than"). These can be represented as either numerical or categorical features.

2. Text features: Text data are frequently transformed into embeddings, which are numerical vectors, or represented as one-hot or multi-hot categorical features.

3. Image features: Image data are preprocessed into numerical arrays, such as raw pixel values (e.g., RGB or HSV) or modified versions of the images created by applying various filters like thresholding, blurring, or equalization.

4. Audio features: Sounds are preprocessed into numerical representations such as frequency components of the audio signal, or Mel-Frequency Cepstral Coefficients (MFCCs).

5. Sequential features: These are features representing time-series data, such as stock prices. Sequential features can be numerical or categorical.

6. Video features: Video features can be represented as sequential image features. Another approach, optical flow features track pixel intensities across video frames.

Insider Tip

Read Google's documentation on their built-in wide and deep algorithm (*Training Using the Built-In Wide and Deep Algorithm | AI Platform Training*, 2023) for practical guidance on when to use categorical or numerical features, vocabulary or hashing, and so on.

Solution 2.7: What is feature selection / importance?

Feature selection is the process of identifying a subset of the most relevant and useful features (predictive variables) from a larger set of features to be used in model building.

One goal of feature selection is to improve the model's predictive performance and reduce the complexity and overfitting of the model by removing irrelevant, redundant, or noisy features. Another goal is to reduce the footprint of the model and streamline the feature hydration process, thereby improving training and serving efficiency.

Feature importance refers to a numerical value or score that indicates the contribution of each feature to the prediction performance of the model. It is used to rank and select the most important features for a given task.

Solution 2.8: How to perform feature selection?

There are three approaches, at a high level, for performing feature selection:

- **Filter:** Features are selected based on statistical tests such as chi-squared test, ANOVA, mutual information, information gain, correlation coefficient, and others.

- **Intrinsic:** Features are selected as part of the modeling process. For instance, the Random Forest method (Palczewska et al., 2013) trains models on subsets of features where the expected fraction of samples contributed by a split is an estimate of the relative importance of the feature. An alternative approach is to incorporate L1 regularization during the modeling process, which reduces weights of less informative features to zero.

- **Wrapper:** A subset of features is selected based on their performance in a model. This usually involves training a model multiple times with different subsets of features. One method is to perturb individual feature values (such as randomly shuffling them) and evaluating the effect on the model's performance. Another method involves omitting features one by one, or in groups. The procedure can be performed bottom-up (Sequential Forward Selection) or top-down (Recursive Feature Elimination), or using non-greedy techniques such as simulated annealing.

When deciding on the best approach, there are certain tradeoffs to consider. For example, Filter methods are straightforward and inexpensive to compute, but they assume that statistical significance equates to improved predictive power. On the other hand, Wrapper methods are computationally intensive, but more directly assess the model's performance. To gain a better understanding of the relative importance of features, ML practitioners often employ a variety of approaches.

Approaches can also be combined, such as Filter and Wrapper. If several features are highly correlated, dropping an individual feature may not impact model performance even if it has a significant contribution to model performance, so highly correlated features should be dropped together.

> ## Insider Tip
>
> An excellent book on this topic is (Kuhn & Johnson, 2019).

Solution 2.9: How would you deal with missing feature values?

Some key questions to ask before imputing, or estimating, missing feature values are:

- Is the training data complete? It's possible that the data became corrupted in some way, and the problem could be resolved by improving the data collection process rather than through imputation.

- What kind of model are you training? Decision trees and ensembles, such as XGBoost, can handle missing values automatically without need for imputation (*Frequently Asked Questions — Xgboost 1.7.5 Documentation*, n.d.).

- Is the data missing at random? Many imputation techniques are only appropriate for scenarios where data are missing at random. Read more about this topic in (Puri et al., 2021). In some cases the data is intentionally missing, and missing values can be simply filled in: for instance, user interaction features (e.g., clicks) often omit values where the count is zero.

- How many values are missing? Visualize the severity of the missing values. For small amounts of missing data, values can be imputed. However, if a significant portion of data is missing at random, it may be better to delete the feature or fix the data collection process.

- What is the distribution for features with missing values? If the distribution is non-Gaussian, such as bimodal, using mean or median imputation will result in poor performance. Studies have also shown that single imputation techniques may underestimate the variance of the data (Alade et al., 2020).

- Are there highly correlated features? In the presence of collinearity with other features, missing features may be deleted entirely. Alternatively, correlation between features can make imputation easier if one or more highly correlated features is present, for instance using tree imputation. You can employ statistical tests such as pointwise mutual information or Pearson's R, or PCA to find underlying correlations.

With that, here are several ways to handle missing feature values in a dataset:

1. **Deletion:** Simply remove the records or instances that contain missing values. This method is useful when there is very little missing data, but it can lead to loss of information if there is a large amount of missing data. Another option is to delete the feature(s) itself.

2. **Mean/Median/Mode:** Replace missing values with the mean, median or mode of the feature. This method is simple and fast but often underestimates variance of the data (Zhang, 2016), produces bad estimates for non-Gaussian distributions (e.g., bimodal distributions), and introduces bias if the data is not missing at random. That said, it is often the de facto method used in ML toolsets, such as BigQuery ML (*Automatic Feature Preprocessing / BigQuery*, 2023).

3. **Interpolation:** In time-series data, missing feature values can be interpolated using adjacent values. For instance, stock prices are not available during weekends. Linear interpolation averages the values from Friday and Monday. An alternative approach is to use the value on Friday (technique called LOCF) or the value on Monday (called NOCB).

4. kNN (aka. "**Hot Deck**"): Replace missing values with values from the k nearest neighbors. This may be resource intensive as kNN requires storing the entire dataset in memory.

5. **Regression:** Train a regression model to predict the missing values based on the other values of other features in the dataset. This approach can also be combined with kNN, for example, the Euclidean distance can be used as a weight. One downside is that regression analysis may underfit the distribution.

6. **Trees:** Decision trees and ensembles are a method of training non-linear models for imputation. The idea is to use trees to identify features that are highly correlated with the missing value and use those features to predict the missing value. Trees are fit on the available features and the prediction is the imputed value.

7. **Multiple imputation:** Multiple imputation involves generating several complete datasets by randomly filling in missing values from an estimated distribution. Each dataset is then used to train a separate model. During inference, the predictions from each model are pooled (e.g., by taking a weighted average) to produce a final estimate. One popular technique is Multiple Imputation with Chained Equations (MICE) (Errickson, n.d.).

Modeling

Solution 2.10: What are some common modeling algorithms? List 3 and compare them.

Three common modeling algorithms seen in industry are (1) logistic regression, (2) gradient boosted trees, and (3) deep neural networks.

Logistic regression:

Popular classification algorithm that models the probability of an event occurring based on one or more input variables (the "features"). In binary logistic regression, the features are combined linearly and then transformed using the logistic function, also called the sigmoid function, to model the probability of the event. In multinomial logistic regression (also called softmax regression), the softmax function is used in place of the logistic function.

The logistic function is defined as:

$$h_\theta(x) = \frac{1}{1 + e^{-\theta^T x}}$$

where x is the input vector, θ is the weight vector, and $h_\theta(x)$ is the predicted probability that the dependent variable takes the value 1 given x.

The weights in the logistic function are estimated from the data by maximizing the likelihood of observing the dependent variable given the inputs and weights. This is equivalent to minimizing the negative log-likelihood, which is expressed as the Log Loss, or Cross-Entropy loss.

Log Loss can be minimized using various optimization algorithms such as gradient descent, stochastic gradient descent, or quasi-Newton methods (e.g., BFGS) (Minka, 2003). During training, the model is repeatedly presented with training examples, and the model weights are updated in the direction of the negative gradient of the loss function with respect to the weights. This process is repeated until the loss converges to a minimum, according to a tolerance threshold.

Logistic regression can be regularized by adding a regularization term to the loss function. The most commonly used regularization techniques are L1 and L2, which add a penalty term to the loss function that encourages small weights.

Pros:
- Simple and efficient algorithm that can be trained quickly even on large datasets.
- Outputs probability estimates, which can be useful in certain applications such as risk assessment or fraud detection.
- Can be easily interpreted, and the weight vector can be used to identify the most important features for the classification task.

Cons:

- Assumes a linear relationship between the input variables and the target variable, which may not always hold true in practice.
- Prone to overfitting if the number of features is much larger than the number of training examples.

Gradient boosted trees (XGBoost is described below):

XGBoost (eXtreme Gradient Boosting) is an ensemble learning algorithm. It uses a gradient boosting framework that trains decision trees iteratively, adding new trees to the model to correct errors made by previous trees.

Commonly used loss functions are:
- Regression: Mean Squared Error (MSE) and Mean Absolute Error (MAE).
- Binary classification tasks: Log Loss (for binary) and Softmax Loss (for multi-class).

In traditional boosting, trees are added by reweighting data samples based on prediction errors of the current ensemble. In contrast, gradient boosting adds new trees by fitting the negative gradient of the loss function with respect to the predictions, also known as the pseudo-residuals.

XGBoost, rather than explicitly fitting the pseudo-residuals, aims to minimize the following objective at each iteration:

$$\sum_{i=1}^{n} l(y_i, \hat{y}_i^{(t-1)} + f_t(x_i)) + \omega(f_t)$$

where $\hat{y}_i^{(t-1)}$ are the predictions of the current ensemble, f_t is the new tree, and ω is a regularizer term. XGBoost applies a Taylor expansion to the objective, reformulating it as:

$$\sum_{i=1}^{n} \left[l(y_i, \hat{y}_i^{(t-1)}) + g_i f_t(x_i) + \frac{1}{2} h_i f_i^2(x_i) \right] + \omega(f_t)$$

where g_i and h_i are first- and second-order gradients of the loss function. The $l(y_i, \hat{y}_i^{(t-1)})$ is usually dropped since it's constant for a given iteration. New trees are grown in a greedy fashion, enumerating over features at each node, and traversing possible splits[1]. The split point is where the sum of loss from the child nodes most reduces the loss in the parent node (the "gain"), and is a function of the sums of first- and second-order gradients on either side.

One of the key innovations of XGBoost is the use of the second-order approximation of the loss function, which improves the accuracy of the gradient descent procedure. This is achieved by adding a second-order Taylor expansion of the loss function to the first-order gradient (Chen & Guestrin, 2016), resulting in more optimal estimates for the new tree.

Another feature of XGBoost is its ability to handle missing values, by assigning each missing value to a default direction in the decision tree, and learning the best direction during training (*Frequently Asked Questions — Xgboost 1.7.5 Documentation*, n.d.). This allows XGBoost to handle missing values without the need for imputation.

XGBoost provides several regularization techniques, such as L1 and L2 (known as alpha and lambda), gamma (the minimum loss reduction to create a tree-split), and max tree depth. Other regularization parameters include learning rate and data subsampling.

Pros:
- State-of-art performance on many regression and classification tasks.
- Robust to missing values and does not require scaling and normalization.
- Performs well on datasets of varying sizes, from small to large.
- Numerous hyperparameters, along with flexible options for parallelization and regularization, are available.

Cons:
- Doesn't support categorical features natively, though there are ways to handle them (*Categorical Data — Xgboost 1.7.5 Documentation*, n.d.).
- Sensitive to outliers as new trees are fit to fix errors made by previous trees.
- Somewhat siloed from other modeling algorithms in industry settings. Integration of training and serving alongside other modeling algorithms can be a hassle.

---

[1] For larger datasets, XGBoost partitions features into quantiles instead of scanning all values.

Deep neural networks (DNN):

Deep neural networks (DNNs) are a class of modeling algorithms that consists of layers of interconnected neurons (also known as "units"). DNNs can learn complex and non-linear relationships between inputs and outputs, making them well-suited for a wide range of tasks.

In a DNN, the units in each layer are connected to the units in the previous and next layers. The inputs to the network are fed into the first layer, and the outputs of the last layer are the predictions of the model. Each unit applies an activation function to the weighted sum of its inputs, and passes the result to the units in the next layer. DNNs can have many hidden layers, which allows them to learn increasingly complex representations of the input data. DNNs with a large number of layers are often referred to as deep learning models.

A variety of loss functions are utilized in DNNs (see ML Fundamentals – Evaluation for a list), popular ones being MSE, Cross-Entropy, and Log-Cosh. DNNs are trained using a process called backpropagation, which involves iteratively updating the weights of the neurons to minimize the difference between the predicted and true outputs. Backpropagation works by computing the gradient of the loss function with respect to the weights of the neurons, and using this gradient to update the weights using a variant of gradient descent, such as stochastic gradient descent (SGD).

DNNs can be regularized to prevent overfitting, by adding L1 or L2 regularization, by using dropout, or with early stopping. Max-norm and batch normalization are other popular techniques.

Pros:
- Learns complex and non-linear relationships between inputs and outputs, and along with XGBoost, achieves state-of-the-art performance on many tasks.
- Scales well to high-dimensional and large-scale datasets, making them well-suited for big data applications.
- Versatility: models come in all shapes and sizes, feature interactions can be modeled explicitly (e.g., with crossing), support for a wide range of features and label types, pre-trained models can be easily transferred to new tasks, and so on.

Cons:

- Computationally expensive to train complex models.
- Requires large amounts of data to train effectively.
- Complex models are prone to overfitting on small to medium datasets.
- Can be difficult to interpret and understand.

In industry, ML practitioners often transition from one modeling algorithm to another, and they may also combine multiple modeling algorithms as well. For example, one might start model development with logistic regression and ramp up to DNNs, as appropriate. XGBoost models are also used in combination with logistic regression (He et al., 2014) and DNNs (Zhu et al., 2017).

Solution 2.11: Deep dive into one. Explain how the algorithm works.

As we described above, logistic regression models the probability of an event occurring based on one or more input variables. In **logistic regression**, the input variables are combined linearly, and transformed using the logistic function (also called the sigmoid function) to model a probability of the event, and then mapped to binary outcomes, such as 0 or 1. The logistic function is defined as:

$$h_\theta(x) = \frac{1}{1 + e^{-\theta^T x}}$$

where x is the input vector, θ is the weight vector, and $h_\theta(x)$ is the predicted probability that the dependent variable takes the value 1 given x.

The logistic regression model is trained using a **maximum likelihood estimation** approach, which involves finding the values of the weight vector that maximize the likelihood of the observed data. The likelihood function is a product of the probabilities of each observation, given the input variables and weights. Maximizing the likelihood is equivalent to minimizing the negative log-likelihood, which is known as the Log Loss (or Cross-Entropy) function, defined as:

$$J(\theta) = -\frac{1}{m} \sum_{i=1}^{m} y_i \log(h_\theta(x_i)) + (1 - y_i) \log(1 - h_\theta(x_i))$$

The goal of the optimization process is to minimize the loss function by finding the optimal values of the weight vector θ. This can be achieved using various optimization algorithms such as gradient descent, stochastic gradient descent, or quasi-Newton methods (e.g., BFGS) (Minka, 2003). During training, the model is repeatedly presented with training examples, and parameters of the weight vector are updated in the direction of the negative gradient of the loss function. This process is repeated until the loss function converges to a minimum.

Logistic regression can be regularized to prevent overfitting by adding a penalty term to the loss function that encourages small weights. The most commonly used regularization techniques are **L1 regularization**, which encourages sparsity by adding the absolute values of the parameters to the penalty term, and **L2 regularization**, which adds the square of the parameters to the penalty term.

Multinomial logistic regression is the generalization of logistic regression to the case of multiple classes. In multinomial logistic regression, the probabilities are estimated using a softmax function, which ensures that the probabilities for all classes add up to 1, defined as:

$$h_\theta(x) = \frac{e^{\theta^{(k)T}x}}{\sum_{j=1}^{K} e^{\theta^{(j)T}x}}$$

The loss function for multinomial logistic regression is defined as:

$$J(\theta) = -\sum_{i=1}^{m}\sum_{j=1}^{K} 1\{y_i = k\}log\frac{e^{\theta^{(k)T}x}}{\sum_{j=1}^{K} e^{\theta^{(j)T}x}}$$

Solution 2.12: What's the loss function? How is it optimized?

Logistic regression is trained using a maximum likelihood estimation approach, which involves finding values of model coefficients (also known as weights) that maximize the likelihood of the observed data given the input variables and weights. The likelihood function is a product of the probabilities of each observation.

Maximizing the likelihood is equivalent to **minimizing the negative log-likelihood**, which is known as the Log Loss (or Cross-Entropy) function, defined as:

$$J(\theta) = -\frac{1}{m} \sum_{i=1}^{m} y_i \log(h_\theta(x_i)) + (1 - y_i) \log(1 - h_\theta(x_i))$$

where y_i is the true label (0 or 1) and h_θ is the predicted probability for the positive class. The multinomial variant of this function is given in the previous answer.

Log Loss in logistic regression can be optimized using **gradient-based optimization** algorithms such as stochastic gradient descent (SGD) or its variants (e.g. mini-batch gradient descent).

The optimization algorithm updates the weights in the direction of the negative gradient of the loss with respect to the weights. The gradient is calculated by taking the derivative of the loss with respect to each weight, which tells us the rate of change of the loss with respect to a small change in that weight. By updating the weights in the direction of the negative gradient, the loss is reduced and the model is trained to make more accurate predictions.

The derivative of the loss function is straightforward to calculate. Since logistic regression uses the logistic, or sigmoid, function the first step of is to find the derivative of the sigmoid function, which is (derivation at (Tanner, 2020)):

$$h_\theta(x)(1 - h_\theta(x))$$

Plugging this in leads to the derivative of the loss function:

$$\frac{1}{m} \sum_{i=1}^{m} (h_\theta(x_i) - y_i)x_i$$

In each iteration of the optimization algorithm, the gradient of the loss is calculated based on a single random sample (for SGD) or a small batch of samples (in mini-batch gradient descent). This is achieved by computing the dot product between the residuals $h_\theta(x_i) - y_i$ and the input variables x_i, and averaging over samples in the batch. Each weight is updated by a product of its gradient and a learning rate, which determines the step size for the update.

The optimization algorithm continues to update the weights until the loss converges to a minimum according to a tolerance threshold, or a maximum number of iterations is reached. The final weights provide a trained logistic regression model that can be used to make predictions on new data.

Solution 2.13: Is there a faster way to optimize the algorithm? What are the tradeoffs?

Second-order optimization methods are optimization algorithms that use information from the second derivative (also known as the Hessian matrix) of the objective function to optimize it. These methods are more efficient than first-order optimization methods (such as gradient descent), as they have a better estimate of the curvature of the objective function, leading to faster convergence and better solutions. Some examples of second-order optimization methods are **Newton's method, BFGS** and **L-BFGS** (Tan & Lim, 2019).

The main downsides of second-order optimization methods compared to first-order methods are:

1. Computational cost: Second-order methods require computation of the Hessian matrix, which can be expensive and time-consuming for large models, though quasi-Newton methods aim to reduce the computational burden.

2. Memory requirements: Storing the Hessian matrix can be memory-intensive for high-dimensional datasets, although there are approaches to approximate the matrix (e.g., L-BGFS).

3. Saddle points: Some second-order methods such as Newton's method are attracted to saddle points, though this can be mitigated with regularization.

For these reasons, first-order methods are often the preferred choice for large-scale problems, especially when there are computational or memory limitations.

Solution 2.14: What are some ways to optimize gradient descent?

Recall that gradient descent takes the form:

$$\theta = \theta - \eta \nabla_\theta J(\theta)$$

where η is the learning rate. We have already discussed techniques like stochastic gradient descent (SGD) which performs a weight update after each sample. However, SGD suffers from high variance in gradience estimation, due to the small sample size, which may lead to overshooting.

Mini-batch gradient descent reduces the variance of the gradient estimation by computing weight update on a small batch of samples (usually between 32 and 256), resulting in smoother convergence.

However, there are still drawbacks, particularly with the learning rate.

- Learning rates that are high lead to large fluctuations in weight updates or even to divergence.
- Learning rates that are low result in slow convergence.
- Learning rates that are fixed or adjusted on a schedule (e.g., annealing) fail to adapt to the model, dataset, or contour of the loss function.
- Learning rates applied uniformly to all weights don't account for feature sparsity.

Here are a few gradient descent optimization algorithms that address these issues:

- **Momentum:** Adds a fraction of the weight update from the previous time step to the current weight update. Can be viewed as adapting to the slope of the loss function. Encourages faster convergence but may also wander in the wrong direction.

- **Nesterov Momentum:** Version of Momentum that computes the gradient after applying the momentum update to the weights. It can be seen as a correction to the momentum, to increase the accuracy of weight updates without sacrificing the speed.

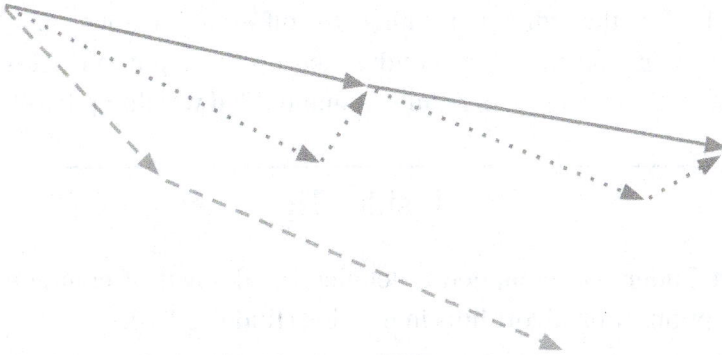

Note. Momentum (dashed) combines the gradient with the previous update. Nesterov Momentum first approximates where momentum will take the parameters and computes the gradient with respect to that position (dotted), resulting in the update (solid).

- **AdaGrad:** Adapts weight updates according to feature sparsity. Features that activate frequently perform smaller weight updates than features that are infrequent. This is achieved by accumulating squared gradients per feature in the denominator of the learning rate, so learning rate decreases the more often features activate. The downside is that the learning rate may be reduced too much before the algorithm converges.

- **AdaDelta (and RMSProp):** Addresses the diminishing learning rates of AdaGrad by allowing the learning rates to speed up again. This is achieved by keeping an exponentially decaying moving average of squared gradients, rather than the entire history of the squared gradient. More memory efficient than AdaGrad. AdaDelta and RMSProp are commonly used by ML practitioners in the industry settings.

- **Adam:** Can be seen as adding momentum to Adadelta/RMSProp. In addition to accumulating an exponentially decaying average of squared gradients in the denominator, Adam also stores an exponentially decaying average of gradients in the numerator, which acts as the momentum term.

In some cases the application of Momentum and Adam should be avoided, such as DNNs that direct training to different regions of the model architecture (e.g., via masking) conditioned on the input variables. Applying Momentum in these scenarios results in unintended weight updates.

Insider Tip

Sebastian Ruder has compiled a detailed breakdown of common gradient descent optimization algorithms in his blog (Ruder, 2016).

Solution 2.15: What's a reasonable procedure for hyperparameter tuning?

There are various methods for hyperparameter tuning, such as grid search, random search, Bayesian optimization, and genetic algorithms.

In **grid search**, a predefined set of hyperparameters are evaluated exhaustively, while in random search, hyperparameters are selected randomly from a predefined search space. These approaches can be inefficient, especially for models with a large number of hyperparameters or ones that take a long time to train.

Bayesian optimization leverages a probabilistic model to approximate the relationship between hyperparameters and the model performance, using an acquisition function that guides the search by balancing exploration (sampling new hyperparameters) and exploitation (evaluating promising hyperparameters).

In a **genetic algorithm**, models represent combinations of hyperparameters ("genes"). The process involves selecting the fittest models from each generation in an iterative manner. The surviving models undergo modification ("mutation") or recombination ("crossover") of their hyperparameters.

Bayesian optimization and genetic algorithms can be effective in finding hyperparameter values for complex models and large datasets.

For **logistic regression**, commonly tuned hyperparameters include:

- Optimization algorithm (aka. "solver")
- Learning rate
- Regularization (aka. "penalty"): L1 and L2

Logistic regression also uses a "C" hyperparameter which controls the amount of regularization applied.

Here are some additional hyperparameters when working with DNNs:

- Number of hidden layers (aka. "depth")
- Neurons (units) per layer
- Embedding size e.g., for text and categorical input features
- Activation functions
- Batch size
- Dropout

XGBoost employs a different set of hyperparameters, the chief one being the number of estimators (trees), or the number of boosting rounds.

The majority of other hyperparameters in XGBoost serve the purpose of regularization:

- Max depth of each tree
- Subsample: Fraction of data used to train on
- Colsample: Fraction of features available to train on
- Learning rate
- L1 (aka. "alpha") and L2 (aka. "lambda")
- Gamma: Minimum loss reduction to create a tree-split

Solution 2.16: What is overfitting? How can you tell if your model is overfitting?

Overfitting is a phenomenon in machine learning where a model is trained to fit the training data too closely, to the extent that it starts to memorize noise or idiosyncrasies of the training data, rather than learning the underlying patterns that would generalize to new, unseen data.

This can lead to a model that performs well on the training data but poorly on new data. Overfitting can occur when a model is too complex (e.g., has too many parameters) relative to the size of the training data, is trained for too long, or model weights become too large. In such cases, the model captures noise or outliers in the training data, which can cause it to make incorrect predictions when presented with new data.

There are several signs and methods to detect overfitting in a machine learning model:

- **Accuracy gap:** If the accuracy of the model on the training data is significantly higher than its accuracy on the validation data, it may indicate overfitting.

- **Learning curve:** A learning curve that shows a rapid decrease in training loss and a slow decrease, or a plateau, in validation loss can also indicate overfitting. Validation loss that inverts – starts to increase – is also a sign of overfitting.

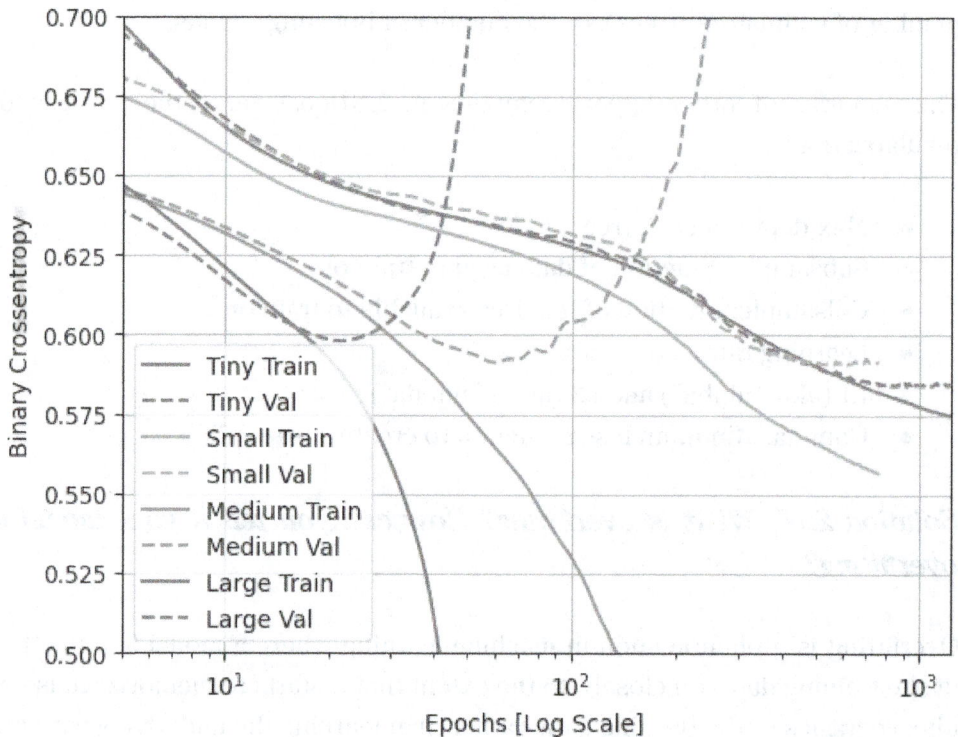

Note. Validation loss going in the wrong direction is a sure sign of overfitting. When validation loss plateaus while training loss improves, the model is close to overfitting. Source: (*Overfit and Underfit,* 2022).

Developing strategies to address overfitting is crucial. Models can often achieve strong performance on the training data, but the objective is to create models that generalize effectively to test data and unseen data.

Solution 2.17: How to deal with overfitting?

There are generally three levers for reducing overfitting:

1. **More complete training data:** Having more complete data necessitates less regularization and enables complex model architectures to reach their potential. However, it's important that the training data contains a comprehensive range of inputs. More data may not be helpful unless it covers novel cases.

2. **Regularization:** Techniques like L1 and L2 incorporate a penalty term into the loss function, decreasing the magnitude of weights, making it more difficult for the model to learn from noise in the training data. Another technique is Dropout, which randomly sets unit outputs in a given layer to zero. The intuition behind Dropout is to avoid "co-adaptation" (Srivastava et al., 2014), which discourages weight updates from systemically fixing errors produced by other units.

3. **Reducing model capacity:** A simpler model is less likely to overfit as it is naturally more constrained in the amount of information it can memorize. If the model can store a limited number of patterns, the training procedure forces it to learn the most important patterns, which increases the model's generalization ability. Reduce model capacity by reducing the number of input variables, the number of layers, and the size of each layer.

Understand that these three levers are complementary: more data may necessitate less regularization, larger capacity may require more regularization, and having more data can allow for larger capacity.

Beyond these key levers, here are some additional techniques:

- **Early stopping:** Interrupts the training process when the validation loss stops decreasing, since this is when the model usually begins to learn more from the noise in the training data rather than the signal.

- **Ensemble methods:** Combining multiple models, such as with bagging or boosting, can also help mitigate overfitting by reducing the variance of the model.

Insider Tip

Read through the Tensorflow tutorial on overfitting and underfitting (*Overfit and Underfit*, 2022) to see an example of the impact of model capacity and regularization on validation loss.

Solution 2.18: Regularization – what is it? List 2 approaches and compare them.

The goal of regularization is to prevent overfitting by reducing the complexity of the model. L1 and L2 regularization are two commonly used techniques which add a penalty term based on the magnitude of the model weights.

L1 regularization, also known as Lasso regularization, adds a penalty term to the loss function proportional to the absolute value of the weights. This leads to sparse models where some weights are exactly equal to zero, effectively reducing the number of features the model uses.

L2 regularization, also known as Ridge regularization, adds a penalty term to the loss function proportional to the square of the values of the weights. This results in small, non-zero weights, which reduces the complexity of the model without making it sparse.

Why does L1 make weights sparse while L2 does not? This is because the gradient of L1 is either -1 or 1 except where the weight is zero, so the penalty moves the value closer to zero by the same increment, regardless of the weight's current value. By contrast, the gradient of L2 is a linear function that decreases to zero as the weight approaches zero, resulting in a penalty that diminishes as the weight value becomes smaller.

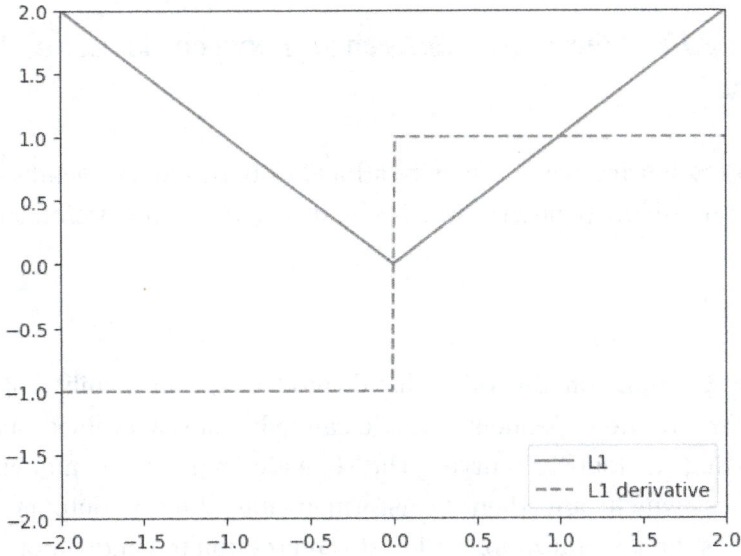

Note. For L1 (solid), the gradient (dashed) moves weights towards zero with the same step size (-1 or 1). This encourages weights to become sparse.

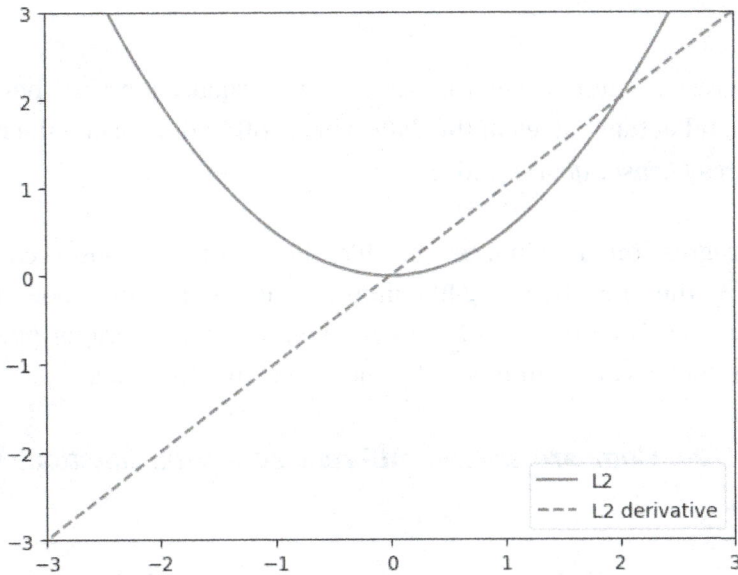

Note. By contrast, with L2 (solid) the magnitude of the gradient (dashed) decreases as weights approach zero. In other words, step sizes get smaller.

In general, L1 regularization is used when the objective is to reduce the number of features the model uses (such as redundant features), while L2 regularization is used to reduce the magnitude of the weights, spreading them out more evenly, without necessarily setting them to exactly zero.

Solution 2.19: What's the difference between linear and logistic regression?

Linear regression models a linear relationship between a dependent variable and one or more independent variables by fitting a best line. Defined as:

$$y = \beta_0 + \beta_1 x_1 + \dots$$

Logistic regression, on the other hand, models the probability of a binary outcome (where the dependent variable can only take two values, such as 0 or 1) by fitting a logistic curve. The logistic regression model outputs probabilities which are then transformed into binary outputs. Softmax regression is the generalization of logistic regression to handle more than two classes. The logistic function is defined as:

$$p = \frac{1}{1 + e^{-(\beta_0 + \beta_1 x_1 + \dots)}}$$

Linear regression minimizes the sum of the squared errors between the predicted and actual values in the data. This is often done using the method of least squares (*Least Squares*, n.d.).

Logistic regression maximizes the likelihood of the observed data by minimizing the negative log-likelihood, known as the Log Loss (or Cross-Entropy) function, which can be achieved with various optimization algorithms such as gradient descent or quasi-Newton methods.

Solution 2.20: Compare several different activation functions in neural networks.

Here are some commonly used activation functions and their characteristics:

- **Sigmoid:** Maps input to the range of 0 to 1, making it useful for producing probabilities (such as for binary classification problems). Can lead to vanishing gradients as the function becomes saturated with large or small values. Not zero-centered, so gradient updates always have the same sign, which may result in slower convergence.

- **Softmax:** Often used as an output layer for multiclass classification problems, mapping input values to a probability distribution over multiple classes.

- **Tanh:** Maps input to the range of -1 to 1, meaning that it can output negative values which may be useful in some contexts. Compared to the sigmoid function, the gradient near zero is notably larger, leading to more substantial updates. However, tanh saturates as well, which makes it prone to vanishing gradients like the sigmoid function. Zero-centered, so it doesn't suffer from zigzagging gradient updates.

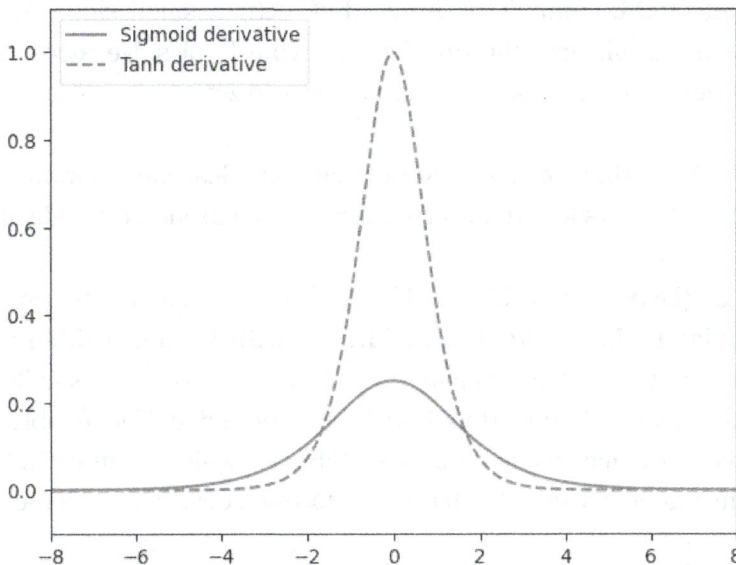

Note. Derivatives of sigmoid (solid) and tanh (dashed). Observe that tanh has larger gradients near zero, while both functions saturate rapidly.

- **Softsign:** Similar to tanh, bounded -1 to 1. Smoother than the tanh function, resulting in less saturation and fewer issues with vanishing gradients. As a result, convergence may be faster. However, computation is more expensive due to complex derivatives.

- **ReLU (Rectified Linear Unit):** ReLU is a piecewise linear function that replaces negative values with 0 and keeps positive values unchanged, which avoids saturation. Gradients do not vanish like they do in sigmoid and tanh. Fast to compute and has been shown to work well in practice for DNNs. However, one issue is the "dying ReLU" problem, which can occur when inputs to the ReLU function become negative, making the unit inactive and causing the gradient to be zero during backpropagation. This problem can be difficult to recover from as a result.

- **Softplus:** Smoother version of ReLU, negative bounded at 0 and positive unbounded. The smoothness and non-zero nature of the gradient improve training stability (Zheng et al., 2015). However, computation is more expensive than ReLU due to complex derivatives (it's the sigmoid function).

- **Leaky ReLU:** Similar to ReLU, but with a small slope for negative inputs, to alleviate the problem of dying ReLUs. Negative values also encourage mean unit activations closer to zero.

- **PReLU:** Variant of Leaky ReLU that has a learnable parameter for the slope of inputs less than zero, rather than a predetermined value.

- **ELU (Exponential Linear Unit):** Popular among ML practitioners. Similar to Leaky ReLU and PReLU, with the main difference being saturation to a fixed negative value as the input gets smaller, making ELU negative bounded and positive unbounded. This enables ELUs to have variance dampening capabilities, which demonstrated faster convergence despite higher computational cost (Clevert et al., 2016).

- **SELU:** Expands the benefits of ELUs – ability to control the mean, to decrease and increase the variance of unit activations – but with theoretical convergence towards zero mean and unit variance (Klambauer et al., 2017). This self-normalizing property supports the training of DNNs with many hidden layers without vanishing or exploding gradients.

- **Swish:** Like ELU and SELU, Swish is an activation function that is negative bounded and positive unbounded. Additionally, it is non-monotonic and smooth. The Google Brain team found these properties to produce superior results to ReLU, ELU, and SELU in experiments (Ramachandran et al., 2017). GELU (Gaussian Error Linear Unit) is another activation function that shares the same characteristics.

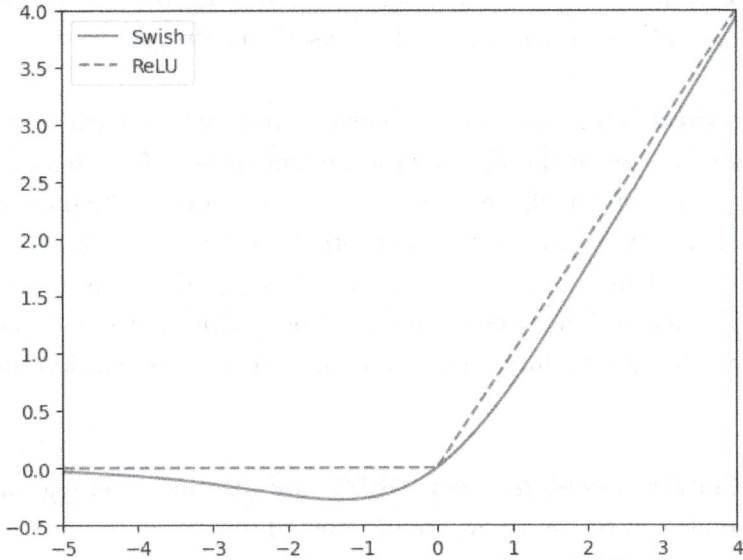

Note. Swish (solid) and ReLU (dashed) activation functions are both positive unbounded – avoiding saturation – and negative bounded. Additionally, Swish is non-monotonic, with negative values for small negative inputs, and smooth, which is useful for optimization.

When choosing an activation function, consider its (1) **zero-centricity**, (2) **computational cost**, and (3) **gradient anomalies** such as vanishing or exploding gradients. As a result of these considerations, effective activation functions often generate both negative and positive values, and are unbounded on the positive side to avoid saturation.

Insider Tip

For an in-depth review of the various activation functions, see (Szandała, 2021).

Solution 2.21: Can you explain the difference between a decision tree, a random forest, and gradient boosted decision trees (GBDT)?

A **decision tree** is an ML algorithm that recursively partitions data into smaller subsets and builds a tree-like model of decisions and their consequences. Each internal node of the tree represents a split on a feature, each branch represents the outcome of the split and each leaf node represents an output.

Criteria for splitting are usually grounded on metrics of "purity", such as the Gini index, or information gain, which is based on entropy.

A **random forest** is an ensemble of decision trees, where each tree is trained on a random subset of the data and a random subset of the features at each split. The predictions of all trees are combined to produce the final prediction, either by majority voting for classification problems or by averaging for regression problems. This combination of many decision trees leads to reduced variance and improved generalization performance, with a drawback of reduced interpretability. The training process is straightforward to parallelize.

Gradient Boosted Decision Trees (GBDT) are also an ensemble of multiple decision trees, where each new tree is trained to correct the errors made by the previous trees. GBDTs add new trees by fitting to the negative gradient of a loss function (e.g., MSE) with respect to the predictions, also known as the pseudo-residuals. The splitting criterion is typically based on the loss function. Unlike random forests, the trees in GBDT are dependent on each other, and the final prediction is made by combining the weighted predictions of all trees. Although trees must be trained sequentially, the construction of an individual tree – particularly the split-finding procedure – may be distributed.

GBDTs aim to take a more principled approach to tree building than random forests: using training loss instead of the information gain heuristic for splitting, employing regularization instead of outright pruning, and so on.

Solution 2.22: What's the difference between boosting and bagging?

Boosting and bagging are two popular techniques used to improve the accuracy of predictive models. Both techniques involve building multiple models and combining their predictions to produce a final output.

A key similarity between boosting and bagging is that they are both ensemble methods that use voting to combine multiple models. In both cases, the goal is to improve the accuracy and reduce the variance of the model.

However, there are several key differences between the two techniques.

- **Boosting** is a sequential process where models are built iteratively, and each subsequent model is trained to improve the performance of the previous ones by focusing on the misclassifications made by the previous models. However, this makes boosting more prone to overfit than bagging.

- In contrast, **bagging** involves building multiple models in parallel, each trained on a different subset of the training data, which improves robustness to outliers and noise. Bagging can be more readily distributed, which means that the training process can be split across multiple machines to speed up the training process.

Solution 2.23: What are some unsupervised learning techniques? How do they work?

Unsupervised learning is a type of ML where the algorithm learns patterns in data without the need for labeled examples. The goal is to discover structure or relationships within the data, such as clustering similar data points together or reducing the dimensionality of the data.

Some popular unsupervised learning techniques are:

- **k-means:** Unsupervised algorithm used for clustering. It works by partitioning a set of data points into k distinct, non-overlapping clusters such that the points within each cluster are as close as possible to each other and as far away as possible from points in other clusters.

- **EM (Expectation Maximization):** Iterative algorithm used to estimate parameters of statistical models. It works by alternating between computing expected values of the missing data given the current estimates of the parameters (the E step) and then updating the parameters to maximize the likelihood of the observed data (the M step). EM has many applications, including in clustering, natural language processing, computer vision, and speech recognition.

- **PCA (Principal Component Analysis):** Statistical technique used to reduce the dimensionality of high-dimensional datasets while maintaining a high degree of information. It works by finding the linear combinations of the original features that explain the most variance in the data. It works by first centering the data, then iteratively finding the directions of maximum variance in the data through the computation of the eigenvectors of the covariance matrix (the principal components).

- **t-SNE (t-Distributed Stochastic Neighbor Embedding):** Algorithm for visualizing high-dimensional data in a low-dimensional space. It works by first measuring pairwise similarities between data points in the high-dimensional space, and then finding a lower-dimensional representation of the data that best preserves these similarities. The algorithm uses a probabilistic approach to map similar high-dimensional data points to nearby points in the low-dimensional space, while keeping dissimilar points far apart.

- **SVD (Singular Value Decomposition):** Reduced-rank approximation used to represent the high-dimensional data in a lower-dimensional space, while minimizing information loss. It works by decomposing the original matrix (a co-occurrence matrix) into three separate matrices – a left, right, and singular value matrix – and the product of these matrices approximates the original matrix. The left matrix is regarded as the "embeddings", while the rank of the approximation is determined by the number of values used from the singular value matrix.

- **Autoencoder:** DNNs used for unsupervised learning that aim to learn a compressed representation of the input data. They work by encoding the input data into a lower-dimensional latent space, and then decoding it back into the original space. Autoencoders have many applications, including in image and video compression, anomaly detection, and dimensionality reduction.

- **VAE (Variational Autoencoder):** The main difference between Autoencoders and VAEs is that VAEs learn a probabilistic distribution of the encoded latent space, while Autoencoders learn a deterministic mapping. VAEs use a variational inference approach to learn this distribution, which involves optimizing a lower bound (ELBO) on the log-likelihood of the data, consisting of a reconstruction term and a regularization term.

- **RBM (Restricted Boltzmann Machine):** Generative models used for unsupervised learning that learn a compressed representation of input data. Consisting of two layers of neurons, one visible and one hidden, where the visible layer corresponds to the input data, while the hidden layer represents a latent representation of the input. The layers are fully connected to one another. The RBM learns weights of these connections that minimize the difference between the input data and reconstructed data, which is generated by feeding outputs of the hidden layer back through the network.

- **GAN (Generative Adversarial Network):** Type of neural network consisting of two parts, a generator and a discriminator. The generator learns to create new data samples that are similar to a given training dataset, while the discriminator learns to distinguish between the generated samples and real data. The two parts are trained together in a game-like process, where the generator tries to fool the discriminator, and the discriminator tries to correctly identify the fake data, resulting in the generator producing more realistic data over time.

Solution 2.24: Describe k-means. How to initialize? What's the stopping criterion?

k-means is an unsupervised algorithm used for clustering. It works by partitioning a set of data points into k distinct, non-overlapping clusters such that the points within each cluster are as close as possible to each other and as far away as possible from points in other clusters.

The standard version of the algorithm proceeds as follows:

1. **Initialization:** Randomly select k data points to serve as initial centroids for the k clusters.

2. **Assignment:** Assign each data point to the nearest centroid based on the Euclidean distance between the data point and the centroid.

3. **Update:** Calculate the mean of all the data points assigned to each centroid and use it as the new centroid for that cluster.

4. Repeat steps 2 and 3 until the centroids **no longer move** (or move within a tolerance), assignments **no longer change** (or change within a tolerance), or a **maximum number of iterations** is reached.

The result of k-means clustering is a partition of the data points into k clusters, each represented by its centroid.

Drawbacks of k-means: manual selection of the value k, sensitivity to initial seeding (Celebi et al., 2013), issues clustering datasets with certain characteristics – high-dimensional datasets, datasets with many outliers. k-means also has trouble with clusters of varying sizes and densities, though k-means Gaussian mixture models addresses this issue (Guestrin, 2007).

Solution 2.25: What are some semi-supervised learning techniques? How do they work?

Semi-supervised learning is a type of machine learning where a model is trained on both labeled and unlabeled data. By leveraging the information in the unlabeled data, the model can improve its performance on the labeled data.

There are several approaches to semi-supervised learning:

- **Induction:** This involves training a model (self-training), or multiple models (co-training), on the available data and then using them to predict missing labels. The downside is that the trained models may reinforce poor predictions.

- **Transduction:** Instead of building a model only on labeled data, consider all the available data when training a model. This can be achieved several ways: (1) clustering algorithms with partial supervision, (2) graph-based methods like label propagation algorithms (LPA), and (3) manifold learning, which encourages neighboring points in a lower-dimensional space to have similar predictions. There are also models that learn with transductive properties, such as the Transductive SVM and the Laplacian SVM.

- **Hybrid:** Extend unsupervised learning with labeled data, and vice versa. For example, Variational Autoencoders (VAEs) are a type of generative model that can incorporate labeled data into the training procedure. In VAEs, the encoder network takes the input data and maps it to a lower-dimensional latent space, where it tries to represent the underlying structure of the data, and the decoder maps it back to the original space.

In semi-supervised learning, labels can provide supervision on the encoder side. For instance, a supervised classifier can be trained on the latent space using labeled data. Alternatively, the decoder network can be conditioned so that it generates samples that are consistent with the labels, such as concatenating labels to the latent representation before passing through the decoder network. Read more about this approach in (Kingma et al., 2014). Another example of a hybrid approach is (Iscen et al., 2019) which alternates between supervised learning and label propagation.

- When the data is unlabeled at the instance level but aggregated labels are available at the group level, several techniques can be employed to leverage group labels to build an instance level classifier. Read more in Advanced ML Questions – Learning Without Labels.

Evaluation

Solution 2.26: What are common loss functions? Compare and contrast.

Common loss functions in machine learning include:

- **Mean Squared Error (MSE):** Average of the squared prediction error. More sensitive to large errors. Gradient decreases as loss moves closer to 0, resulting in more precise convergence as training progresses. Also known as L2 loss.

- **Mean Squared Log Error (MSLE):** Average of the squared logarithmic differences between the predicted and actual values. Compresses large values, which makes MSLE more robust to outliers than MSE. However, there are some quirks. MSLE measures relative error between the predicted and actual values, not the absolute scale of the error. Penalizes underestimation more than overestimation.

- **Mean Absolute Error (MAE):** Average of the absolute prediction error. More robust to outliers. Useful when the magnitude of error for outliers is not a major consideration. Gradient does not decrease with loss, so adding a learning rate is important. Also known as L1 loss.

- **Mean Absolute Percentage Error (MAPE):** Average of the absolute prediction error, expressed as a percentage of the actual value. Similar to MSLE, only measures relative error between the predicted and actual values, not the absolute scale. Useful when dealing with data with varying scales. Avoid actual values of zero.

- **Huber loss:** Hybrid of MSE and MAE. Squared error for small differences, absolute error for larger differences. The cutoff is determined by the hyperparameter δ (delta). More robust to outliers than MSE, yet retains MSE's better precision when loss is small. The choice of δ is important.

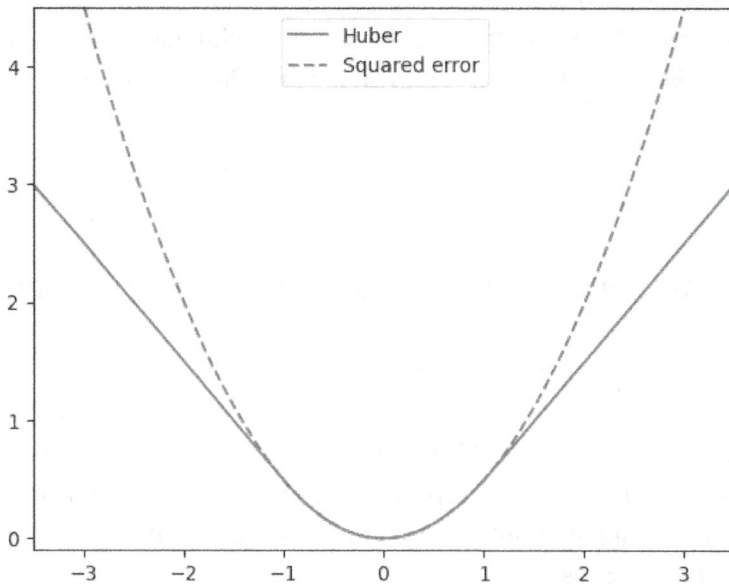

Note. Plot of Huber loss (solid) versus squared error loss (dashed). The Huber loss is linear for larger values.

- **Log-Cosh loss:** Logarithm of the hyperbolic cosine of the prediction error. Similar to Huber loss but without the δ hyperparameter, Log-Cosh behaves like squared error for small values and absolute error for larger values. Twice differentiable, which is useful for algorithms like XGBoost.

- **Poisson loss:** Used in regression problems where the goal is to predict count data, such as the number of events in a given time period. Measures prediction error assuming distribution of events follows a Poisson distribution and that they occur independently.

- **Cross-Entropy (or Log Loss):** Used in classification problems, or regression problems where the actual value is between 0 and 1 (e.g., a probability). Measures the error between the predicted probability of the positive class and the actual value:

$$-\frac{1}{m} \sum_{i=1}^{m} y_i log(\hat{y}_i) + (1 - y_i)log(1 - \hat{y}_i)$$

This loss function is used in logistic regression. Read this worked out example comparing Cross-Entropy loss with MSE on the same data (McCaffrey, 2013).

- **Kullback-Leibler Divergence (KLD):** Measure of the difference between two probability distributions, or the relative entropy. Similar conceptually to Cross-Entropy with several differences. First, KLD is always non-negative. Second, when the two distributions are identical, KLD is zero, whereas Cross-Entropy is equal to the distribution entropy. Cross-Entropy is more often used in practice as they solve equivalent optimization problems (Siddiqui, 2022), with the notable exception of Variational Autoencoders (VAE), where KLD is used as a regularization term (Prokhorov et al., 2019) in the loss function.

- **Hinge loss:** Absolute prediction error, except where the prediction for the actual class label greater than a margin incurs zero loss. Can be viewed as trying to maximize the margin between the decision boundary and actual values, and commonly used in Support Vector Machines (SVMs) as a result. While Hinge loss can produce accurate models, it is not as adept at estimating probabilities as Cross-Entropy loss.

Solution 2.27: How to determine whether a loss function is convex?

A loss function is strictly convex if it satisfies either the first-order or second-order condition for convexity. Intuitively:

1. **First-order condition:** If the first derivative of the function, also known as its gradient, is a monotonically increasing function. Alternatively, one can say that the function's tangent line (first-order Taylor approximation) is a global underestimator for the function.

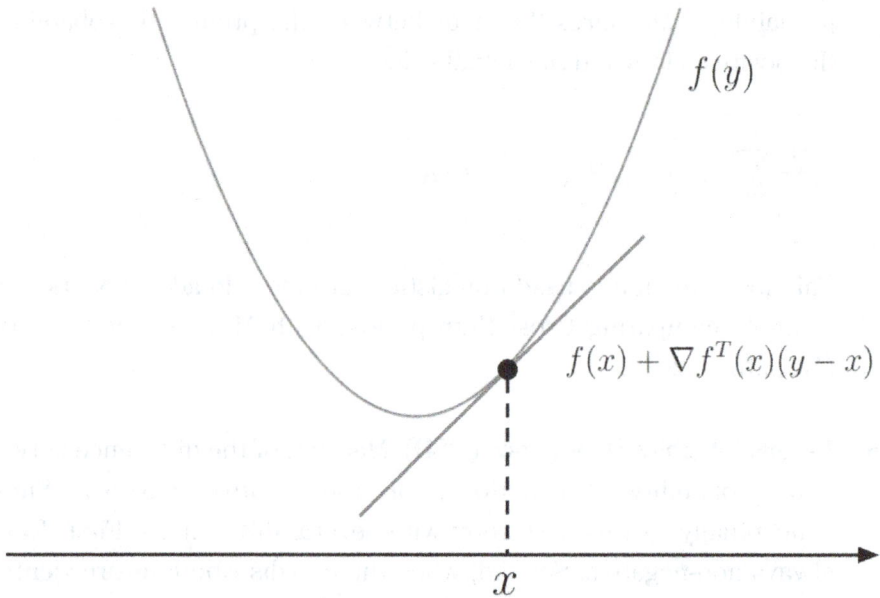

Note. Under the first-order condition, the tangent line should be a global underestimator of the function.

2. **Second-order condition:** If the second derivative of the function is always positive.

Furthermore, the unique global minimum of a strictly convex function is guaranteed to occur at the point where its gradient is equal to zero.

Solution 2.28: How to evaluate a classifier model? List 3 metrics and describe when to use them.

There are many metrics that can be used to evaluate model performance, depending on the type of problem and the evaluation goals. Some of the most commonly used metrics include:

- **Accuracy:** Proportion of correct predictions among all predictions. Use when the specific type of error is not a significant concern, such as when classes are relatively balanced.

- **Precision:** Proportion of true positives among all positive predictions. Use when the goal is to minimize the occurrence of false positives.

- **Recall:** Proportion of true positive among all actual positive cases. Use when the goal is to minimize the occurrence of false negatives.

- **F1 Score:** Harmonic mean of Precision and Recall. Use when sensitive to either low Precision or low Recall.

- **Precision@k:** Version of Precision metric that is more pertinent for ranking problems. Measures the proportion of true positives among the top-k results returned by the system.

- **AUC (or PR AUC):** Precision vs Recall curve. Useful for visualization and thresholding. PR space is preferred to ROC when the number of positives is few, because a large change in false positives only leads to a small change in False Positive Rate in ROC analysis (Davis & Goadrich, 2006).

- **ROC (or ROC AUC):** True Positive Rate vs False Positive Rate curve. ROC space is particularly useful when the positive class is either the majority class or when the classes are relatively balanced.

- **DCG (and nDCG):** Graded relevance measuring the value (or "gain") of retrieved results, discounted by the position of each result. nDCG is a normalized version of DCG which bounds the metric between 0 and 1. Commonly used in learning-to-rank problems where there is variance in the relative value of every result.

In many cases, metrics are used together to get a better understanding of the model's performance. Metrics sensitive to positives are the most popular for retrieval and ranking tasks, such as F1 Score, PR AUC, and nDCG.

Solution 2.29: How to evaluate the quality of a regression model?

Below are several commonly used evaluation metrics for regression:

- **Mean Absolute Error (MAE):** Calculates the average absolute difference between the predicted and actual values. Expressed in the same units as the dependent variable, making it easier to interpret.

- **Mean Squared Error (MSE):** Computes the mean of the squared differences between the predicted and actual values. Squaring the differences has several benefits. First, it eliminates the possibility of negative differences canceling out positive differences. Second, it penalizes large errors more heavily than small ones, which makes it more sensitive to outliers.

- **Root Mean Squared Error (RMSE):** Square root of the mean of the squared differences. Shares benefits with MSE, however, interpretation is more intuitive than MSE since value is scaled to that of the dependent variable.

- **Root Mean Squared Logarithmic Error (RMSLE):** Similar to RMSE, but it is applied to the logarithms of the predicted and actual values instead. More robust to outliers than RMSE. Measures relative error between the predicted and actual values, not the absolute scale of the error. Underestimation is penalized more than overestimation (Saxena, 2019).

- **R-squared:** Measures the ratio of residual sum of squares to the total sum of squares. Also known as "coefficient of determination" or "goodness of fit". May be more intuitive than other metrics, since it's expressed as a percentage.

- **Mean Absolute Percentage Error (MAPE):** Measures the average percentage difference between the predicted and actual values, relative to the actual values. Scale independent, useful when comparing series of different scales. Avoid values of 0 in the dependent variable.

Solution 2.30: Why not optimize a model directly on evaluation metrics?

Models are not directly optimized on evaluation metrics for several reasons:

- **Non-differentiable:** Some evaluation metrics, such as Accuracy or F1 score, are not differentiable. Differentiability is required for optimization using gradient-based methods.

- **Non-convex:** Direct optimization of evaluation metrics may lead to optimization difficulties, such as non-convexity and local minima.

- **Impractical:** Some evaluation metrics, such Precision or F1 score, require many samples to generate reliable values. Other evaluation metrics such as DCG require inputs to be grouped by query. This may be impractical for data extraction, transformation, and loading (ETL), or for model training.

A related question is, *"Why not use the model's loss function as the evaluation metric?"*

Loss is in fact often used as one evaluation metric (Log Loss in particular), however, typically it's better to have a separation of concerns. This gives model development the freedom to explore various loss functions, while focusing evaluation on metrics that are most intuitive or informative for the given task.

Solution 2.31: If your model is performing poorly, how to debug and improve performance?

Here are several steps that can be taken to debug and improve model performance:

1. **Define the problem:** Clearly define what is considered as "poor performance". Is the model compiling? Are there runtime issues? Is the loss not converging, or simply too high? Are model predictions outside of expected bounds?

2. **Visualize the data:** Plot the data to check for patterns, outliers, corruption, and other issues that could be affecting model performance. Determine whether the dataset is being sampled properly, or if there are any ingestion issues. Check the data before and after preprocessing. For instance, missing values might be too

pervasive, handled incorrectly, or numerical features are not properly normalized. Read more about data validation in (*TensorFlow Data Validation | TFX*, 2023).

3. **Check model variables:** By variable, we mean a tensor whose value can be changed via operations (*Introduction to Variables*, 2022). Check variable scoping and proper reuse of variables. Verify variable names and shapes.

4. **Step through the model:** Inspect the model state at each layer for several steps. Print the outputs of all tensor operations, including outputs of activation functions. It is common to discover problems such as incorrect tensor operations, outliers, NaNs, and improper inputs at this stage.

5. **Loss:** Verify the loss computation is correct. Check the learning rate, gradient computation and layer weights. After several steps, verify optimizer behaviors like momentum.

6. **Simplify the model:** If model performance is still difficult to troubleshoot, simplify all components of the model. Ingest fewer features. Use a simple optimizer like SGD. Use fewer parameters, layers, and fewer tensor operations. Once the model is converging and metrics are moving in the right direction, incrementally add complexity back and verify once more.

7. **Debugging with TensorBoard:** Use TensorBoard to visualize the training process, such as loss over time, to help identify issues with the model. For instance, if the model shows signs of overfitting, apply regularization or early stopping.

8. **Model tuning:** To get better performance, experiment with various components of the model:

   - Feature selection
   - Feature preprocessing, see (*Working With Preprocessing Layers*, 2022)
   - Training label
   - Loss function

- Layer activations
- Hyperparameters
- Model architecture

Insider Tip

See (*Keras Debugging Tips*, 2020) for more debugging suggestions.

---

3. ML Coding

There are generally three types of questions that are asked in the ML Coding interview:

1. Implement a familiar ML algorithm.
2. Write code solving a Probability or Statistics question.
3. Traditional Software Engineering coding question – not directly related to ML.

Below, we discuss patterns you can apply to solve coding questions for (1) and (2). Since (3) is more of a catch-all for Software Engineering coding questions, broad coverage is beyond the scope of this guide. That said, we will review several SWE question templates that show up repeatedly in ML interviews.

Our main focus in this chapter is to help you formulate a plan to tackle these coding questions. Whenever appropriate, such as when demonstrating a specific approach, we will provide solutions in the form of code. In other instances, we may direct you to code solutions in alternative resources.

What Matters Most to Interviewers

In a coding interview, interviewers prioritize several aspects of the candidate's code, which we rank below in order of importance.

1. The first and foremost aspect that the interviewers care about is **whether the code solves the problem or not**. This is because the ultimate goal is to solve real-world problems efficiently and effectively. In many cases, candidates may come up with partial or incorrect solutions. This can happen due to a variety of reasons, such as an inadequate understanding of the problem, errors in logic, or lack of attention to detail. In such cases, even if the candidate has other positive qualities, it can become difficult to overcome an invalid solution.

Therefore, it is crucial for candidates to focus on understanding the problem statement thoroughly before attempting to write the code. It is preferable to have a functional solution rather than hyper-optimizing the code and getting it entirely wrong.

2. The second aspect is the use of **reasonable data structures and algorithms**. The interviewers look for code that uses data structures and algorithms that are appropriate for the given problem. For example, if the problem involves storing key-value pairs, using a hashmap for storing the mappings would be a reasonable choice. Similarly, if the problem requires adding and removing elements in order, using queues and stacks would be a reasonable choice.

   These data structures have known time complexities and can be used to solve a wide range of problems. It is important for the candidate to understand the trade-offs between different data structures and algorithms and choose one that is appropriate for the given problem.

3. The third aspect is the **cleanliness of the code**. The interviewers look for code that is easy to understand and maintain. Descriptive and intuitive variable names can make the code more understandable and reduce the need for comments. The layout of loops and conditionals is another important aspect of code structure. If the code is not well organized, it can be difficult to follow the logic of the code, leading to errors and inefficiencies.

4. The fourth aspect is the candidate's **communication skills**. The interviewer looks for the candidate's ability to reason about the code. They might ask questions like the time and space complexity of the code, why a particular data structure was used, or ask the candidate to walk through the algorithm.

5. The fifth aspect is testing. Interviewers appreciate candidates who **proactively test their code**. It goes a long way if the candidate can test the main success scenarios and a few edge cases. Testing the main success scenarios involves testing the code with input values that are expected to produce the correct output. These inputs should cover the most common and straightforward cases.

Testing the edge cases involves testing the code with input values that are expected to produce unexpected or boundary cases. This demonstrates that the candidate has thought about potential edge cases and has taken steps to ensure that the code works as expected in those cases. This builds confidence in their coding abilities and demonstrates their attention to detail.

Implement an ML Algorithm

These questions lead with a discussion about a simple ML algorithm or evaluation metric, followed by some clarifications (e.g., stopping criteria, the mathematical formula if needed, etc.), and then jump straight into code.

In this session the interviewer may ask a couple of questions related to ML Fundamentals to prep the coding question, but is generally not interested in diving deep there, so feel free to ask details if you're fuzzy on the math. For example, if asked to implement the information gain metric, you are not expected to recall the exact formula by memory, and the interviewer should provide it without penalty.

Practice Interview

Here are some example ML algorithm coding questions:

- 7.1: What is k-means?
  - Follow ups:
    - 7.2: How to initialize?
    - 7.3: What's the stopping criterion?
    - 7.4: Can you implement it?

- 7.5: What is k-nearest neighbor?
  - Follow ups:
    - 7.6: What distance metric to use?
    - 7.7: Can you implement it?

- 7.8: What is a decision tree?
  - Follow ups:
    - 7.9: How are splits determined?

- 7.10: What's the stopping criterion?
- 7.11: Can you write the code for information gain?

• 7.12: Can you implement linear regression from scratch?

• 7.13: Code up an evaluation metric, such as nDCG or AUC-ROC.

Study Strategy

The key to improving your ability to implement ML algorithms is through some practice. Here are some suggestions to aid you.

1. Refresh yourself on simple, common ML algorithms:
   ○ Linear regression, logic regression, naive bayes, k-means, k-nearest neighbor, d-trees, and random forest.

2. Do the same for common evaluation metrics:
   ○ Mean absolute error, mean squared error, cross-entropy, f-score, AUC-ROC, average precision, recall@k, and nDCG.

3. Practice coding several of these algorithms from scratch. Although you may generally use any language of preference, it's recommended you learn to write these algorithms in Python, as it's most commonly adopted in industry, and knowledge of math libraries like NumPy will make algorithmic coding much easier.

Spend time learning to write vectorized versions of these algorithms with NumPy, it will save you significant interview time and coding effort, and win points with your interviewer as well. Learning how to use **broadcasting** (*Broadcasting — NumPy V1.24 Manual*, n.d.) is particularly helpful when comparing items or lists of different sizes.

Take the **k-nearest neighbor** algorithm, for example. With plain Python, your code may look something like this:

```
def k_nearest_neighbors(query, candidates, k):
  # compute Euclidean distances by looping through all candidates
  distances = []
  for i in range(len(candidates)):
    diff = 0
```

```
    for j in range(len(query)):
        # sqrt is not necessary
        diff += (candidates[i][j] - query[j])**2
        distances.append(diff)

    # get sorted indices
    indices = sorted(range(len(distances)), key=lambda k: dist[k])
    return indices[:k]
```

Using broadcast with NumPy is cleaner and more efficient:

```
def k_nearest_neighbors(query, candidates, k):
    # assumes np.arrays are passed in
    diff = candidates - query
    distance = sum(diff**2, axis=-1)

    # np.argsort(dist)[:k] works fine too
    return np.argpartition(distance, k)[:k]
```

another version that's even shorter:

```
def k_nearest_neighbors(query, candidates, k):
    distance = np.linalg.norm(candidates - query, axis=1)

    # np.argsort(dist)[:k] works fine too
    return np.argpartition(distance, k)[:k]
```

The Machine-Learning-Collection github (Persson, n.d.) has code samples for many of the above ML algorithms. Try coding up several ML algorithms from scratch and compare your solutions with those in the github – keep in mind, there isn't a single correct method for implementing these algorithms, and the code references serve as a resource to explore alternative or more optimal implementations.

Solution 7.1-7.4: k-means

k-means is an algorithm used to partition a dataset into distinct clusters based on similarity between data points. It aims to minimize the sum of squared distances between data points and their corresponding cluster centroids. To initialize k-means, we first specify the desired number of clusters k. Random initialization is a common approach, where initial centroids are randomly chosen from the dataset. Alternatively, we can use a more advanced technique like k-means++, which aims to spread out the initial centroids. The stopping criterion for k-means is typically defined by either a maximum number of iterations or a threshold for the change in centroid positions.

Here's an implementation with maximum number of iterations:

```python
def kmeans(input, k, max_iters=100):
  # randomly initialize k centroids
  centroids = input[np.random.choice(
      range(len(input)), size=k, replace=False)]

  for _ in range(max_iters):
    # assign each data point to the nearest centroid
    distances = np.linalg.norm(
        input[:, np.newaxis] - centroids, axis=2)
    labels = np.argmin(distances, axis=1)

    # update centroids
    new_centroids = np.array(
        [input[labels == i].mean(axis=0) for i in range(k)])

    if np.allclose(centroids, new_centroids):
      break

    centroids = new_centroids

  return centroids, labels
```

Solution 7.5-7.7: k-nearest neighbor

k-nearest neighbor (kNN) is an algorithm used for classification and regression tasks. It finds the k nearest data points in the dataset to a given query to predict the label or value of the query. The most commonly used distance metrics in kNN are Euclidean distance and Hamming distance (for discrete variables). Other distance metrics, like cosine similarity, can also be used based on specific requirements.

The sample code for k-nearest neighbor is given above.

Solution 7.8-7.11: Decision tree

A decision tree is an algorithm represented by a flowchart-like structure where each internal node represents a feature, each branch represents a decision rule based on that feature, and each leaf node represents the predicted value. Splits in a decision tree are determined using various criteria, with information gain being one commonly used measure. Information gain quantifies the reduction in entropy in the dataset achieved by splitting it based on a particular feature. The attribute that maximizes information gain is chosen as the split point at each node. Stopping criteria could be based on a maximum depth limit, minimum number of instances required in a node, or when further splits do not improve the classification accuracy significantly.

Here's the code for information gain:

```python
def entropy(labels):
    _, counts = np.unique(labels, return_counts=True)
    probs = counts / len(labels)
    entropy = -np.sum(probs * np.log2(probs))
    return entropy

def information_gain(features, labels, split_index):
    feat_split = features[:, split_index]
    unique_values, counts = np.unique(
        feat_split, return_counts=True)
    probs = counts / len(feat_split)

    weighted_entropies = [
      (count / len(feat_split)) *
      entropy(labels[feat_split == value])
      for value, count in zip(unique_values, counts)
    ]

    return entropy(labels) - np.sum(weighted_entropies)
```

Solution 7.12: Can you implement linear regression?

For linear regression, use the normal equation $\theta = (X^T X)^{-1} X^T y$ to minimize the cost function (least square).

```python
def linear_regression(features, labels):
  # add a column of ones to features for the bias term
  feat_with_bias = np.c_[
    np.ones((features.shape[0], 1)),
    features
  ]

  # use the normal equation to compute weights
  weights = np.linalg.inv(
    feat_with_bias.T.dot(feat_with_bias)).dot(
      feat_with_bias.T).dot(labels)

  return weights
```

Solution 7.13: Code up an evaluation metric, e.g., nDCG.

Here's code based on the $2^{rel_i} - 1$ definition of relevance for nDCG:

```python
def ndcg(predictions, labels, k):
    # Calculate ideal dcg. Use rank + 2 since rank starts at 0
    ideal_labels = sorted(labels, reverse=True)
    ideal_dcg = sum((2 ** label - 1) / math.log2(rank + 2) \
                    for rank, label in enumerate(ideal_labels[:k]))

    # Calculate the dcg from predictions
    pred_indices = sorted(range(len(predictions)),
                          key=lambda x: predictions[x],
                          reverse=True)
    pred_labels = [labels[i] for i in pred_indices]
    dcg = sum((2 ** label - 1) / math.log2(rank + 2) \
            for rank, label in enumerate(pred_labels[:k]))

    if ideal_dcg != 0:
        ndcg = dcg / ideal_dcg
```

```
else:
    ndcg = 0.0

return ndcg
```

Probability & Statistics Questions

Fortunately, the ML interview does not typically involve as rigorous a focus on probability and statistics as might be encountered in a Data Science interview. The interviewer may briefly touch upon fundamental concepts like "p-value". Probability and statistics concepts are instead woven into the interview process in a more general sense, such as when evaluating one's familiarity with ML fundamentals.

It is not uncommon to get a coding question involving the process of iteratively sampling data and subsequently determining the final state or outcome. There are two main reasons why this is assessed. First, sampling is a widely utilized technique for such purposes as data collection and model training. Second, it serves to evaluate the candidate's basic understanding of probability theory.

Practice Interview

Here are some sample questions you might encounter:

- 7.14: What is reservoir sampling?
    - 7.15: Can you implement it?
    - 7.16: Is there a more optimal way to implement it?
    - 7.17: How to adapt the solution to weighted reservoir sampling?

- 7.18: Draw lottery balls with replacement. Each ball has a value between 1 and N. Continue to draw lottery balls until a final value of V or more. What's the probability that I have a final value of U or less?

- 7.19: Given a NxN chessboard and a knight in the initial position (i, j). The knight can take up to K moves. If the knight leaves the chessboard, it can no longer reenter. What is the probability that the knight remains on the chessboard after K moves?

Study Strategy

Reservoir sampling:

Solution 7.14: What is reservoir sampling?

Reservoir sampling is a technique for selecting a random sample of k items from a large set of n items, where n is either unknown or too large to process in its entirety. The technique works by maintaining a reservoir of k items, and selecting items from the input stream randomly, with a decreasing probability of selection as more items are seen.

Solution 7.15: Can you implement it?

```python
class Reservoir:
  def __init__(self, size):
    self.size = size
    self.reservoir = []

    # initialize count to -1 as it gets
    # incremented to 0 on first try_add
    self.count = -1

  def try_add(self, value):
    self.count += 1

    if self.count < self.size:
      self.reservoir.append(value)
      return True

    # sample incoming items with decreasing probability
    else:
      insertion_idx = random.randint(0, self.count)
      if insertion_idx < self.size:
        self.reservoir[insertion_idx] = value
        return True
      else:
        return False
```

Solution 7.16: Is there a more optimal way to implement it?

One disadvantage of the above implementation is that it requires generating a random number for every item in the input, even those that are ultimately discarded. This means that, for large inputs, the probability of selecting an item that is not already in the reservoir becomes very small, and most of the random numbers generated by the algorithm are wasted.

To optimize the algorithm for large inputs, we can take advantage of the fact that the interval of acceptance for each item follows a **geometric distribution**. This means that we can calculate the number of items to skip over before the next acceptance, enabling us to quickly move to the next item to accept into the reservoir. This implementation is called Algorithm L and details can be found in (Li, 1994).

Insider Tip

A Python implementation of Algorithm L can be found in this blog (Steadman, 2020).

Solution 7.17: How to adapt the solution to weighted reservoir sampling?

Weighted reservoir sampling is a variant where each item in the input is associated with a weight that represents its relative probability of being selected. To compute the acceptance probability for each item, we first calculate the sum of weights for all items seen so far. We then divide the weight of each item by this sum to obtain its relative weight. The probability of accepting an item is then proportional to its relative weight.

```python
class WeightedReservoir:
  def __init__(self, size):
    self.size = size
    self.reservoir = []
    self.total_weight = 0

    # initialize count to -1 as it gets
    # incremented to 0 on first try_add
    self.count = -1

  def try_add(self, value, weight):
    if weight <= 0:
      return False
```

```
    self.count += 1
    self.total_weight += weight

    if self.count < self.size:
      self.reservoir.append(value)
      return True

    else:
      # add item with probability proportional
      # to its relative weight
      random_weight = random.randrange(0, self.total_weight)

      if random_weight < weight:
        insertion_idx = random.randrange(0, self.size)
        self.reservoir[insertion_idx] = value
        return True
      else:
        return False
```

Probability questions:

Dynamic programming is a frequently useful technique for solving coding questions that involve calculating the probability of certain events occurring after a series of steps.

Here are typical procedures for solving such problems using dynamic programming:

1. Set up the initial state: This is the starting point for the problem. For example, in the knight problem, initialize all squares with the probability that the knight stays on the chessboard after zero moves.

2. Take incremental steps: This involves defining some transition rules for going from one state to the next. For example, in the knight problem, the incremental step is to explore all the moves the knight can make to a new position on the chessboard.

3. Accrue the probability from previous states into next states: This involves computing the probability of the current state based on the probabilities of previous states. For example, in the knight problem, the probability of the knight being inside the chessboard after k moves

depends on its previous position and its probability of being inside the chessboard after *k-1* moves.

4. Determine probability at the end state: This involves computing the final probability of the event(s) we're interested in. For example, in the lottery balls problem, the final probability of the ball being *U* or less is the sum of all probabilities for values between *V* and *U*.

Here are some code examples to help illustrate the steps above:

Solution 7.18: Draw lottery balls with replacement. Each ball has a value between 1 and N. Continue to draw lottery balls until a final value of V or more. What's the probability that I have a final value of U or less?

To solve the lottery balls question, we can define *prob[k]* as the probability that the sum of all drawn lottery balls equals *k*. In order to determine the probability of any specific value *prob[k]*, we tally up the probabilities of all valid values that could reach *k*:

$$prob[k] = (prob[k-1] + prob[k-2] + \ldots + prob[k-N]) / N$$

Then, to calculate the probability that the total sum is *U* or less, we sum up the probabilities for all values between *V* and *U*, since *V* is the stopping criterion. For readability, in the code below, we use min_val to represent *V* and max_val to represent *U*.

```python
def probability_max_val_or_less(max_val, min_val, num_options):
    if (max_val <= 0 or min_val <= 0 or
        max_val < min_val or num_options <= 0):
        return 0.0

    if max_val >= min_val + num_options:
        return 1.0

    prob_sum = 1.0
    prob = [prob_sum] + [0.0] * max_val

    for idx in range(1, max_val + 1):
        # prob[idx] represents the sum of all
        # the probabilities of the elements that can
        # reach the value idx, normalized by num_options
```

```
      prob[idx] = prob_sum / num_options

      # maintain a sliding window such that prob_sum contains
      # the sum of at most num_options elements
      if idx - num_options >= 0:
        prob_sum -= prob[idx - num_options]

      # accrue probabilities for each potential draw
      # stop accruing when no more draws can be made
      if idx < min_val:
        prob_sum += prob[idx]

  return sum(prob[min_val:])
```

Solution 7.19: Given a NxN chessboard and a knight in the initial position (i,j). The knight can take up to K moves. If the knight leaves the chessboard, it can no longer reenter. What is the probability that the knight remains on the chessboard after K moves?

For the knights question, let *prob[x][y][k]* be the probability that the knight remains on the chessboard after *k* moves, starting from position *(start_x, start_y)*. The base case is when *k=0*, in which case the probability is 1.

For each subsequent *k*, we can calculate *prob[x][y][k]* by summing the probabilities of all the valid moves the knight can make from *(start_x, start_y)* at the *k-1*th move. To calculate the probability of a single move, we need to check if the target position is within the bounds of the chessboard. If it is, we add the probability of that move to the current position to the running sum.

```
N = 8  # size of the board
directions =
[(-2,-1),(-2,1),(-1,-2),(-1,2),(1,-2),(1,2),(2,-1),(2,1)]
num_directions = len(directions)

def probability_on_chessboard(start_x, start_y, num_moves):
  if num_moves <= 0:
    return 1.0

  prob = [[[0] * (num_moves + 1)
          for _ in range(N)]
          for _ in range(N)]

  # for 0 moves, the probability is 1
  for x in range(N):
```

```
      for y in range(N):
        prob[x][y][0] = 1.0

  # take moves incrementally
  for move in range(1, num_moves + 1):

    # compute the chances that this move ends inside the board
    for x in range(N):
      for y in range(N):
        prob_sum = 0.0

        for dx, dy in directions:
          new_x = x + dx
          new_y = y + dy

          # if the move ends inside the board
          # accrue the probability mass
          if (new_x >= 0 and
              new_x < N and
              new_y >= 0 and
              new_y < N):
            prob_sum += prob[new_x][new_y][move - 1]

        # normalize by the number of directions
        prob[x][y][move] = prob_sum / num_directions

  return prob[start_x][start_y][num_moves]
```

Hash Table & Distributed Programming

Hash table questions are not frequently asked in ML interviews, but if they do come up, they often serve as a precursor to follow-up questions about distributed computing (e.g., MapReduce).

This is due to the fact that the MapReduce programming model is utilized to extract and aggregate information from large volumes of logs and datasets, which is a common occurrence in real-world industry situations.

Practice Interview

Here are a few sample hash table questions which can be extended to distributed implementations:

- 7.20: Create a co-occurrence matrix from a corpus of text with window size of W.

- 7.21: Create a tf-idf dataset from a corpus of text, which outputs the format:

    term   document   tf-idf score

Study Strategy

Hash table coding problems generally involve aggregating counts over keys, often in an incremental manner. For example, when calculating tf-idf, group the terms in each document and store the counts in a hash table to compute term frequency. To compute document frequency, group the terms from the term frequency hash table and store the count of documents. Finally, the tf-idf values can be computed by iterating over the terms and documents.

The challenge comes when thinking about how to extend these implementations to distributed programming. When extending any coding problem to distributed programming, it can be helpful to think about how to code it up in a **functional programming** style. Functional programming is well-suited for distributed programming for several reasons:

- **Immutability:** Functional programming emphasizes the use of immutable data structures, which means that once a value is set, it cannot be changed. This property is crucial in distributed systems, as it eliminates the need for complex synchronization mechanisms to handle shared mutable state.

- **Statelessness:** Functional programming discourages the use of stateful objects, making it easier to reason about the behavior of a program in a distributed context. Stateless functions can be easily parallelized without worrying about hidden state or side effects.

- **Referential transparency:** Functions in functional programming are referentially transparent, meaning that their outputs are solely determined by their inputs. This allows for better caching and memoization, which can lead to performance improvements in distributed systems.

- **Higher-order functions:** Functional programming languages support higher-order functions, which are functions that accept other functions as arguments or return them as results. This enables a more modular and composable approach to building distributed systems.

- **Fault tolerance:** The immutability and statelessness of functional programming make it easier to implement fault-tolerant systems. Since functions do not depend on shared mutable state, it becomes simpler to recover from failures, such as node crashes, by re-executing the failed function with the same inputs.

Insider Tip

Read more about functional programming through Scala's resources (*What Is Functional Programming? | Scala 3 — Book*, n.d.) on the topic.

For example, here is some code that calculates the sum of even integers in an array after doubling their values. Java is used for illustrative purposes.

Imperative style

```
int[] arr = {1, 2, 3, 4, 5};
int sum = 0;
for (int i = 0; i < arr.length; i++) {
    if (arr[i] % 2 == 0) {
        sum += arr[i] * 2;
    }
}
```

Functional style

```
int[] arr = {1, 2, 3, 4, 5};
int sum = Arrays.stream(arr)
    .filter(x -> x % 2 == 0)
    .map(x -> x * 2)
    .reduce(0, Integer::sum);
```

Adopting this perspective can help with structuring the flow in a distributed environment.

With that said, let's dive into the practice interview questions above. Now, MapReduce itself is a complex topic that comprises numerous topics. For simplicity, we will focus on the main stages involved.

- **Map stage:** The input data is split into chunks that are processed by map tasks in a parallel manner. Each map task reads the input data and converts it into (key, value) pairs.

- **Partitioning, sorting and shuffling:** The (key, value) pairs from the map tasks are partitioned and sorted based on their keys, and then shuffled to be sent to the appropriate Reducer tasks. This stage is responsible for grouping together all pairs with the same key.

- **Reduce stage:** The shuffled (key, value) pairs are processed by reduce tasks in a parallel manner. Each reduce task processes all the values for a given key and produces aggregated results for the corresponding key.

Solution 7.20: Create a co-occurrence matrix from a corpus of text with window size of W.

There are two common approaches to calculate co-occurrence counts in MapReduce: the Pairs approach and the Stripes approach (Lin & Dyer, 2010). Below we describe the Pairs approach.

In the Pairs approach, for each word in a given window, we emit key-value pairs representing all possible word pairs in the window. Then we count the number of times each word pair occurs together within the window.

Here are the steps to implement the Pairs approach:

- Map: The input data is a set of documents. For each document, split the text into individual words. Then, for each pair of words in a window, generate a key-value pair with the key being the word pair and the value being 1.

- Reduce: The input data is the output of the map stage. For each word, we sum up the counts for all the word pairs produced by the mapper. The output is a set of key-value pairs where the key is the word pair and the value is the co-occurrence count.

The pairs approach, while straightforward, can generate a large number of key-value pairs during the Map stage. An alternative method is the Stripes approach, where the Map stage creates a key-value pair with the word as the key and a hashmap of all other words that co-occur with that word, along with their respective counts, as the value.

Insider Tip

To see code for implementing the Pairs and Stripes approaches, check out this blog (Bejeck, 2012).

Solution 7.21: Create a tf-idf dataset from a corpus of text.

Now that we have a basic understanding of how MapReduce works for co-occurrence counts, we can move on to the next problem of computing tf-idf scores. There are several variations to the solution, a simple one is given below:

The approach first generates the term frequency (tf) of each term in each document, where the input is a document, and the output of the mapper is ((term, doc), 1). The reducer then either sums up the raw counts, or produces the document-length normalized counts to obtain the tf.

The inverse document frequency (idf) is then calculated, where the input is ((term, doc), tf), and the output of the mapper is (term, 1) for each document per term. The reducer sums up the counts to get the total number of documents containing the term, and then calculates the idf using the formula log(number of docs / count).

Finally, the tf and idf values are joined on the term, and the input is (term, ((doc, tf), idf)). The output of the mapper is ((term, doc), tf*idf), which gives the tf-idf score for each term in each document.

To summarize, the process can be divided into three stages:

1. tf:
   - Input: document.
   - Mapper output: ((term, doc), 1) for every occurrence.

- Reducer sums up the counts ((term, doc), tf).
    - Alternatively, reducer can produce the document-length normalized counts ((term, doc), tf).
- In practice, another mapper may reformulate the tuple as (term, (doc, tf)) to simplify the joining process below.

2. idf:
    - Input: ((term, doc), tf).
    - Mapper output: (term, 1) for every occurrence, since (term, doc) is unique.
    - Reducer sums up the counts as df and computes (term, log(number of docs / df)), which is (term, idf).

3. tf-idf:
    - Join tf dataset with idf dataset on term.
    - Input is (term, ((doc, tf), idf).
    - Output of mapper is ((term, doc), tf*idf).

Insider Tip

Explore the code for this and how it aligns with functional programming principles by referring to Spotify's Scala implementation on github (*Big-Data-Rosetta-Code/TfIdf.scala*, n.d.).

Other Coding Questions

In addition to the questions outlined previously, ML interviews may also ask traditional Software Engineering coding questions. As the subject of coding questions is extensively covered in numerous books, we will not repeat that content. Rather, we'll identify the types of traditional coding questions that are more frequently encountered in ML interviews and direct you to additional resources for practice and review.

Here are the traditional coding question types commonly found in ML interviews:

1. Graph questions

2. String questions
3. Array questions

Practice Interview

Sample graph questions:

- 7.22: Given a reference to a node in an undirected graph, perform a deep copy of the graph.

- 7.23: Given a reference to the root node in a directed graph, check whether the graph contains a cycle.

Sample string questions:

- 7.24: Given a list of keywords, find the shortest snippet of text containing all the keywords.

- 7.25: Find the longest substring without repeated words.

- 7.26: Given two strings, check whether s is a subsequence of t. For example: s="abc" and t="a1b2c3", return True.

- 7.27: Find and replace: given a string, replace all the substrings s with the substring t.

Sample array questions:

- 7.28: Given a 2-dimensional array of 0s and 1s, find the number of islands. An island is a group of connected 1s (up, down, left, right).

- 7.29: Given a 2-dimensional array of 0s and 1s, write a function that dilates, that is it sets every coordinate adjacent (up, down, left, right) to an existing 1 to the value of 1.

  o Example:
     [0 0 0]
     [0 1 0]
     after dilating would be

$$[\,0\ 1\ 0\,]$$
$$[\,1\ 1\ 1\,]$$

- 7.30: Given an array of integers, determine whether there is a majority element, that is an element that occupies over half of the indices.
    - 7.31: Does it make a difference if the array were sorted?

- 7.32: Given an array of integers, find out whether any three integers sum up to 0. This is also known as the "3-sum" problem.

Study Strategy

Graph questions:

There is an underlying strategy for tackling many graph-based coding problems. The strategy involves traversing the graph, either in a depth-first or breadth-first manner, and using some data structures to keep track of visited nodes and other information.

To summarize:

1. Traverse the graph using either DFS or BFS.

2. Use data structures such as a hashmap or a set to keep track of visited nodes.

3. Use additional data structures, such as in the case of detecting cycles, a container to keep track of the nodes on the search path.

Let's apply this strategy to solve a couple of the practice coding questions.

Solution 7.22: Given a reference to a node in an undirected graph, perform a deep copy of the graph.

In the case of the deep copy of an undirected graph, we can traverse the graph and create a new graph with the same structure as the original graph. To achieve this, we use a hashmap to keep track of visited nodes and to map the original nodes to the new nodes in the new graph.

```
class Node:
  def __init__(self, val = 0):
    self.val = val
    self.neighbors = []

visited = {}

def clone_graph(node: Node) -> Node:
  if node in visited:
    return visited[node]

  clone_node = Node(node.val)
  visited[node] = clone_node

  for neighbor in node.neighbors:
    clone_node.neighbors.append(clone_graph(neighbor))

  return clone_node
```

Solution 7.23: Given a reference to the root node in a directed graph, check whether the graph contains a cycle.

In the case of detecting cycles in a directed graph, we can use DFS to traverse the graph and keep track of all visited nodes as well as the nodes in the current search path. If we reencounter a node in the search path, it means that there is a cycle in the graph.

```
class Node:
  def __init__(self, val = 0):
    self.val = val
    self.neighbors = []

# stores all the nodes that have been visited
visited = set()

# stores only nodes that are being explored
search_path = set()

def has_cycle(node: Node) -> bool:
  if node in search_path:
    return True

  if node in visited:
    return False

  visited.add(node)
  search_path.add(node)
```

```
    for neighbor in node.neighbors:
      if has_cycle(neighbor):
        return True

    search_path.remove(node)
    return False
```

The purpose of the two data structures can be demonstrated in the following test cases:

No cycle

```
node1 = Node(1)
node2 = Node(2)
node3 = Node(3)
node4 = Node(4)
node1.neighbors = [node2, node3]
node2.neighbors = [node4]
node3.neighbors = [node4]
```

In the above example, the code visits node4 twice, but there is no cycle. Therefore, search_path will remove node4 and node2. However, when node4 is reached again via node3, it will no longer be explored because of its existence in visited.

Cycle

```
node1 = Node(1)
node2 = Node(2)
node3 = Node(3)
node4 = Node(4)
node1.neighbors = [node2, node3]
node2.neighbors = [node4]
node3.neighbors = [node4, node1]
```

In this case, the code visits node4 twice again, but there is a cycle which is discovered when node3 reencounters node1, as node1 is still in the search_path (node1 → node3 → node1).

String questions:

The **two pointer approach** can be a useful technique for solving various types of substring problems. This approach involves the following steps:

1. Initialize a hashmap to store information about characters or words in the query. This depends on the exact problem.

2. Initialize two pointers, Begin and End, to point to the beginning of the string.

3. Move the End pointer towards the end of the string until a desirable condition is met. This desirable condition will be different for each problem.

4. When the desirable condition is met, move the Begin pointer towards the end of the string until the desirable condition is no longer met.

5. Update the match if it is better than the best solution thus far (e.g., shorter, or longer), depending on the problem.

6. Repeat steps 3-5 until the End pointer reaches the end of the string.

Let's use the above framework to solve the shortest matching snippet problem:

Solution 7.24: Given a list of keywords, find the shortest snippet of text containing all the keywords.

Following the two pointer approach, the concrete steps are as follows:

1. Initialize a hashmap to store the frequency of keywords in the query.
2. Initialize two pointers, Begin and End, to the beginning of the string.
3. Move the End pointer towards the end of the string until all the keywords are present in the substring.
4. When all the keywords are present, move the Begin pointer towards the end of the string until any of the keywords are missing from the substring.
5. Update the match if it is shorter than the current best match.
6. Repeat steps 3-5 until the End pointer reaches the end of the string.

This is an implementation for the shortest matching snippet problem. Note that this code assumes that the input is already split into words and does not perform any text preprocessing:

```
def shortest_matching_snippet(input, keywords):
  # store the count of each keyword
  keyword_counts = {}
  for keyword in keywords:
    keyword_counts[keyword] = keyword_counts.get(keyword, 0) + 1

  begin, end = 0, 0
  count = len(keywords)
  min_window = float('inf')
  min_begin = 0

  # move the end pointer until we have a valid window
  while end < len(input):
    if input[end] in keyword_counts:
      if keyword_counts[input[end]] > 0:
        count -= 1
      keyword_counts[input[end]] -= 1

    # if we have a valid window, move the begin pointer
    while count == 0:
      if end - begin + 1 < min_window:
        min_window = end - begin + 1
        min_begin = begin

      if input[begin] in keyword_counts:
        keyword_counts[input[begin]] += 1
        if keyword_counts[input[begin]] > 0:
          count += 1

      begin += 1

    end += 1

  # if no valid window was found, return an empty string
  if min_window == float('inf'):
    return ''

  return input[min_begin:min_begin + min_window]
```

This approach can be used to solve many similar problems: for instance, to find the *longest* snippet of text containing all the keywords, simply modify step 5 to update the match only if it's longer than the current best match.

Solution 7.25: Find the longest substring without repeated words.

To find the longest substring without repeated words, let's make a few adjustments to the two pointer approach:

- Step 1: The hashmap stores the last seen index of each word.
- Step 3: Expand End until a repeated word is found.
- Step 4: Move Begin to remove the repeated word.
- Step 5: Update the match if it's longer than the current best match.

Solution 7.26: Given two strings, check whether s is a subsequence of t.

To solve the subsequence coding problem, we can simplify the two pointer approach. We don't need to keep a hashmap or track the length of the match. We can simply move the End pointer forward until we find a matching character. Once we find a match, we move the Begin pointer forward until we no longer have a match.

```
def is_subsequence(text, query):
  len_query, len_text = len(query), len(text)
  begin, end = 0, 0

  while begin < len_query and end < len_text:
    if query[begin] == text[end]:
      begin += 1
    end += 1

  return begin == len_query
```

Solution 7.27: Find and replace: given a string, replace all the substrings s with the substring t.

In terms of general string search (e.g., find and replace), two efficient algorithms are Boyer-Moore and Knuth-Morris-Pratt (KMP). You don't need to memorize details, except to know that both algorithms have in common the idea of preprocessing the query string to create tables that can be used during the search to avoid unnecessary character comparisons. However, they differ in the specific types of tables they create and the way they use them during the search.

For instance, **Boyer-Moore** makes use of two preprocessing steps before starting the search. The first step involves creating a "bad character" table that is used during the search to quickly shift the query to align with a mismatched character in the text. The second step involves creating a "good suffix" table that helps in finding the longest suffix of the query that matches a prefix of the text. These two tables enable Boyer-Moore to skip over many irrelevant characters.

Insider Tip

We suggest reading the Wikipedia article on string searching algorithms (*String-Searching Algorithm*, n.d.) as a way to gain a general understanding of the topic.

Array questions:

Array-based coding problems encompass a variety of problem types and do not have a single definitive approach. The sample problems provided illustrate only a few of the possible scenarios that can be encountered.

For 2-D array problems, a reasonable strategy involves traversing the array row by row and column by column. When we reach a cell of interest, such as an "island" or a "pixel" in the sample questions, we **investigate the adjacent cells** to accomplish the desired outcome.

Solution 7.28: Given a 2-dimensional array of 0s and 1s, find the number of islands.

One approach to solving the island problem can be to use a depth-first search (DFS) algorithm to traverse the 2-D array and count the number of islands. Specifically, if an element is a 1, increment num_islands by 1, and start a DFS traversal from that element to find all connected 1s.

In the DFS traversal, mark the current element as visited and explore its adjacent cells (up, down, left, right). If an adjacent cell is also a 1 and has not been visited yet, mark it as visited and explore its adjacent cells recursively. Once the DFS is complete, go back and continue traversing the array until all elements have been visited.

```
def num_islands(grid):
    if not grid:
        return 0

    num_islands = 0
```

```
    rows = len(grid)
    cols = len(grid[0])

    for x in range(rows):
      for y in range(cols):
        if grid[x][y] == 1:
          num_islands += 1
          dfs(grid, x, y, rows, cols)

    return num_islands

def dfs(grid, x, y, rows, cols):
    if (x < 0 or x >= rows or
        y < 0 or y >= cols or grid[x][y] != 1):
      return

    # mark cell as visited to avoid double counting
    grid[x][y] = 0

    dfs(grid, x - 1, y, rows, cols)
    dfs(grid, x + 1, y, rows, cols)
    dfs(grid, x, y - 1, rows, cols)
    dfs(grid, x, y + 1, rows, cols)
```

Solution 7.29: Given a 2-dimensional array of 0s and 1s, write a function that dilates.

To solve the dilate problem, we also traverse the 2-D array row by row and column by column, similar to the approach used in the islands problem. Whenever we encounter a 1 in the array, we are tempted to set its adjacent cells to 1.

However, this approach is flawed as it can lead to assigning more 1s than necessary, including some that were previously 0. To avoid this issue, we first set the adjacent cells to 2, and then iterate over the array again to set all 2s to 1s, thereby dilating the original 1s without introducing new 1s.

1. Traverse the input array row by row, column by column.

2. For each element that is equal to 1, set its adjacent cells to 2. The adjacent cells are those above, below, to the left, and to the right of the current element.

3. Traverse the input array again and set all elements that are equal to 2 to 1.

```python
def dilate(grid):
    rows, cols = len(grid), len(grid[0])

    # set adjacent cells to the value 2 temporarily
    for x in range(rows):
        for y in range(cols):
            if grid[x][y] == 1:
                if x > 0 and grid[x-1][y] == 0:
                    grid[x-1][y] = 2
                if x < rows-1 and grid[x+1][y] == 0:
                    grid[x+1][y] = 2
                if y > 0 and grid[x][y-1] == 0:
                    grid[x][y-1] = 2
                if y < cols-1 and grid[x][y+1] == 0:
                    grid[x][y+1] = 2

    # set all 2s to 1s
    for x in range(rows):
        for y in range(cols):
            if grid[x][y] == 2:
                grid[x][y] = 1

    return grid
```

Insider Tip

If you're interested in learning more about dilating by k, you may find this blog post (Ostermiller, n.d.) by Stephen Ostermiller informative.

When solving 1-D array problems, it's worth considering the **benefits of having a sorted array**. For example, take the majority element problem:

Solution 7.30: Given an array of integers, determine whether there is a majority element.

When dealing with the majority element problem, an unsorted array requires a linear time solution that iterates through the array and uses a hashmap to count the frequency of each element. The majority element is the element that appears more than half the length of the array. However, with a sorted array, we can find the majority element more efficiently in O(log N) time. Let's see how.

Solution 7.31: Does it make a difference if the array were sorted?

If the given array is sorted, we can take advantage of certain properties. Specifically, if there exists a majority element, it must occupy the middle of the array. Here are the steps:

1. Locate the candidate element, which is the value at the middle index. For arrays with an odd number of elements, the middle index may be positioned to the left or right of the exact middle of the array.

2. Since the array is sorted, we can efficiently find the leftmost occurrence of the candidate element by performing a binary search.

3. Check whether the element at Left + N/2 is equal to the candidate element. If there is a majority element, then the candidate element must also occur at the index Left + N/2. Otherwise, there is no majority element.

```python
def majority_element(sorted_arr):
  size = len(sorted_arr)

  if size == 0:
    return None

  # if the array contains one element, it is the majority
  if size == 1:
    return sorted_arr[0]

  # candidate is the middle element
  mid = size // 2
  candidate = sorted_arr[mid]

  # find the leftmost occurrence of the candidate
  left = binary_search(sorted_arr, 0, size, candidate)

  # check if the candidate occurs more than n/2 times
  if (left + size // 2 < size and
      sorted_arr[left + size // 2] == candidate):
    return candidate
  else:
    return None
```

```
def binary_search(arr, start, end, target):
  while start < end:
    mid = (start + end) // 2
    if arr[mid] < target:
      start = mid + 1
    else:
      end = mid
  return start
```

Solution 7.32: Given an array of integers, find out whether any three integers sum up to 0.

Sorting the array can also be helpful in solving the 3-sum problem. By sorting the array, you can apply a modified version of the two pointer approach that we discussed earlier to solve this problem.

In this implementation, we use the left and right pointers to find all unique triplets that sum to zero. If the sum of the current triplet is less than zero, we increment the left pointer to increase the sum. If the sum is greater than zero, we decrement the right pointer to decrease the sum. If the sum is zero, we add the triplet to the result list and increment the left pointer while decrementing the right pointer to find all other possible triplets with the same first element. We skip duplicate elements to avoid redundant triplets.

```
def three_sum(arr):
  size = len(arr)
  arr.sort()
  result = []

  for idx in range(size - 2):
    # if the current number is the same as the
    # previous one, skip it to avoid duplicates
    if idx > 0 and arr[idx] == arr[idx - 1]:
      continue

    left = idx + 1
    right = size - 1

    while left < right:
      # calculate the sum of three elements
      total = arr[idx] + arr[left] + arr[right]

      if total < 0:
        # if sum is less than zero, move the left
        # pointer to the right to get a bigger sum
```

```python
            left += 1
        elif total > 0:
            # if the sum is greater than zero, move the right
            # pointer to the left to get a smaller sum
            right -= 1
        else:
            # if the sum is zero, add triplet to the results
            result.append([arr[idx], arr[left], arr[right]])

            # skip duplicates
            while left < right and arr[left] == arr[left + 1]:
                left += 1
            while left < right and arr[right] == arr[right - 1]:
                right -= 1
            # move left and right pointers to next unique elements
            left += 1
            right -= 1

    return result
```

4. ML System Design: Part 1

In **ML System Design: Part 1**, we will (a) introduce a framework for tackling system design questions, and (b) walk through a comprehensive example of a system design question.

The ML System Design interview session consists of one end-to-end applied ML modeling question that covers the entire ML practitioner workflow. Recapping the steps of the ML practitioner workflow, introduced earlier in Prerequisites:

1. Offline data exploration
2. Offline creation of features
3. Offline creation of dataset, or join features with existing dataset
4. Offline model training
5. Offline model evaluation
6. Offline model hyperparameter tuning
7. Online hydration of features
8. Online serving the model
9. Online periodic model refresh

For this question, the interviewer typically starts with, *"We would like to build a system that [performs a prediction task]"* and then asks you to walk through the construction of that ML system from initial design through launch. There are many possible variations that may be asked in the ML System Design interview session, here are several examples.

"We would like to build a system that …"

*   Extracts company names from financial documents.
*   Identifies topics discussed in news articles.
*   Classifies products into a taxonomy.
*   Merges duplicate products in a catalog.
*   Analyzes the sentiment of products on the web.
*   Recognizes bot traffic patterns.
*   Infers user demographics.
*   Finds users that are similar to one another.

- Generates concise summaries of documents.
- Shows ads on a search results page.
- Recommends content based on user behavior.
- Understands natural language commands.
- … and many more.

Design Framework

It may be tempting to jump straight into the modeling part when answering an ML System Design question, such as recommending the use of a specific ML algorithm with certain features. However, this is not the right way to approach the problem. Instead, it is important to recall the ML practitioner workflow and organize your response accordingly. When answering these questions in an interview, structure your response into sections following the general outline below:

1. **Clarify the problem:** Why do we want to do this? Who are the end users? How will they be consuming this data? What metrics do we expect to move? Besides this, understanding the operational parameters of the problem will help inform design decisions later in the model building process, such as size of the dataset, latency requirements, and so on.

2. **High-level design:** ML systems are complex and involve more than just model building. The process of producing desired outputs involves a series of steps that need to be considered. This includes identifying the inputs and candidate outputs of the system, as well as understanding the intermediate stages that the data undergoes during the transformation process into the final outputs. For example,

   - In recommender systems, there is (a) a candidate fetch stage, (b) filters and other business logic, (c) a pre-ranking stage to reduce burden on full ranking, (d) full ranking, and (e) reranking e.g., with heuristics applied in post-ranking.

   - For information extraction tasks, stages may include (a) content classification, (b) entity extraction, followed by (c) entity resolution which itself involves a separate candidate fetch and ranking flow.

3. **Data collection & processing**: Data collection is a crucial aspect of designing ML systems and demands careful attention. What kind of data do we need? Where does the data come from? How much data? To ensure that the training data accurately represents a wide range of items, it may be randomly sampled or stratified to ensure diversity. Additionally, data must be denoised to remove outliers, duplicates, and missing values. And then there's the issue of labeling, annotators may be hired and trained, and where labels are available from user interactions, serving bias must be dealt with.

4. **Feature engineering**: Feature engineering includes exploring datasets, prototyping inputs, selecting relevant features while considering operational impacts, and transforming the data for model training. It can be challenging because the datasets and corresponding dataflows can be very large and complex, knowledge of the problem domain is required to create useful features, and experimenting with feature combinations to optimize model and serving performance can be time-consuming.

5. **Modeling & evaluation**: To design a successful ML model, practitioners must navigate various challenges. These challenges include experimenting with various model architectures, handling dataset quality and bias issues, dealing with model fit (overfitting and underfitting) and hyperparameter tuning, balancing model and dataset size with computational resources and training time, and selecting appropriate evaluation metrics. Additionally, it's not always clear what the training objective and evaluation metrics should be, as offline goals (e.g., minimize the loss) and online goals (e.g., maximize user engagements) can differ.

6. **Deployment & serving**: Deploying a model can be challenging due to various factors such as latency and infrastructure impacts, and added system complexity. In some cases, deploying a model may require system redesign and optimization to maintain the overall performance. Monitoring and maintenance is a major concern when deploying and/or serving a model. The system also needs to support an online experimentation framework, which involves procedures for model

update and rollback. Creating new models or modifying existing models could also affect the quality of training data and perpetuate biases.

By adhering to this framework for answering ML System Design questions, you can effectively guide your response, address all critical aspects of the system, and highlight your understanding of the complex aspects of system design and execution.

Practice Interview

Let's now walk through a practice interview for recommender systems, or RecSys for short. Recommender systems recommend content that is tailored to individual user preferences, leading to a more personalized experience.

Recommender systems come in various forms and are widely utilized across numerous industries. Some well-known examples include:

- YouTube feed
- Instagram Reels
- TikTok feed
- Twitter feed
- Google News
- LinkedIn: People You May Know
- Netflix movie and TV show recommendations
- Amazon product recommendations
- Online advertisements

The list of interview questions provided below is rather comprehensive, so it is important to note that in an actual interview, only a third or so of these questions may be asked due to time constraints.

Try to answer as many questions as you can on your own before consulting the Interview Solutions section!

Prompt: *"We would like to build a system that recommends content to users tailored to their individual interests and preferences."*

Clarify the Problem

4.1: Why would we want to recommend content to the user?

4.2: What metrics do we expect to improve?

4.3: What kinds of content should we recommend?

4.4: How to blend different types of content (e.g., in-network, out-of-network, ads)?

4.5: Describe operational parameters of this recommender system (e.g., latency).

High-Level Design

4.6: Describe the high-level design for this recommender system.

4.7: How to generate recommendations for new users and items, aka. the cold start problem?

Data Collection

4.8: What datasets do we need to collect to build this system?

4.9: How to collect these datasets?

4.10: What sorts of biases might be found in the dataset?

4.11: How to mitigate serving bias?

4.12: What about position bias?

Candidate Generation

4.13: Where do candidates come from? List potential sources.

4.14: What are the benefits and drawbacks of each source?

4.15: Describe how candidate generation works at a high-level.

4.16: What are some algorithms for generating candidates?

4.17: How might you develop an embedding approach to generate candidates?

4.18: At scale, candidate generation cannot score every potential candidate in real-time. What are some ways to solve this problem?

4.19: How to index newly created content?

4.20: Suppose we need to limit the number of candidates that survive to ranking. How should we merge and prune candidates from different algorithms?

4.21: Why not use the candidate generator to rank items?

Pre-Ranking

4.22: What is a pre-ranking (or light ranking) model? What does it do?

4.23: What should the pre-ranking model learn?

4.24: Describe some evaluation metrics for this model.

4.25: What are some suitable algorithms for this model?

4.26: Suppose we need to pre-rank a large number of candidates. How to optimize the model to support this?

Feature Engineering

4.27: What features to use? What are their intuitions?

4.28: How to handle textual or id-based features?

4.29: What about counting features? Problems with using counting features?

Modeling & Evaluation

4.30: What should the heavy ranking model learn?

4.31: What are some reasonable modeling algorithms?

4.32: Describe what your model architecture might look like.

4.33: What if the model predictions need to be calibrated?

4.34: What are some appropriate evaluation metrics and why?

4.35: How to balance multiple objectives, e.g., Likes versus Subscribes?

4.36: Should we build one multi-task model or combine multiple smaller models?

Deployment & Serving

4.37: How to enable the model to serve real-time requests?

4.38: What can we cache in the serving system and where?

4.39: How often to update the model?

4.40: How does online experimentation (A/B testing) work?

4.41: How should the server support model experimentation?

4.42: Describe some ideas for model experiments.

4.43: Suppose we would like to predict which offline evaluation metrics improve online metrics (e.g., engagement). How to go about this?

4.44: How to debug if online experiment performance drops over time?

Interview Solutions

Clarify the Problem

Solution 4.1: Why would we want to recommend content to the user?

By aiding users in discovering engaging content amidst a vast amount of data, recommender systems offer several benefits:

1. **Relevance:** Recommender systems recommend items that are tailored to individual users' preferences, leading to a more personalized experience for users.

2. **Discoverability:** Recommender systems make it easier for users to discover new items and can save them time and effort from searching. It also becomes more convenient for user content to be discovered by others.

3. **Increased engagement:** By providing relevant recommendations, recommender systems can increase engagement, driving user retention and organic growth.

4. **Increased revenue:** Recommender systems can directly contribute to increased revenue, as users are more likely to purchase items they are interested in.

5. **Better understanding of customer behavior:** The data collected by recommender systems can provide valuable insights into customer behavior and preferences, which can be used to improve products and services.

Recommender systems play a significant role in various industries. Research conducted in 2013 found that recommender systems accounted for 35% of Amazon's consumer purchases and 75% of the content consumed by Netflix subscribers (MacKenzie et al., 2013). By 2016, this figure was 80% (McAlone, 2016).

Solution 4.2: What metrics do we expect to improve?

Consumer:

From the consumer standpoint, our main goals are to improve the following metrics:

- **User retention**, such as daily and monthly active users, time spent, and churn rate.

- **Positive and negative engagements**, including clicks and reports.

- **User state progression**, which involves converting light users into medium and heavy users.

- **Subscriptions**, also known as "follows", which increase the density of the network of producers and consumers.

Balancing these metrics, such as determining the relative importance of each metric and achieving a balance between positive and negative engagements, is influenced by business objectives and data science research.

Revenue:

When it comes to revenue, the objectives are more complex. Driving an increase in revenue could potentially lead to negative consequences, such as higher costs for advertisers, which may result in churn. The primary factors to evaluate are:

- **Impression** count, which may fluctuate based on several factors. These factors include the efficiency of the recommendation pipeline (e.g., latency), effectiveness of budget pacing, and the type and quality of the ads displayed.

- **Cost-per-engagement**, where engagements may include impressions and clicks.

- **Monetizable engagements**, which measures the effectiveness of ad relevance. A higher value of this metric indicates that the ads are more relevant and engaging to users.

Generally speaking, the primary objective is to improve **monetizable engagements**, indicating an improvement in ad relevance, while maintaining revenue levels or increasing them. This strikes a balance between user objectives (relevant ads) and business objectives (competitive ad auctions).

If revenue and engagements can be increased simultaneously, it is even more advantageous. However, it is crucial to ensure that the rise in cost-per-engagement is proportional to the improvement in ad relevance.

Solution 4.3: What kinds of content should we recommend?

Consumer:

For the consumer, there are two types of content that the system should recommend:

1. **Non-personalized content:** Non-personalized content may include popular content (frequently engaged with or highly rated by a large number of users), trending content (recently gained popularity), and new content (recently added to the platform). Content may also be popular or trending within specific categories, geographies, or topics.

2. **Personalized content:** Content that is specifically tailored to the user's preferences, taking into account their personal traits and previous interactions. This includes content that is both in-network (specific to the user's current network of connections) and out-of-network (specific to the user's interests and preferences).

Other factors to consider include:

- **Diversity:** Provide a diverse range of content to cater to different user interests and avoid creating a filter bubble. A recommender system should cover a broad range of topics and sources.

- **Serendipity:** Refers to the degree to which the system recommends unexpected or surprising content to the user. The system should include some serendipitous recommendations to keep the user engaged and interested.

Revenue:

On the revenue side, the objective is to display the highest scoring ads while evaluating the following factors:

- Positive and negative predicted **engagements**
- **Bids:** Advertisers employ various strategies, such as max bid and target bid, to place their bids (*Bidding Strategies Overview*, n.d.).
- **Budget pacing:** Campaigns may need to be throttled to ensure smooth spending.
- **Boosting:** Certain types of ad products may be subsidized for business purposes.
- **Revenue share:** This is applicable for ad formats such as video ads (*AdSense Revenue Share - Google AdSense Help*, n.d.).
- Additional **bid optimizations**, such as secondary ad objectives (*Create an App Installs Campaign*, n.d.).

In addition to this, contextual information should be considered. For instance, it is necessary to avoid recommending ads that could potentially conflict with or be deemed offensive to the surrounding organic content. It is also crucial to avoid repeatedly showing the same ad or advertiser to users.

Solution 4.4: How to blend different types of content (e.g., in-network, out-of-network, ads)?

There are several ways that one might blend different types of content. Some of these approaches include:

1. **Interleaving:** This involves alternating between different types of content, such as organic and sponsored content. Interleaving can be non-uniform, such as showing a specific amount of organic content per ad. The interleaving can also be weighted based on factors like relevance and popularity. While this approach can help to diversify recommendations, it is often heuristic-driven and may bias towards certain types of content.

2. **Heuristics:** This involves prioritizing and limiting certain types of content based on factors like diversity, seasonality, serendipity, and business priorities. For example, the system may show fewer ads to new users.

3. **Separated:** This approach recommends one type of content before switching to another, or different types of content in distinct parts of the user interface, such as displaying ads at fixed locations. This can provide a smoother user experience and allow for more targeted recommendations.

4. **Clustered:** This approach groups content into clusters based on shared characteristics or features, such as topics. The system then recommends content from each cluster to provide a diverse set of recommendations on different topics. This can help surface new topics that the user may be interested in.

5. **Global ranking:** This approach ranks all types of content as a hybrid list in a single, unified recommendation. Alibaba developed one such technique (Wang et al., 2019b). This can converge towards an optimal balance of user and revenue objectives, but may not be effective for all types of content. For example, ranking organic and sponsored content together can be a challenge, as it requires determining the relative value from organic content (user engagement and retention) from that of ads (revenue).

6. **Reinforcement learning:** Develop a framework for adapting the insertion strategy for different content types (e.g., organic vs ads) based on interactions with users. Bytedance, the makers of TikTok, designed a two-level system which generates an initial list of recommendations, followed by a decision on where to insert ads (Zhao et al., 2020).

Multiple approaches can be combined, such as using a unified model that ranks both in-network and out-of-network content, with heuristics determining how much content from each type is ranked, or with interleaving applied to the result.

Solution 4.5: Describe operational parameters of this recommender system (e.g., latency).

The operational parameters of a recommender system will vary depending on the specific use case. For example, systems that send emails or push notifications have significantly different latency considerations than those that provide recommendations in real-time.

Here are some general operational parameters to consider:

1. **Latency:** The time it takes for the system to generate and deliver recommendations. In a real-time recommender system, low latency is desirable to ensure that users receive timely and relevant recommendations. Latency varies based on system complexity but p99 is typically low 100s of milliseconds due to multiple stages, including candidate, pre-ranking, and full ranking. Pinterest developed a recommender system with a p99 of only 60ms (Eksombatchai et al., 2018). In non real-time systems like email and push notifications, latency is determined by cycle time, which refers to the time it takes to produce recommendations for all users. This can be measured in minutes or even hours.

2. **Throughput:** Refers to the system's ability to process a high volume of requests and deliver recommendations quickly and efficiently. The anticipated throughput of a real-time recommender system depends on several factors such as the platform's active user base, their usage frequency, time of day and year, user interaction patterns, and system design. A figure of several 100s of requests per second for every million users – which refers to recommendation requests sent from clients – is not uncommon.

3. **Number of candidates:** Refers to the total number of items that are considered for recommendation. These candidates are retrieved upstream via candidate generation, and further processed to determine the best items to show to the user. The size varies based on the type and domain of the content, and the content catalog's size: such as tens to hundreds of thousands for ads, or millions for users to follow (Goel et al., 2015). The above-mentioned Pinterest recommender system has a catalog in the billions.

4. **Number of results:** This parameter refers to the actual number of recommended items that are shown to the user. This number is determined by factors such as the user interface and the type of content being recommended. Push notifications, for instance, may only produce one result. A real-time feed (videos, news, posts, etc.) on the

other hand might generate a list of several dozen results for the user to choose from.

High-Level Design

Solution 4.6: Describe the high-level design for this recommender system.

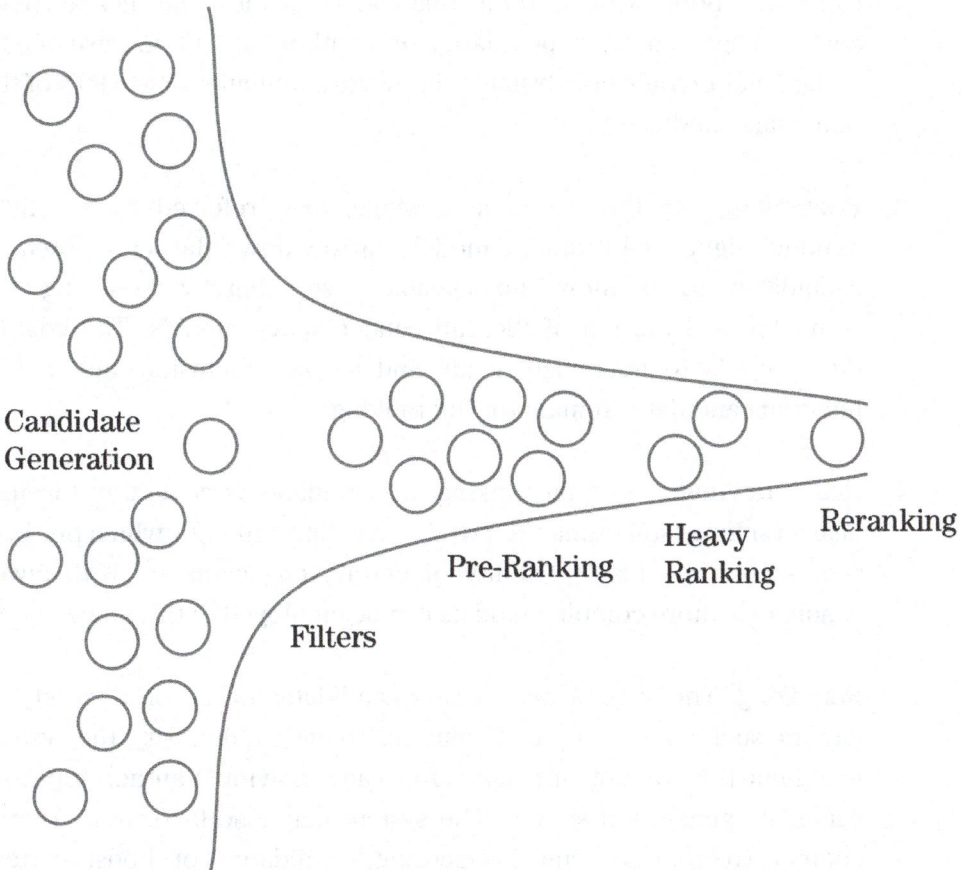

Recommender systems typically use a multistage cascading architecture, or "funnel", with the following components:

1. **Candidate generation:** The recommender system begins by reducing a vast content catalog to a significantly smaller group of candidates to rank. Different candidate generators can be used, each producing its own distinct set of nominees. The candidate generator for YouTube produces few hundred or thousand potential candidates from a catalog

of billions (*Recommendation Systems Overview / Machine Learning*, 2022), a yield typical in the industry due to the number of subsequent filtration and ranking stages. In ads, this process may also be called "selection" as the system identifies candidates based on specific targeting criteria such as demographics and interests.

2. **Filters:** Filters are employed to narrow down the candidates to a relevant subset of items. This involves assessing each item in the candidate pool with criteria related to quality and health (e.g., content's age, language, popularity, and author) and in the case of ads, budget and privacy constraints. This stage eliminates 20% to 90% of the remaining candidates.

3. **Pre-ranking:** At the pre-ranking stage, also referred to as "light ranking", lightweight ranking models narrow down the set of potential candidates to a more manageable size, thereby lessening the computational burden of the subsequent heavy models. The goal of this stage is to maximize recall, and by its conclusion, only a few hundred candidates remain for full ranking.

4. **Heavy ranking:** The final ranking of candidates is generated through heavy ranking, sometimes referred to as "full ranking", which predicts scores such as the probability of certain engagements. With fewer candidates, more complex models can be employed in this stage.

5. **Reranking:** The system may rerank candidates based on a variety of factors, such as diversity or freshness. To ensure diversity, the system may limit the amount of content from any individual author, topic, or candidate generation source. The system may also favor more recent content (freshness), cull low-scoring candidates, or boost certain candidate types. Additionally, reranking can be done for performance reasons, such as with a lightweight model on the client utilizing only local device features. In ads, predictions from heavy ranking must be combined with the advertiser bids along with other elements[2] to be reranked for auction.

---

[2] There are many additional factors to running an ad auction, such as campaign budget and spend-through, revenue share, and other business rules.

Insider Tip

Here is some additional reading on industrial recommender system designs:

- YouTube: Deep Neural Networks for YouTube Recommendations (Covington et al., 2016)
- Baidu: Towards the Next Generation of Query-Ad Matching in Baidu's Sponsored Search (Fan et al., 2019)
- Alibaba: Cascade Ranking for Operational E-commerce Search (Liu et al., 2017)
- Snapchat: Machine Learning for Snapchat Ad Ranking (*Machine Learning for Snapchat Ad Ranking*, 2022)
- Instagram: Core Modeling at Instagram (Bredillet, 2019)

Insider Tip

Read through Google's course on recommender systems (*Introduction | Machine Learning*, 2022), which goes over high-level concepts.

Solution 4.7: How to generate recommendations for new users and items, aka. the cold start problem?

The cold-start problem is characterized by the absence of behavioral interactions. As most recommender system models heavily rely on user-user and user-item engagements, the system may struggle to generate relevant recommendations. To address this issue, there are several techniques that can be employed:

Data collection techniques:

- **New user onboarding flow:** When a new user signs up, they may not have sufficient data for the recommender system to personalize recommendations. Therefore, it's important to have a comprehensive onboarding flow that gathers as much information as possible about the user's preferences, demographics, and interests. The data collected can establish an initial user profile that is partially personalized. This profile can be bootstrapped with behavioral interactions over time to enhance its accuracy.

- **Heuristics:** Based on the limited information available for new users, heuristics can be used to provide recommendations. One approach is to take the average of the embeddings of users or items with similar parameters (*Collaborative Filtering Advantages & Disadvantages | Machine Learning*, 2022). Alternatively, display non-personalized content, such as popular or trending items, and diverse content. As user engagements are collected, gradually transition to more personalized recommendations.

- **Learning period:** Increase the visibility of new items and users on the platform by boosting their presence in recommendations. This boost can be decayed over time or other signals, such as engagement levels. While this method won't directly help with the user onboarding flow, it aids in making new users and items more discoverable.

- **Contextual bandits:** A systematic approach that selects items in a sequential manner, taking into account contextual information of the user and item (Li et al., 2010, Zhou & Brunskill, 2016). The algorithm adjusts its strategy based on user feedback, to maximize long-term user engagements. For example, the Upper Confidence Bound (UCB) algorithm balances exploration and exploitation by recommending items that have the highest upper confidence bound on reward given the available context – historical and context features of the user and item. As users interact more with the system, the algorithm gains more certainty about the users' preferences and can provide increasingly personalized recommendations.

Modeling techniques:

- **Fallback models:** These models provide recommendations when there isn't enough data available to employ the primary model. The system can monitor feature coverage fed into a model and if it is lower than a threshold, it can have fallback options that are less accurate but only use high-coverage or dense features, such as contextual features. Instagram (Bredillet, 2019) and Facebook (He et al., 2014) have applied this technique to recommend content for new users.

- **Collaborative models:** Interpolate between content-forward modeling techniques in cold start, such as collaborative topic regression with

Latent Dirichlet Allocation (LDA) (Wang & Blei, 2011) or collaborative deep learning with stacked denoising autoencoders (Wang et al., 2015), and conventional modeling techniques when historical features are available. One drawback of this approach has been the complex formulation of the objective function.

- **Hybrid models:** Combine user behavioral information and latent content information using deep learning approaches. Examples include DeepMusic (Oord et al., 2013) and YouTube (Covington et al., 2016), which use hybrid methods for generating recommendations. Heterogeneous information networks, such as TwHIN (El-Kishky et al., 2022), can improve cold-start for candidate generation by incorporating diverse types of data.

- **Dropout:** Force the model to apply dropout, reconstructing input from a corrupted version. The aim is to train a model that can still produce accurate representations even when parts of the input data are missing. DropoutNet (Volkovs et al., 2017) is an example of a model that utilizes this approach, improving its performance in cold-start scenarios.

Data Collection

Solution 4.8: What datasets do we need to collect to build this system?

A recommender system typically requires **user-item interaction data**, such as clicks, purchases, or follows, in order to make recommendations. This data is used to train models that can predict a user's preferences and suggest items they are likely to be interested in. The more data that is available, the more accurate the recommendations can be. Additionally, contextual features, such as demographic data about users, and item metadata, such as category or freshness, can also be used to improve the recommendations.

Apart from this fundamental dataset, other important datasets in a recommender system include:

- **Candidate generation:** For candidate generation algorithms, the training data typically consists of positive examples, or instances where the correct answer is known, and negative examples, or instances where the correct answer is not in the candidate list. Since user-item interactions are typically very sparse, candidate generators do not train on all of the negatives, or only on the positives. Instead, candidate generation algorithms conduct what is known as negative sampling. Negative sampling involves selecting a small subset of items that are not relevant to use as negative examples. The goal of negative sampling is to provide a representative sample of negative items to optimize the training procedure.

- **Pre-ranking:** Pre-ranking models typically engage in knowledge distillation. For knowledge distillation, the training data typically consists of the inputs to the model, along with the outputs produced by the teacher model (e.g., the heavy ranking model) for those inputs. During training, the student model is optimized to produce outputs that are similar to the teacher's outputs.

  Unlike in heavy ranker training, the pre-ranking model does not need ground truth labels from user engagements. As a result, there are more options for collecting the data to train the model. One approach is to sample from all of the input candidates to the pre-ranking model and ask the heavy ranker to score them all offline. By doing this, the heavy ranking model can score all the candidates, including those that were not served to users. This powerful approach not only facilitates various model training and evaluation techniques, but also forms the basis for a robust counterfactual reasoning framework, which we discuss next.

- **Counterfactual reasoning framework:** Counterfactual reasoning is a technique to estimate the effect of changing one or more variables in a system. In the context of a recommender system, this means estimating how a user would have behaved if a different set of candidates were presented, and using that estimate to minimize regret.

  Counterfactual reasoning is particularly valuable in recommender systems as there are numerous steps through which candidates may be downranked, boosted, or filtered out. For instance:

  1. Heuristics used to merge and prune candidate generator outputs.
  2. Application of various filters, such as exclusion of content that is old, avoiding consecutive display of items by the same author, language matching, and so on.

3. Ranking performance of the pre-ranking model.
4. Rules around boosting some types of content over others.
5. Candidates may be reranked for diversity or reasons.

Traditionally, improving a recommender system involved conducting a series of online A/B experiments to make individual component tweaks. However, online experiments can be time-consuming and limited in number, requiring prioritization.

Instead, the counterfactual reasoning framework can be employed offline to tackle this challenge. One approach is to allow all generated candidates for a sample of requests to survive until heavy ranking and annotate each step where a candidate is scored, reranked, or filtered out. Mark the candidates ultimately served. Since all candidates receive a score from the heavy ranker, it's possible to compute the amount of regret that each heuristic, filter, or model contributed to the system. This enables rapid offline experimentation.

While the heavy ranker cannot be considered flawless as it only serves as an estimation of actual user engagement, this framework can help pinpoint potentially fruitful paths for improving the system. These directions can then be validated through online A/B experiments to either support or disprove the hypotheses.

Solution 4.9: How to collect these datasets?

Collecting training data for recommender systems can be a challenging task. The data must be representative of the users and items, it must be large enough to train a robust model, and it must be constructed in a way that minimizes the impact of bias. Let's examine some data collection techniques in several stages of the recommender system.

Candidate generation:

In the candidate generation stage, negative sampling is used in place of optimizing against all items, which is too expensive, or only positive items, which may result in the overprediction of negative items (a phenomenon called "folding"). Negative sampling generates items that are unlikely to be engaged by the user, assisting training algorithms in distinguishing between positive and negative items. Here are some techniques for negative sampling:

1. **Uniform sampling:** Randomly selects items that are not in the user's history as negative samples (Rendle et al., 2009). It is simple and easy to implement, but it may not force the model to effectively distinguish between positive items and negatives that resemble positives.

2. **Popularity-based sampling:** Samples negative items based on their popularity, where less popular items are preferred over highly popular items (Lerer et al., 2019). It can help models differentiate between niche and well-known items, but may result in over-penalization of popular items.

3. **Popularity-dampened sampling:** Dampens the popularity of negative items when sampling (*What Is Candidate Sampling*, n.d.). It can be useful in promoting the discovery of less popular or less known items, but it may also miss some popular items that are still relevant to the user. An example of this is node2vec (Grover & Leskovec, 2016).

4. **Faraway negative sampling:** Selects negative items that are dissimilar to positive items, or items with lower scores. Although this approach seems intuitive by treating nearby nodes as positives and distant ones as negatives, it may also produce uninformative negative samples, much like random sampling.

5. **Hard negative sampling:** This is a popular contemporary approach. Selects negative items that are similar to positive items, or those that are likely to be relevant, such as items with high scores (Zhang et al., 2013). It can help to avoid recommending irrelevant items that are similar to positive items, but it can also be prone to false negatives. There are a number of techniques for this. For instance:

   ○ A common technique is to sample negative examples in a way that gives higher model scores a greater likelihood of being selected. Examples of this are PinSage (Ying et al., 2018) and RotatE (Sun et al., 2019).

   ○ Monte Carlo Negative Sampling (MCNS) (Yang et al., 2020) is a technique that utilizes a random walk to identify negative samples through a balance of exploration and exploitation. The negative samples are selected in proportion to their predicted model scores.

- Generative Adversarial Networks (GAN) define an adversarial learning framework for selecting negatives. KBGAN (Cai & Wang, 2018), for instance, involves using a softmax-based model as the generator to sample negatives likely to confuse the discriminator, and a margin-loss based model as the discriminator. However, this may be inefficient for generating a substantial number of negative samples.

Pre-ranking:

When constructing a training dataset for a pre-ranking (light ranking) model using the knowledge distillation strategy, there are several options to consider:

1. **Biased:** Sample candidates that survive the pre-ranking stage, or from served candidates.

  - Pros:
    - Easy to collect, since these candidates are logged downstream.
    - Allows the model to learn from stronger candidates.

  - Cons:
    - The model will fail to distinguish weaker candidates.
    - Dataset does not accurately represent the input data the model receives.
    - Creates an unfavorable feedback loop for the pre-ranking model.

2. **Uniform:** Sample input candidates completely at random.

  - Pros:
    - Provides an accurate representation of the input data.
    - Most diverse in terms of the training data the model encounters.

  - Cons:

- Inability to evaluate ranking metrics, which are typically the most informative for pre-ranking models.
- Limitations on training options, such as listwise ranking methods, or training on top-n pointwise labels.

3. **Request-level:** Sample all input candidates for a given request or query.

- Pros:
  - Provides an accurate representation of the input data.
  - Unconstrained in terms of training options, evaluation metrics, counterfactual reasoning, and so on.

- Cons:
  - Request diversity will suffer, particularly when the number of candidates per request is large.
  - The model may overtrain on sub-populations of weak or clickbaity candidates that have little representation in the final results.
  - Often the most challenging method to implement in production systems.

In practice, it may be beneficial to use a combination of these approaches to construct a more comprehensive training dataset. For example, the uniform dataset can be used for training, while the request-level dataset can be used for evaluation. Alternatively, the request-level dataset can be subsampled to boost request diversity or to reduce the incidence of spurious candidates. It's important to consider the trade-offs of each approach and how they impact the performance of the model.

Ranking:

In a heavy ranking model, the training loop typically involves a stream of data from candidates that are served to users. This data is then fed back into the model, causing it to update and improve its ranking algorithm over time. When it comes to collecting and using training data for heavy ranking models, there are several important considerations:

- **Update frequency:** Data freshness is an important factor to consider when collecting training data for ranking models. There are several ways to update ranking models, including batch, online, or continuous updates. See the ML Infrastructure Design – Offline section for a more detailed description of these options. Depending on the update method used, the data collection process may differ. For batch updates, the data collection process typically involves running offline jobs to aggregate logs and other data into a training repository, which is then used to train the model. In contrast, continuous updates require a continuous stream of data to be sent back to the model in real-time, which can involve more complex data processing and storage infrastructure.

- **Delayed feedback:** In many real-time systems, user interactions are only labeled after a possibly long and random delay (Ktena et al., 2019). For example, in a recommender system, a user may not click on an item until seconds or minutes later. In an extreme case, ad products such as mobile app promotions will not have labels for days or even weeks (*Machine Learning for Snapchat Ad Ranking*, 2022) (if ever! See Advanced ML Questions – Learning Without Labels). Naive strategies which consider any data point a negative example until a positive label becomes available tend to underpredict those instances. There are several strategies for combating this problem which are discussed in the Advanced ML Questions section.

- **Negative sampling:** The number of positive samples is typically much smaller than the overall pool of served candidates, leading to a severe class imbalance problem. For example, in a mobile app promotion scenario, the probability of an ad impression leading to an installation on the user's device may be <0.01%. This class imbalance can lead to a training dataset that is skewed towards negative examples, which can negatively impact the performance of the model. To address this issue, sampling strategies can be employed during the data collection process, which we described earlier in ML Fundamentals – Datasets. Oversampling and downsampling are commonly used methods to balance the class distribution. Another approach is cost-sensitive training. Negative sampling is often employed in practice. Read more about negative sampling techniques in the preceding question.

- **Explore / exploit:** In a heavy ranker, the model only has access to labels for items that are served to users. This creates a potential feedback loop issue, where the model gets to select its own training data. This can lead to various biases in the dataset, such as position bias and serving bias, which can affect the performance of the model over the long-term. To mitigate these biases, it is important to incorporate some level of exploration into the training process. These problems and solutions are discussed in greater detail in the following questions.

Solution 4.10: What sorts of biases might be found in the dataset?

There are various biases that can be found in a training dataset for recommender systems. Some of them are as follows:

1. **Position bias:** Occurs when the items at the top of the list are more likely to be clicked or selected by users, leading to an overemphasis on the importance of those items. This can happen because users may not scroll down to see other items or may believe that the items at the top are more relevant.

2. **Presentation bias:** Occurs when the presentation of the items influences the user's decision (Yue et al., 2010). For example, if certain items are presented with more attractive images or descriptions, they may receive more clicks or engagement than other items.

3. **Trust bias:** Occurs when users have a high level of trust in the recommender system, leading them to only consider the first few results or to only select particular items recommended by the system (O'Brien & Keane, 2006).

4. **Serving bias:** Also known as algorithmic bias, this is the tendency of a system to recommend items similar to those that have historically performed well (e.g., been clicked or consumed), in an attempt to exploit the training data. This can lead to the perpetuation of biases in the model, as it may not accurately reflect the full range of user preferences and experiences.

Solution 4.11: How to mitigate serving bias?

Recommender systems are updated in a training loop to improve prediction accuracy and adjust to evolving user preferences. However, this creates a feedback loop where the model selects its own training data, leading to serving bias. This causes the model to potentially learn from noise and fail to explore promising candidates.

This exploitation/exploration trade-off is a critical concept in recommender systems. To create an unbiased dataset, items may be uniformly shown to users; however, excessive exploration results in a poor user experience.

There are several ways to mitigate serving bias in recommender systems. Here are some popular ones:

1. **ε-greedy exploration:** One simple way to mitigate serving bias is to add some random data to the training dataset. The ε-greedy exploration strategy recommends the item with the score with a probability of 1-ε, while uniformly selecting other items at random with a probability of ε. Despite its simplicity, this approach often outperforms more advanced methods like bandit approaches in industrial recommender systems.

2. **Contextual bandits:** Thompson sampling and UCB (Upper Confidence Bound) and Thompson sampling are two contextual bandit algorithms used to address the exploration-exploitation dilemma. Thompson sampling is a probabilistic approach that selects items by randomly sampling from the posterior distribution of the model prediction and selects the items with the highest values. UCB selects items with the highest upper confidence bound, which it computes by adding an uncertainty estimate to the model's prediction, thereby promoting exploration. These approaches have been adopted by Twitter (Guo et al., 2020), Yahoo (Li et al., 2010), and Google (Chen et al., 2019a).

3. **Causal inference:** Causal inference methods aim to estimate the causal effects of alternate actions on outcomes of interest. In the context of recommender systems, this can involve using randomization strategies to obtain accurate counterfactual estimates and performing importance sampling to reweight the data. Microsoft applied such techniques for the ad prediction (Bottou et al., 2013) task.

4. **Learning period:** Boosting new items such as new users, ad campaigns, products, etc. with a decay based on time or other signals like engagements can help to mitigate serving bias effects on the cold start problem. This involves giving higher weights to newer data and gradually decreasing the weight over time. However, this approach

does not address other problems caused by exploitation, such as learning from spurious signals or a lack of diversity or exploration of content.

Theoretically, ranking models should be trained solely on unbiased datasets. However, in reality, the exploration dataset may be too small and may also contain other types of biases depending on the sampling strategy employed. In practice, during training, models often learn from a combination of exploration and exploitation data.

Solution 4.12: What about position bias?

These are some effective ways to mitigate position bias in ranking models for recommender systems:

1. Adding randomness to the position of items can help mitigate position bias during the development stage of a new ranking model. By **randomly shuffling** the positions of the items in the recommendations, the model can learn to identify relevant items independent of their position. However, this approach may degrade user experience.

2. **Add positional features:** Incorporate positional features (Chapelle & Zhang, 2009), such as the position of an item in the list, into the model (Zinkevich, 2023). These features can help capture the effect of position bias. During serving, set all items to have position of 1 to negate the impact of position.

3. **Model position bias:** Develop a model that accounts for position bias by modeling item examination and relevance separately, and then applies position bias as a normalizer or regularizer. This approach assumes that item examination depends on the position, while relevance depends on the context and item. Position bias can be modeled globally (same for all all queries), segmented based on query type, or generalized (train a model to predict position bias). Then, the ranking model can be trained to optimize the inverse propensity weighted score to account for the effect of position bias. See examples from Microsoft (Richardson et al., 2007, Craswell & Taylor, 2008), TripAdvisor (Li, 2020), and Google (Wang et al., 2018, Wang et al., 2016b).

4. **Multi-task model:** Incorporate features contributing to position bias as a wide component in a multi-task ranking model, where each task optimizes for different objectives of the ranking. This can help the model learn to account for the effect of position bias in each task without relying on random experiments to obtain the propensity score. See how YouTube implements this approach (Zhao et al., 2019).

5. **Adversarial training:** Define an auxiliary task that predicts the position of items in the training data. Later, during the backpropagation phase, negate the gradient passed into the model to combat the influence of the position feature on model predictions. This approach is commonly implemented in domain adaptation (Tzeng et al., 2017) and machine learning fairness (Beutel et al., 2017) tasks.

Candidate Generation

Solution 4.13: Where do candidates come from? List potential sources.

Candidate generation in recommender systems is the process of selecting a set of items that could be recommended to a user. There are several sources from which candidates can be generated, including non-personalized sources, personalized in-network sources, and personalized out-of-network sources.

Non-personalized sources:

Non-personalized sources are those that are not specific to the user's interests and preferences. These sources can include:

- **Popular content:** Items that are frequently engaged with or highly rated by a large number of users.

- **Trending content:** Items that have recently gained popularity and are being engaged with or rated more often than usual.

- **New content:** Items that have been recently added to the platform and have not yet been rated or engaged with by many users.

- **Trending content for certain areas:** Items that are trending within specific categories, geographic locations, or topics.

Personalized in-network sources:

Personalized in-network sources are those that are specific to the user's current network of connections and activities. These sources can include:

- **In-network content:** Items that are generated by users or businesses that the user is currently following or connected to.

- **Historical content:** Items that the user has previously consumed or engaged with, such as items they have rated highly or added to their favorites.

Personalized out-of-network sources:

Personalized out-of-network sources are those that are specific to the user's interests and preferences but are not necessarily generated by their current network of connections. These sources can include:

- **Content-based filtering:** Items that are similar to items that the user has previously interacted with or shown interest in. This can be based on characteristics such as genre, keywords, topics, media, or other metadata.

- **Collaborative filtering:** Items that are recommended based on the similarity of the user's preferences to those of other users in the system. This can be based on items that other users have interacted with or shown interest in that are similar to the user's own interests.

By default, when discussing candidate generation in recommender systems without specifying the sources, they are referring to **Personalized Out-of-Network** sources.

Solution 4.14: What are the benefits and drawbacks of each source?

Here are some benefits and drawbacks of each source.

Non-personalized sources:

Benefits:

- Can provide a good starting point for new users who have not yet provided any personal information or ratings.
- Can be helpful for users who are looking for popular or trending items in general, regardless of their specific interests.

Drawbacks:

- May not be tailored to the user's specific interests, resulting in less relevant recommendations.
- Can be biased towards certain types of content or popular trends, leading to limited diversity in recommendations.

Personalized in-network sources:

Benefits:

- Can be highly relevant to the user's specific interests and preferences, as they are based on the user's current connections and activities.
- Can provide opportunities for discovery of new items and users within the user's existing network.

Drawbacks:

- Can be limited by the user's current network, resulting in less diverse recommendations.
- May not be effective for new users who do not yet have a well-established network.

Personalized out-of-network sources:

Benefits:

- Can provide highly personalized recommendations that are tailored to the user's specific interests and preferences.
- Can be effective for users who are looking to discover new items and expand their interests beyond their current network.

Drawbacks:

- Can require significant user data and processing power to generate recommendations based on user similarity or content-based filtering.

- May result in a "filter bubble" effect where users are only recommended items that are similar to what they have interacted with in the past, limiting diversity in recommendations.

Solution 4.15: Describe how candidate generation works at a high-level.

Here are the steps of candidate generation for recommender systems:

1. **Fetch sources:** The first step in candidate generation is to fetch sources that can act as seeds for generating candidates. These sources could be user embeddings, content, and other users that have been recently engaged with. For example, a recommender system for a music streaming service might fetch sources such as the user's listening history, songs on the user's playlists, and artists that the user follows.

2. **Generate candidates:** The next step is to use one or more candidate generation algorithms to generate candidates. There are various algorithms that can be used for candidate generation, including graph-based algorithms, deep neural network techniques, and many others.

3. **Filter candidates:** After generating candidates, the next step is to merge and prune them so that a reasonable number survive to the pre-ranking stage. This is important because too many candidates can lead to longer processing times and reduced recommendation quality.

Candidates can be generated from different sources using different algorithms, making this stage many-to-many. For example, a graph-based algorithm might be used to generate candidates based on songs the user recently listened to, while a deep neural network technique might be used to generate candidates based on artists that the user follows.

For example, Twitter applies dozens of combinations to generate candidates for their recommender systems (*The-Algorithm/CR-Mixer*, n.d.).

Solution 4.16: What are some algorithms for generating candidates?

At a high-level, candidate generation can be performed with several different approaches, including:

1. **Neighborhood-based methods:** These methods leverage user preferences between items or other users to generate candidates. Examples of neighborhood-based methods are Slope One and Pearson R. Slope One is an item-based method that predicts the rating of an item by considering the differences in ratings between pairs of items that users have rated. Pearson R is a user-based method that computes the correlation coefficient between the user and other users to identify similar users and recommend items based on their ratings. These methods do not learn embeddings.

2. **Graph-based methods:** These methods model the relationships between items or users as a graph and use graph algorithms to generate candidates. For instance, a graph-based approach might identify similar items or users based on the connections between them and generate candidates accordingly. There are numerous approaches for this:

   - Amazon (Smith & Linden, 2017) has applied content-based filtering based on association rule mining (Agrawal et al., 1993), or co-visitation counts, for many years.
   - YouTube did the same (Davidson et al., 2010).
   - Twitter leveraged the concept of hubs and authorities in a graph structure (Sharma et al., 2016).

   There are also graph-based methods that produce user and item embeddings, known as "graph embeddings", which we will explore in the next answer.

3. **Latent methods:** These methods use algorithms like matrix factorization and deep neural networks (DNNs) to generate candidates. These methods capture latent relationships that are not directly observable in the data and use them to make predictions. There are numerous approaches, such as:

   - Yahoo (Grbovic et al., 2015) applied neural language modeling techniques for product recommendations.

- PinSage (Ying et al., 2018), developed by Pinterest, is a Graph Convolutional Network (GCN) which aggregates feature information from local graph neighborhoods (such as a user's one-hop neighborhood) using neural networks.
- Google (Yi et al., 2019) uses a two-tower approach to generate item recommendations. We will explore this type of technique in greater depth below.

There are also hybrid approaches, such as the PinSage example above, which combine both content-based information and graph structure.

Solution 4.17: How might you develop an embedding approach to retrieve candidates?

We will now examine three embedding techniques that utilize the methods mentioned earlier: one that utilizes matrix factorization, another that makes use of deep neural networks, and a third that employs graph-based methods.

Matrix factorization:

Through much of the 2010s, a popular approach for candidate generation was matrix factorization (MF) (Koren, 2008). For example, Facebook implemented MF for item recommendation in 2015 (Ilic & Kabiljo, 2015). Matrix factorization methods learn embeddings for users and items by decomposing the rating matrix into low-rank matrices.

One technique for computing the embeddings is through **singular value decomposition (SVD)**, where a low-rank approximation is used to represent the user-item interaction matrix in a lower-dimensional space while minimizing information loss. It works by decomposing the original matrix into three separate matrices – a left, right, and singular value matrix – where the product of these matrices approximates the original matrix. The left matrix is regarded as the embeddings.

Another approach is **weighted matrix factorization**, where an objective function consists of two terms: one for minimizing the error over observed pairs and another for minimizing the error over unobserved pairs. By incorporating the weights into the objective function, the weighted matrix factorization approach can handle datasets with a high degree of sparsity.

Here is an objective function for weighted matrix factorization, where A is the sparse user-item interaction matrix, $\langle U_i, V_j \rangle$ is an inner product of the user and item embeddings, and w_0 is a hyperparameter that balances the two terms.

$$\min_{U \in \mathbb{R}^{m \times d}, \ V \in \mathbb{R}^{n \times d}} \sum_{(i,j) \in \text{obs}} (A_{ij} - \langle U_i, V_j \rangle)^2 + w_0 \sum_{(i,j) \notin \text{obs}} (\langle U_i, V_j \rangle)^2$$

Optimization techniques such as **stochastic gradient descent (SGD)** and **weighted alternating least squares (WALS)** are used to optimize the embeddings. WALS is an optimization technique that alternates between updating the user and item embeddings.

MF techniques have faced a challenge in effectively incorporating user and item features. Certain methods, including SVDFeature (Chen et al., 2012) and the Factorization Machine (Rendle, 2010), have been developed to capture up to second-order feature interactions.

Deep neural networks:

Recent studies have demonstrated the effectiveness of deep neural networks (DNNs) in improving recommendation accuracy over MF techniques (He et al., 2017). Due to their highly nonlinear nature, DNNs are capable of capturing complex feature interactions more efficiently than conventional MF methods.

There are several types of DNNs that can be used to generate embeddings in recommender systems, popular ones including sequence models, graph neural networks, and Two Towers.

- **Sequence models**, such as neural language models, can be used to create user and item embeddings for candidate generation. By treating a user's interaction history as a sequence of "words" (i.e., items), a neural language model can learn embeddings that capture the sequential dependencies between items and the user preferences. Recent advancements have led to the development of models that can leverage attention mechanisms and transformers to generate embeddings. Furthermore, these models can incorporate user and item features in their model structure, enabling them to learn more accurate embeddings that capture both the temporal and contextual aspects of the data. This technique has been applied at AirBnb (Grbovic & Cheng, 2018), Criteo (Vasile et al., 2016), and Etsy (Zhao et al., 2018). A related method was adopted by Yahoo for news embeddings (Okura et al., 2017).

- **Graph neural networks**, such as Graph Convolutional Networks (GCNs), are a type of network designed to handle graph-structured data. GCNs learn to gather and combine feature information from local neighborhoods of nodes by performing convolutions recursively. A convolution operation aggregates feature information from a node's immediate neighbors and transforms it into a dense representation. By stacking layers of convolutions, graph information can be propagated across distant parts of the graph, allowing GCNs to capture both local and global graph structure. Unlike purely content-based DNNs, GCNs can leverage both content information and graph structure to generate user and item embeddings. PinSage and PinnerSage (Pal et al., 2020) are examples of this.

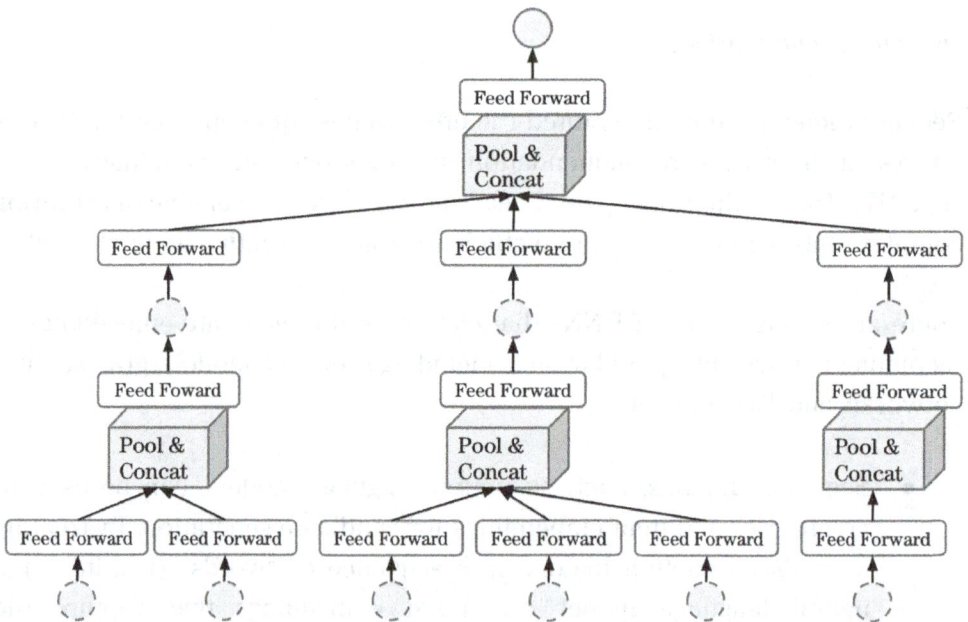

Note. Visualization of a single node's embedding in a depth-2 GCN. Each dashed node represents a neighboring node in the graph. The node's neighbors are processed incrementally through convolution operations. Each convolution operation consists of a pooling step, a concatenation, and a feed forward network.

> ### Insider Tip
>
> For a survey of graph neural networks, read (Wu et al., 2019).

- The **Two Tower architecture**, also referred to as SplitNet or vector-product models, divides a DNN into two sub-networks that process user and item features separately, and there are no crossing features between them. The output of each network is a fixed-size vector that represents the user and item embeddings, respectively. The score can be computed with different similarity functions, such as an inner product or hadamard product. The Two Tower design offers a notable advantage in that it allows for the independent embedding of new users and items. This is made possible by the isolation of the user and item towers from each other, which is particularly useful in scenarios where there is a constant influx of new users and items. This approach has been adopted by Google (Yi et al., 2019) and Twitter (Wong, 2022) for candidate generation.

> ### Insider Tip
>
> Here are a few other DNN-based approaches for further reading:
>
> - SDNE (Wang et al., 2016a) is an example that incorporates high-order proximity in the node embedding objective.
> - More advanced methods use stacked denoising autoencoders to learn node embeddings (Cao et al., 2016).
> - Self-supervised techniques train graph encoders (graph neural networks) through actions such as perturbing and reconstructing the graph (Wu et al., 2023a).

Graph embeddings:

Graph embeddings, also known as network embeddings, is a technique used to convert the nodes of large networks into compact low-dimensional representations.

One such approach is **SimClusters** (Sataluri et al., 2020), which is a community-based graph embedding approach developed by Twitter. These embeddings are used extensively for candidate generation throughout Twitter. In SimClusters, the embedding dimensions are represented by communities with similar followers; they represent groups of users with similar interests or preferences. It works this in this sequence:

1. Follow Graph: Create a follower-followee (also known as consumer-producer) matrix, also known as the Follow Graph.

2. Producer-Producer Similarity: From the Follow Graph, create a producer-producer matrix, computing the cosine similarity between pairs of producers in the Follow Graph based on the fraction overlap between their followers.

3. KnownFor matrix: Densify the Follow Graph into k communities by applying the Metropolis-Hastings algorithm, yielding the KnownFor matrix. This is a lower-dimensional representation of the producer-producer matrix, and it represents the similarity between a producer and the followers of a particular community.

4. User embeddings: to compute user embeddings, multiply the Follow Graph with the KnownFor matrix. They represent the similarity between a user and each community (specifically, the followers of that community), based on who that user follows. These embeddings are also known as user "InterestedIn" embeddings.

5. Item embeddings: compute by aggregating the InterestedIn vector of each user who likes the item (e.g., a tweet). Other interactions can also be used.

Insider Tip

Read more details about Twitter's SimClusters algorithm on github at (*The-Algorithm/src/scala/com/twitter/simclusters_v2*, n.d.).

Another popular technique is using **Heterogeneous Information Networks (HINs)** (Shi et al., 2016). HINs allow us to model networks that contain multiple types of entities (e.g., users, items) and various types of relations (behavioral interactions) among them. In such networks, each entity and relation is represented by an embedding vector.

To generate graph embeddings, the HIN employs a scoring function to triples consisting of the source entity, relation type, and target entity. One such approach is TransE (Bordes et al., 2013), where the scoring function takes the source entity's embedding, translates it by the relation's embedding, and scores it with the target entity's embedding via an inner product. In other words, the scoring function tries to capture the similarity between the embeddings of the entities connected by the relation.

To train the model, the HIN employs a pairwise margin-based ranking criterion. The goal of this criterion is to differentiate between positive observed triples and negative unobserved triples. Negative samples are created by corrupting one of the entities in the positive triple. Twitter has successfully applied HINs (El-Kishky et al., 2022) to represent user and item embeddings for several candidate generation tasks.

There are other graph embedding methods, such as LINE by Microsoft (Tang et al., 2015) which maximizes the probability of observing first- and second-order edges in a graph, given their embeddings. All of these techniques provide scalable and effective ways to embed the nodes of a network into a lower-dimensional space.

Solution 4.18: At scale, candidate generation cannot score every potential candidate in real-time. What are some ways to solve this problem?

When dealing with large-scale recommender systems, it is often infeasible to score every potential candidate in real-time. To address this issue, here are some potential solutions:

- One popular approach is to use **approximate nearest neighbors (ANN)** to efficiently find the top candidates for each user. ANN is a technique that enables efficient searching of high-dimensional spaces by approximating the distances between points. Here are a few popular methods for implementing ANN:

    - **Locality Sensitive Hashing (LSH):** Efficiently search high-dimensional spaces by hashing similar items to the same bucket with high probability, while data points with low similarity are likely to fall into different buckets. One popular technique involves random projections, called SimHash. SimHash works by generating binary hash codes based on the sign of the inner product between random vectors and the item vector.

- o **Inverted File Index with Product Quantization (IVFPQ):** Designed to handle high dimensional data by compressing and quantizing the data into compact codes. The data is first partitioned into subspaces. Each subspace is quantized by clustering to find centroids, and the data points are assigned to the nearest centroid's codeword for each subspace. The resulting codes are stored in an inverted file index. To search, find the nearest neighbors using the inverted file index by applying the product quantizer to the query vector.

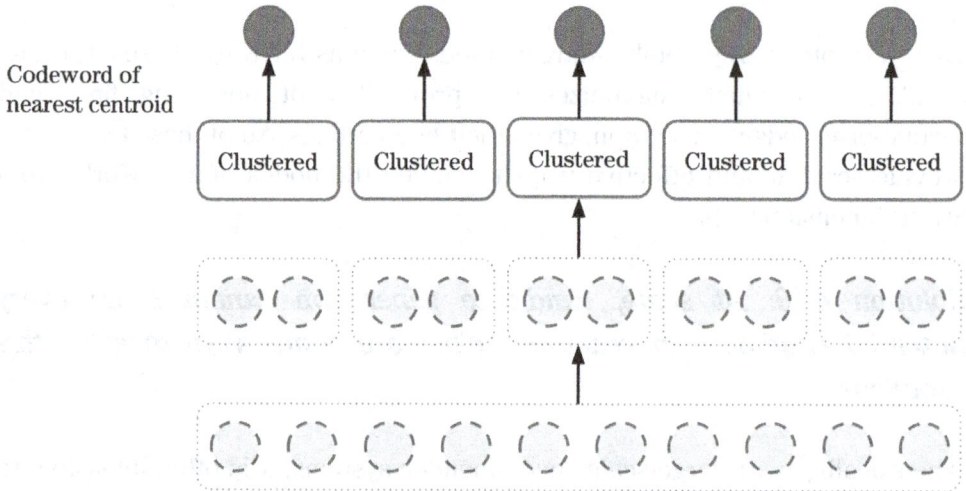

Codeword of
nearest centroid

| Clustered | Clustered | Clustered | Clustered | Clustered |

Note. Illustration of product quantization. The original vector is partitioned into subspaces, each subspace is clustered, and the centroids of sub-clusters are represented by codewords.

- o **Hierarchical Navigable Small World (HNSW):** Constructs a graph of high-dimensional items with a high clustering coefficient, meaning that nearby nodes tend to be connected to each other, and low diameter, which is the shortest path length between any two nodes, allowing for efficient traversal. In HNSW, the graph is constructed in a hierarchical manner, with each layer representing a different level of resolution (Malkov

& Yashunin, 2020). The top layer contains a small number of highly connected nodes, which are connected to a larger number of less connected nodes in the layer below. This allows for efficient and accurate nearest-neighbor search.

Insider Tip

For an illustration of clustering coefficient, diameter, and how navigable small worlds are constructed, watch the NetSci 10-1 Small World Model Youtube video (*NetSci 10-1 Small World Model*, 2020).

- Another approach is to perform exhaustive scoring offline, **precomputing** and storing a list of the top candidates for each user or item. This can be effective for related-item recommendations, where the pool of candidate items is comparatively smaller and more stable.

Solution 4.19: How to index newly created content?

In many instances, it can be quite straightforward to incorporate new content into the system without the need for model retraining.

- **Matrix factorization:** The matrix factorization approach enables the system to quickly generate an embedding for new users or items. With a small number of behavioral interactions, the system can just solve the following equation, which corresponds to one iteration in WALS (*Collaborative Filtering Advantages & Disadvantages / Machine Learning*, 2022):

$$\min_{v_i \in \mathbb{R}^d} \|A_i - U v_i\|$$

where A is the user-item matrix, U is the embedding matrix, and v_i is the embedding for the new user or item.

- **DNNs:** The Two Tower approach offers a particularly seamless solution, as passing the new user or item features through the corresponding tower in the DNN and saving the resulting embedding is all that is required. This architecture is purposefully designed to function irrespective of user and item interdependence.

- **Graph embeddings:** In the SimClusters approach, the process is also straightforward since the communities are already predetermined. For users, all that is required is the collection of their follow graph and its multiplication with the existing KnownFor matrix to produce the user's InterestedIn embedding. It is not essential to retrain the KnownFor matrix that represents all communities frequently, since user interests in aggregate do not change rapidly. For items, the process is equally straightforward - one just needs to aggregate the InterestedIn embeddings of the users that have engaged with the item.

Solution 4.20: Suppose we need to limit the number of candidates that survive to ranking. How should we merge and prune candidates from different algorithms?

There are several ways to merge and prune candidates that are generated from several different candidate generation sources and algorithms.

1. **Heuristics:** Use a heuristic to limit the number of candidates from each algorithm or to prefer some algorithms over others. This can be based on the performance of the algorithms on a test set or some prior knowledge about the algorithms. However, the drawback of this approach is that it may not take into account the relative quality of the candidates across algorithms or the overlap between the candidates from different algorithms.

2. **Thresholding:** Adjust the number of candidates from each algorithm based on a threshold defined by the scoring function from that algorithm. However, this approach still does not take into account the relative quality of the candidates across algorithms.

3. **Universal score:** Develop a universal score by calibrating the scoring functions across all algorithms. This involves normalizing the scores from each algorithm based on a teacher model like the heavy ranker prediction. The advantage of this approach is that it takes into account all algorithms while selecting the best candidates from each algorithm. However, some may argue that the scoring function of the candidate generator should not be optimized for ranking. Another drawback is that recalibration can create additional work for ML practitioners.

4. **Regression:** Perform a linear regression based on the scoring function of each algorithm. The dependent variable can be based on a teacher model like the heavy ranker prediction. One drawback of this approach is that most candidates will not be scored by all algorithms. Another drawback is that introducing new algorithms can be slowed down as a result of this approach.

5. **Light ranking:** A fifth approach is to send all the candidates to a very fast light ranker (pre-ranker). The pre-ranker uses more complex models and features that better capture context and user preferences. However, there are drawbacks to this approach. The pre-ranker might be optimized for ranking and not effective in ensuring diversity, which is one aim of using multiple candidate generation algorithms. Moreover, it may not be capable of handling all candidates generated by all algorithms.

Solution 4.21: Why not use the candidate generator to rank items?

While candidate generators do compute a score or similarity measure between items, it is not recommended to rely on them for ranking candidates. Here are some reasons why:

- **Multiple candidate generators** may be used in a system, and their scores may not be directly comparable. Thus, a separate ranking model may be necessary to combine the scores and generate a final ranking.

- The ranking task involves considering a smaller pool of candidates, which allows for the use of **more complex models** and features that better capture context and user preferences. This can lead to more accurate and personalized recommendations.

- The **scoring function** used by the candidate generator may not be optimized for the ranking task, which requires taking into account factors such as optimizing for multiple objectives (such as clicks and likes) and reducing negative engagements. A separate ranking model can be designed to address these factors and optimize for the ranking objectives.

Pre-Ranking

Solution 4.22: What is a pre-ranking (or light ranking) model? What does it do?

A pre-ranking, also known as a light ranking, model is typically a simplified version of a heavy (or full) ranking model. The model is used to quickly rank candidates in advance of the heavy model's application, with the objective of screening for the top candidates. The pre-ranking model primarily focuses on optimizing recall or cumulative gain, as explained in answers below.

The pre-ranking model is employed in situations where the latency of the recommender system is critical, such as in real-time or interactive applications, but also has utility in non real-time recommender systems such as push notifications to reduce overall compute and cycle time.

In order to rapidly evaluate candidates, pre-ranking models employ a reduced set of features and simpler models compared to full ranking models. Through this approach, typically 25% to 90% of candidates are eliminated, thereby allowing the full model to be more complex. A pre-ranking model that sustains a high level of recall or cumulative gain can thus enable the system to generate a more accurate set of recommendations overall.

Solution 4.23: What should the pre-ranking model learn?

Pre-ranking models most commonly use **knowledge distillation**. Knowledge distillation is a technique used to transfer knowledge from a large, complex model (called the teacher model) to a smaller, simpler model (called the student model). The idea is to train the student model to mimic the outputs of the teacher model, rather than trying to train the student model from scratch using the original training data.

The process of knowledge distillation (Ba & Caruana, 2014) involves using the outputs (e.g., probabilities) of the teacher model as the targets for the student model during training. The student model is then trained to minimize the difference between its own outputs and the target outputs. With knowledge distillation, the teacher model can transfer rich information to the student model, while being faster to train and suitable for deployment in resource-limited environments.

The main drawback of knowledge distillation is exactly that same dependence on the teacher model: if the teacher model is not well-trained or is over-parameterized, the distilled knowledge will be erroneous as well.

Another approach is for the pre-ranking model to learn from **ground truth labels** directly, as the full ranker does. However, there are several arguments against this:

- Collecting ground truth for all samples is impractical due to candidates being eliminated during the pre-ranking stage. While it's feasible to collect training data by including eliminated candidates in the final results, this results in a relatively smaller dataset and may lead to underperformance of the recommender system, particularly when considering other exploration conducted by the full ranking model.

- The training data may be imbalanced in ways that's biased towards full ranking tasks due to several factors. First, many recommender systems have several full rankers and only one or two pre-rankers at most, which means the pre-ranking model needs to compress the knowledge from the ensemble. Second, the full ranker training data may be sampled in a way that skews the input distribution to a specific full ranker, which is dissimilar to the input distribution for the pre-ranking model.

- Correlation between stages can be beneficial for reducing system error in aggregate. Furthermore, improvements in the full ranker propagate back to the pre-ranking stage automatically.

That said, it is possible to incorporate ground truth into the knowledge distillation procedure. For example, ground truth labels may be integrated into the training data (Tang & Wang, 2018). The training loss can also be modified to account for ground truth labels (Hinton et al., 2014), or weighted by the sample's significance in relation to the ground truth.

Solution 4.24: Describe some evaluation metrics for the model.

Pre-ranking models aim to maximize the recall of the input candidate pool to retain the top candidates for the full ranker. There are various ways to measure this, depending on factors such as the ultimate user experience:

- **Normalized cumulative gain:** Also known as "cumulative gain ratio", this is a metric that evaluates the model's ability to identify the best subset of candidates. It is equivalent to the normalized discounted cumulative gain (*Discounted Cumulative Gain*, n.d.) metric but without the position penalty. The gain is determined based on the full ranking prediction, such as the probability of certain engagements, or the predicted revenue of a candidate in ads, excluding elements such as bid and budget pacing parameters that are provided at inference time.

- **Top-k recall:** Evaluates how well the pre-ranking model can identify the top-k candidates, where k is a specified number. For example, if k=1, it measures the model's ability to consistently identify the best candidate, even if it means overlooking the second or third best candidate. This metric is particularly relevant in cases where only one recommendation is presented to the user, like in a push notification, where getting the best recommendation right is essential.

- **Expected top-k loss:** Smoother version of top-k recall that assesses the difference in the gain value of the top-k candidates. This metric is beneficial in predicting the potential loss in engagements or revenue that may arise from utilizing the pre-ranker as a replacement for fully ranking all the candidates.

Solution 4.25: What are some suitable algorithms for this model?

Heuristics to Logistic Regression:

Over the years, the development of pre-ranking models has undergone several iterations. Initially, non-personalized methods like **heuristics** such as averaging predicted engagements or interleaving candidate sources and algorithms were employed, but they were later replaced by **logistic regression** models that were quick to train and could be readily updated through continuous learning (McMahan et al., 2013).

Logistic Regression to Two Tower:

The logistic regression approach was dominant for several years before being eventually supplanted by **Two Tower architectures**, also known as SplitNet or vector-product. These models consist of two parallel sub neural networks, with one network receiving target features while the other receives candidate features, and no crossing features between them. At the end of each network is a fixed-size vector representing the target and candidate embedding respectively. Efficient predictions are made at serving time by retrieving the embeddings and performing an inner product. This approach has been successfully employed in various platforms like YouTube (Covington et al., 2016), Twitter (Dilipkumar & Chen, 2019), and Alibaba (Wang et al., 2020).

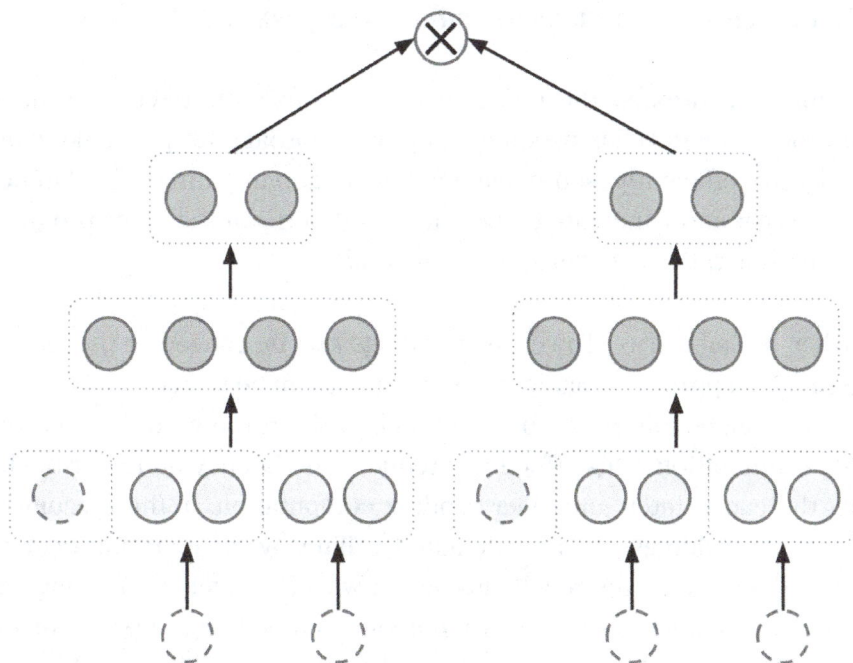

Note. Illustration of the Two Tower network. Each tower takes its respective input features and converts sparse features (dashed, white) into embeddings. These embeddings are concatenated with dense features (dashed, gray) and then fed through fully connected layers. The final layer from each of two towers is combined, usually with an inner product. In some cases, a sigmoid function is then applied to convert the output to a probability. There are numerous variations, for instance Twitter uses a Hadamard product (Wang, 2020) instead of the inner product.

Two Tower to Lightweight DNNs:

Despite the success of the Two Tower approach, one major drawback was its inability to use crossing features, which are often essential for optimal performance of recommender systems and often rank at the top of feature importance analysis.

To balance between speed and accuracy, **lightweight DNNs** have emerged as a viable alternative. These models can approach the speed of Two Tower by employing various optimization techniques, such as caching and model compression. One example of these models is Alibaba's COLD model (Wang et al., 2020), which incorporates a Squeeze-and-Excitation (SE) (Hu et al., 2018) block to dynamically adjust the complexity of the model architecture.

Solution 4.26: Suppose we need to pre-rank a large number of candidates. How to optimize the model to support this?

As previously mentioned, the Two Tower model (also referred to as SplitNet or vector-product model) has become a popular approach for pre-ranking due to its ability to efficiently score candidates at serving time. The latency to produce target and candidate embeddings and perform the inner product can be measured in the single digits of milliseconds.

To further optimize Two Tower, **embeddings can be cached or precomputed**. In the caching approach, candidate embeddings can be stored in a large cache, while target embeddings can be computed early in the request, even before candidate generation. This effectively reduces the latency on the critical path to only the cache fetch and inner product computation. In the precomputing approach, embeddings are precalculated offline by enumerating over users and candidates. This approach has its downsides, such as making model updates more cumbersome due to potential embedding version mismatch issues. Additionally, the cycle time to update the embeddings could result in staleness.

To improve upon the accuracy of the Two Tower model, which is limited by its inability to utilize crossing features, DNNs may be employed. However, since traditional DNNs are generally slower than the Two Tower approach, optimizations must be applied to reduce prediction time:

- **Parallelism** can be achieved at every stage of the process. Ranking requests can be split up into several queries, and sharding is a way to distribute ranking requests while maintaining an efficient cache strategy. Another way to achieve parallelism is by fetching features simultaneously or grouping them to minimize network calls needed to hydrate them. Predictions can be executed in parallel by adjusting the batch size.

- **Optimizations can be made to the inputs**. Inputs can be densified by concatenating features. Additionally, features can be compressed by storing dense embedding representations of target and candidate features during training. Only the embeddings are required during serving and can be directly fed into the model's inner layer.. Separately, in the Alibaba COLD model, features are represented in a column-based format that is cache-friendly.

- To minimize feature hydration latency, **features can be cached at multiple levels**, including in memory and at the datacenter level, to achieve a balance between latency and hit rate. When hydrating target features, which occurs before candidate generation, **crossing features can be prefetched** in a non-blocking manner. However, since features cannot be fetched for all candidates, only the top-k candidates are hydrated, while the remaining crossing features can be backfilled after candidate generation. In a time-critical situation, they could be dropped at a cost to accuracy.

- The **model architecture can be optimized** by reducing the size and computational complexity of the model, while retaining accuracy. Popular techniques for achieving this include quantization, and model compression techniques such as pruning and low-rank factorization. Furthermore, efficient model architectures, such as the Squeeze-and-Excitation (SE) block introduced in the Alibaba COLD (Wang et al., 2020) model, can be applied.

- Finally, there are some ideas for combining the Two Tower model and concepts above. One such method is to utilize a **three-way split network** that can be trained on target, candidate, and crossing features. The embeddings for both target and candidate can be obtained using one of the standard approaches for the Two Tower model. Additionally, the crossing features can be prefetched and/or backfilled in the manner described earlier. This results in a faster inner product that does not require a prediction call to the model server.

In cases where the aforementioned techniques do not yield the desired results, it is possible to **cache pairwise model scores** or even **precompute** them all offline. However, it is important to note that these methods come with certain drawbacks. Caching scores can incur significant storage costs and may not always achieve a satisfactory hit rate if the time-to-live (TTL) is low. On the other hand, precomputing scores offline can result in delays that may not be amenable to shifts in data distribution.

Feature Engineering

Solution 4.27: What features to use? What are their intuitions?

There are a number of different features that can be used in ranking models for recommender systems. The main feature types include:

- **Target features:** Features that describe the user.
- **Candidate features:** Features describing items that the user might be interested in.
- **Crossing features:** Features that describe the interaction between the user and items.

Numeric features are used heavily throughout industry recommender systems, commonly in the form of historic features such as a user's previous interactions. Historic features are often the most important features (He et al., 2014).

When it comes to historic features, there is a wide range of options available: these include raw counts, decayed counts, windowed counts, durations, ratios, time since events, and binary counting features like *"has done X in Y time window"*.

Taking a closer look at each of these feature types:

Target features:

Features representing the user include **demographics** such as age, gender, and language, as well as relevant **keywords** and the user's **interests** which may be represented by embeddings.

Additionally, there are **request-level features** which include where the content is displayed, such as the specific page of the user interface, the originating query (if applicable), the device, the client, the carrier, the user's network condition, geographic location, time of day, day of week, and so on.

Numeric features representing the **user's past actions**, such as how often they use the product, when they last used the product, and how much content they consume. These features can capture both historic and recent engagements. There are also numeric features that represent the user's presence on the product, such as their subscribers.

Embedding features are commonly used, such as those representing the user itself, embeddings for content comprising the user's recent engagement history, content that seeded the recommendation, embeddings of their subscribers, and so on.

Revenue (ad) models may incorporate additional features, such as the average bid depth, bid value, click-through rate, fill rate[3], and network valuation provided by platforms such as Vungle.

Candidate features:

Firstly, **static attributes** of content include its id, category, features extracted from its text and media, the size, the format, and more. There are also static attributes of the author and/or advertiser, such as advertiser type and scale.

Like target features, candidate features also heavily consist of **numeric features** such as the content's recency, as well as historic and recent engagements. There are also **embedding features** representing the content, the content's category, and so on.

Similar features can also be constructed for the content's **author**, and the **advertiser** and **ad campaign**, when applicable.

Additionally, revenue (ad) models use **metadata features** like the type of ad product, the bid type, and currency. They also include features specific to the ad product: for example, for mobile app promotions there are features for app details, app installs, app category, and more.

Crossing features:

---

[3] Fill rate is defined as the ratio of ads impressed divided by the number of total ad requests.

Crossing features play a key role in capturing the user's historical and recent interactions with the content and its author. When it comes to ads, these features can track the user's interactions with the ad itself, the ad campaign, and the advertiser. For example: How much content by this author has the user consumed? When was the last time the user consumed content by this author? How many times has the user interacted with this ad, or campaign, or advertiser?

Moreover, it is possible to cross features by means of inner products within the model architecture. Here are some common methods for crossing features in the model architecture:

- **Explicit crossing:** Primarily used in logistic regression and can also be found in Google's Wide & Deep (Cheng et al., 2016). Since explicit crossing can result in a large number of features, it's important to use domain knowledge or feature selection algorithms to limit the number of crossed features.

- **Embedding crossing:** Involves crossing the embeddings generated by input preprocessing. This technique is employed in recommender systems such as Huawei's DeepFM (Guo et al., 2017a) and Facebook's DLRM (Naumov et al., 2019).

- **Deep crossing:** The Deep & Cross Network (Wang et al., 2017) developed by Google, as well as DCN v2 (Wang et al., 2021), use a technique known as deep crossing, where each cross layer is a function of interactions between the previous cross layer and the original concatenated embedding layer.

Insider Tip

Here are some resources to learn more about the features commonly used in industry recommender systems:

- Ranking Tweets with TensorFlow (Twitter) (Zhuang et al., 2019)
- Multi-Task Learning of Graph-based Inductive Representations of Music Content (Spotify) (Saravanou et al., 2021)
- Leaving No One Behind: A Multi-Scenario Multi-Task Meta Learning Approach for Advertiser Modeling (Alibaba) (Zhang et al., 2022)

- Real-time Short Video Recommendation on Mobile Devices (Kuaishou) (Gong et al., 2022)
- Deep Neural Networks for YouTube Recommendations (Covington et al., 2016)

Solution 4.28: How to handle textual or id-based features?

In deep neural networks (DNNs), there are various methods for preprocessing textual and id-based features:

- If the input has low cardinality it's possible to use a **one-hot encoding**, also referred to as the vocabulary (for textual) or identity (for id-based). As a rule of thumb, low cardinality may be seen as having a number of unique values less than 20% of the dataset size or less than the square root of the dataset size (*Training Using the Built-In Wide and Deep Algorithm | AI Platform Training*, 2023).

- For inputs with higher cardinality, the **hashing trick** can be applied to reduce the dimensionality of the input vector. The hashing trick involves applying a hash function to the features and using the resulting hash values as indices. Besides consuming less memory, the hashing trick facilitates model updates on unseen values without altering the input vector's definition or shape, but may result in collisions.

- **Embeddings** are used to represent categorical features as continuous-valued vectors in a lower-dimensional space. Embeddings are particularly useful when capturing the relationships between input values is important (such as in recommender systems!). However, embeddings may overgeneralize, especially for id-based features that are sparse and high rank.

Embeddings are widely used in practice, with both Google's Wide & Deep and Facebook's DLRM recommender system utilizing them for every categorical feature. A common practice is to use one embedding per input feature, with the embedding dimension typically set between 5 and 100, and the ceiling set to the square root of the number of unique values in the input.

Solution 4.29: What about counting features? Problems with using counting features?

Because counting features can get quite large, it's important to standardize them in some way. Failure to do so can lead to several problems during the training process, such as (1) the loss may fluctuate due to significant differences in the input feature ranges, resulting in slow or unstable learning and (2) the model may become vulnerable to noise in the data, resulting in poor performance on new data.

There are several ways to preprocess numeric features in DNNs:

- **Log transformation:** Involves calculating either the natural logarithm or the logarithm of one plus the feature value (log1p). This approach is efficient to compute and is particularly suitable for features that adhere to a power law distribution. However, it does not handle negative values.

- **Z-score scaling:** Converts each value to a standard score, by subtracting from the mean and dividing by the standard deviation. Has the benefit of zero-centricity for normally distributed features, and is a good choice if outliers are not extreme. However, it can be computationally expensive to compute on larger datasets, necessitating sampling.

- **Bucketing:** Also known as binning or discretizing, involves the partitioning of each numeric feature into discrete bins via one of several methods, such as the use of quantile boundaries or the application of minimum description length (MDL) (Fayyad & Irani, 1993), which leverages information gain to identify optimal splits. Bucketing is a valuable technique for datasets characterized by skewed feature distributions. However, note that this approach results in a loss of information.

- **Clipping:** Constrains the range of a feature by bounding all values above and below designated thresholds. This strategy is particularly useful in scenarios where outliers are extreme. Clipping is often employed in conjunction with other preprocessing techniques.

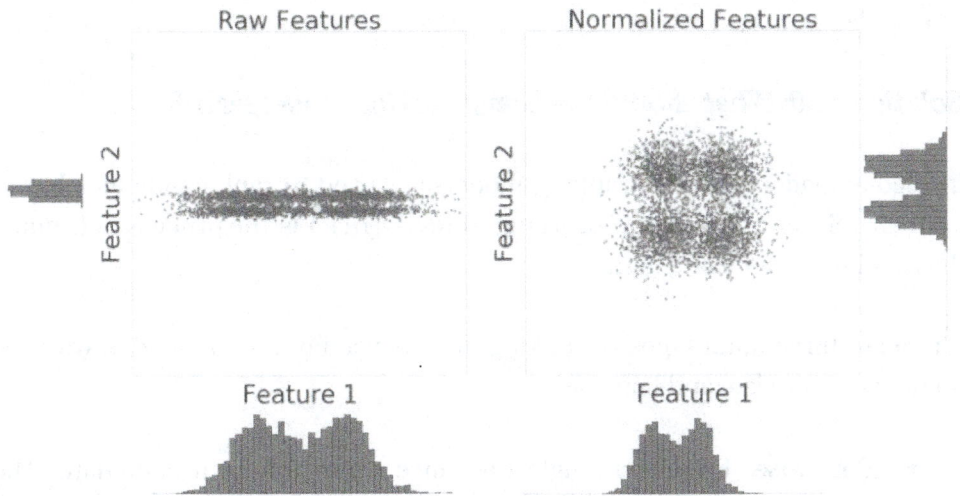

Raw Features **Normalized Features**

Note. After applying z-score scaling (normalization), features on the x- and y-axes have the same scale. Source: (*Prepare Data | Machine Learning*, 2022).

Performing multiple preprocessing techniques is also a viable option. It is possible to combine techniques, or generate multiple versions of a feature, such as creating both bucketed and z-score scaled versions.

All three techniques are used in practice. For instance, Google's Wide & Deep uses z-score scaling, Huawei's DeepFM uses discretization, and Google's Deep & Cross Network uses log transformation. It is worth noting that for these models, the same preprocessing technique is applied across all numeric features.

Another approach to preprocess numeric features involves applying a multilayer perceptron (MLP) directly to the features and utilizing the output of the hidden layer as the input for the remaining network layers. While this approach is not widely adopted in industry, it is utilized by Facebook's DLRM recommender.

Insider Tip

Test your understanding of various numeric preprocessing techniques with this quiz (*Transforming Your Data: Check Your Understanding | Machine Learning*, 2022) in Google's course on data prep.

Modeling & Evaluation

Solution 4.30: What should the heavy ranking model learn?

In recommender systems, ranking models are used to rank candidates based on their relevance to a user. Learning-to-Rank (LTR) is the process of training the ranking model using data.

There are three main types of ranking models used in recommender systems: pointwise, pairwise, and listwise.

- **Pointwise:** Predict a single relevance score for each candidate. The score is then used to rank candidates in descending order of preference. Sigmoid cross entropy is a popular loss function. Pointwise models are straightforward to implement and scale well, but they have the disadvantage of not capturing relationships between candidates and how they compare to each other in terms of relevance to the user. Nonetheless, pointwise models are widely used in many applications.

- **Pairwise:** Distinguish between preferred and non-preferred candidates. These models learn to compare two candidates at a time and predict which one the user would prefer. The indicator function-based pairwise logistic loss function is commonly used. The pairwise approach allows the ranking model to learn the relative preferences of candidates, which is more consistent with the human nature of ranking. Pairwise ranking models have been shown to outperform pointwise models in some real-world applications (examples: Google (Pasumarthi et al., 2019), Tencent (Ren et al., 2019)), but are computationally more expensive to train and serve.

- **Listwise:** Optimize a function that takes into account the entire list instead of just pairwise comparisons or single-item predictions. ListNet (Cao et al., 2007) and ListMLE (Xia et al., 2008) are two popular listwise loss functions. ListNet is a probabilistic loss function that optimizes the Kullback-Leibler divergence between the predicted ranking and the ideal ranking. ListMLE, on the other hand, is a maximum likelihood-based loss function that maximizes the probability of the ideal ranking. Listwise models require a significant amount of training data and computational resources to learn effectively.

Insider Tip

Tensorflow libraries make it easy to switch between these approaches (*Listwise Ranking*, 2022) with minimal modifications to the underlying code.

Solution 4.31: What are some reasonable modeling algorithms?

Pointwise LTR models are widely used in recommendation systems to predict the relevance of items to individual users. Below is a summary of the evolution of pointwise models in the industry:

1. **Logistic regression:** In years past, logistic regression was the most popular modeling algorithm (Ackerman & Kataria, 2021) used for pointwise ranking models due to its simplicity and interpretability. Logistic regression models are easy to implement, scalable, and can be efficiently updated through continuous learning.

2. **Gradient boosting:** Over the years, tree-based models such as XGBoost gained popularity (Xia et al., 2017) due to their ability to capture non-linear feature interactions and handle missing values. XGBoost is a gradient boosting algorithm that uses decision trees as base models and optimizes a differentiable loss function to minimize the prediction error. XGBoost has shown to outperform traditional machine learning algorithms such as logistic regression and random forests in many real-world applications (See "Machine Learning Challenge Winning Solutions" at (*Awesome XGBoost*, n.d.)).

3. **Hybrid:** For a while, boosted trees and logistic regression were used together in recommender systems. Boosted trees capture complex, nonlinear relationships between features. Paths from the root to leaf nodes are designated as binarized derived features. These derived features are then fed into a linear classifier, which learns the weights corresponding to the paths through the trees. Companies such as LinkedIn and Facebook (He et al., 2014) successfully implemented this approach.

4. **Deep neural networks (DNNs):** More recently, DNNs have become the most popular modeling algorithm for pointwise ranking models in

industry (Gupta et al., 2020). DNNs are powerful models that can learn complex non-linear relationships between input features and output labels. DNNs have the capacity to process vast amounts of data without suffering from performance saturation and can be tailored to fit specific problem domains, which enables them to outperform other machine learning algorithms in a wide range of tasks.

Solution 4.32: Describe what your model architecture might look like.

Historically, **logistic regression** has been a popular choice for industrial-scale recommender systems due to its simplicity, scalability, and interpretability. Sparse features that have been binarized and encoded using a one-hot technique are utilized to train logistic regression models. To achieve memorization, the sparse features are often crossed, which can require manual feature engineering and is a disadvantage of the technique. Logistic regression models also have had limited capacity to capture complex patterns within the data.

Subsequently, **DNNs** were adopted to improve the generalization capability over logistic regression models by learning low-dimensional dense embedding vectors for each feature. This approach reduced the need for extensive feature engineering. However, DNNs struggle to learn effective low-dimensional representations of sparse interactions between target-candidate features, especially in the case of niche items.

As a result, Google introduced the **Wide & Deep architecture** (Cheng et al., 2016), which uses a combination of linear models and DNNs to achieve both memorization and generalization in a single model. This sparked a trend in pointwise ranking models with the use of crossing models, such as Google's Deep & Cross Network (DCN) (Wang et al., 2017) and DCN v2 (Wang et al., 2021), and **factorization machines**, such as DeepFM (Guo et al., 2017a) and xDeepFM (Lian et al., 2018). These models combine the strengths of linear and neural approaches with additional techniques for capturing interactions between features. The result is a highly flexible and expressive model that can capture complex patterns in the data.

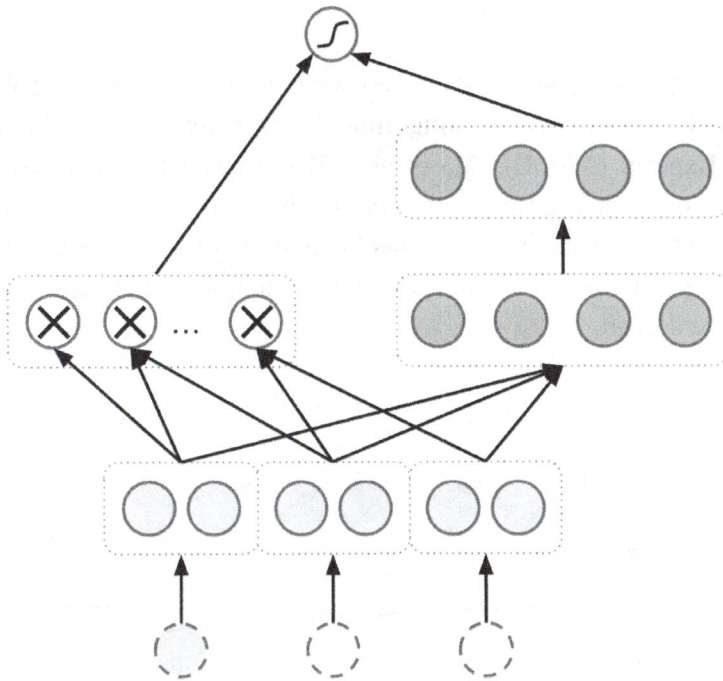

Note. A simplified view of the DeepFM network. The Inner Product units capture second-order feature interactions. In the actual DeepFM network, there is also an Addition unit that captures first-order features.

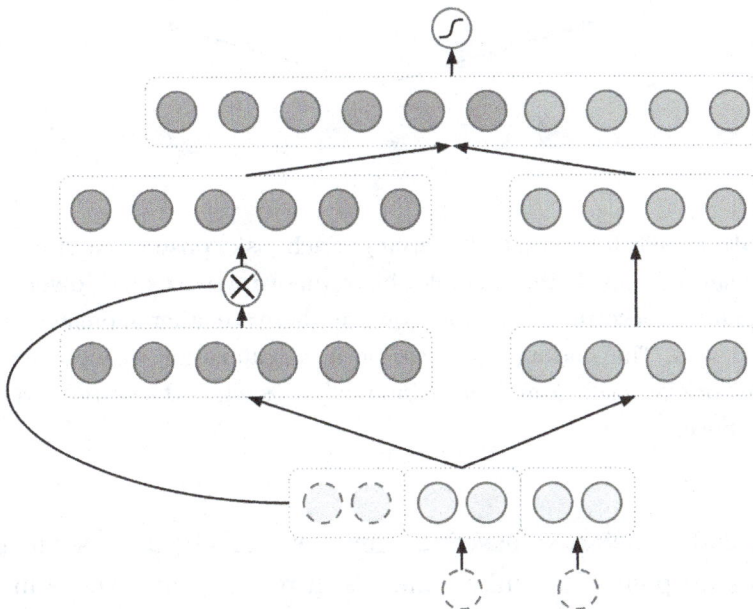

Note. In DCN and DCN v2, each cross layer is a function of interactions between the previous cross layer and the embedding layer. In DCN v2, the cross layer uses the Hadamard product to model the interaction.

More recently, there has been a growing interest in **multi-task learning** approaches for pointwise ranking models. One example is the Multi-gate Mixture-of-Experts (MMoE) (Ma et al., 2018) approach, which uses a gating mechanism to learn multiple sub-models that are specialized for different tasks or objectives. This approach has been shown to be effective at learning multiple tasks at the same time. For example, a model might learn to optimize both clicks and likes.

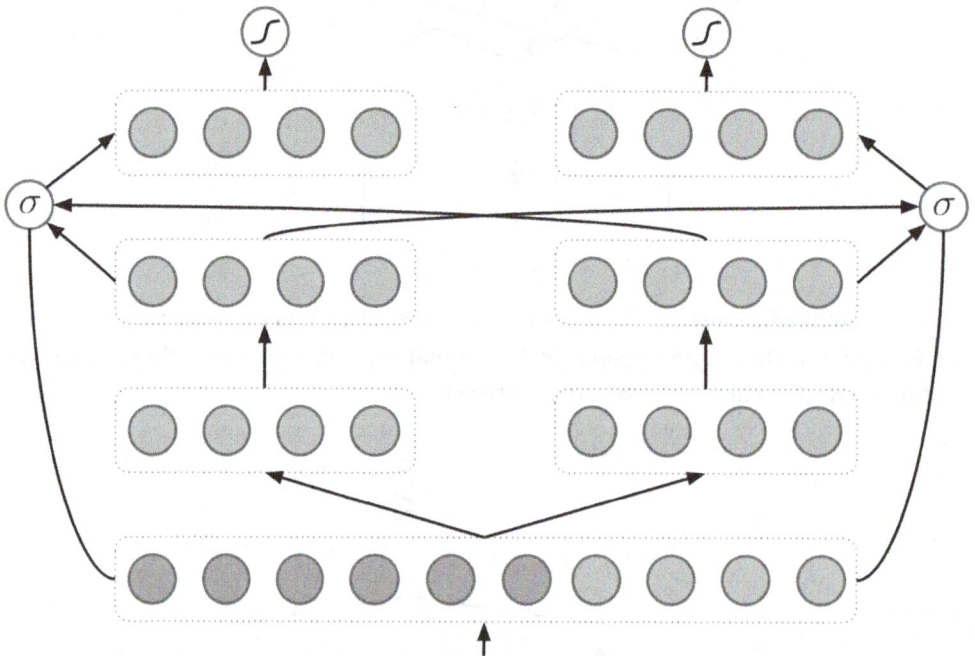

Note. MMoE module for multi-task learning. Each task consumes a different gate to combine expert outputs. In the example above, there are two expert towers, and gates are represented by a softmax function, however there are other implementations such as weighted sum. The bottom layer can be a concatenation of input features and embeddings, or can result from feature interactions, such as the output layer obtained from DCN above.

Attention and **transformer-based models** have emerged as some powerful approaches for pointwise ranking models in recent years. These models are designed to capture long-range dependencies between features and can be used to represent sequences, such as user behavior: historic interactions, recent interactions, and real-time interactions.

Key Terms

The **attention mechanism** is a technique used in neural networks to focus on relevant parts of input data. The attention mechanism consists of three elements: the key, query, and value.

Specifically:

- The **key** vector represents an input element (for example, a current user interaction).

- The **query** vector represents the element we want to focus attention on (for example, a previous user interaction).

- The **value** vector represents the information we want to extract for the query element (for example, the semantics of the query interaction).

The key and query are used to compute a **similarity score**, indicating how much focus to place on each element. This is typically done using a dot product. The resulting scores are then passed through a **softmax function** to create a probability distribution over the keys, which indicates how much each key is relevant to the query.

This softmax distribution is then used to weight the value vectors, which represent the information associated with each query. The **weighted value vectors are then summed up** to create the output of the attention layer for the current input. This output is then passed onto the feedforward network for further processing.

In **multi-headed attention**, the model maintains multiple sets of key, query, and value vectors. Each of the weight matrices are separately initialized. This enables the attention mechanism to capture a diverse set of interactions between input elements.

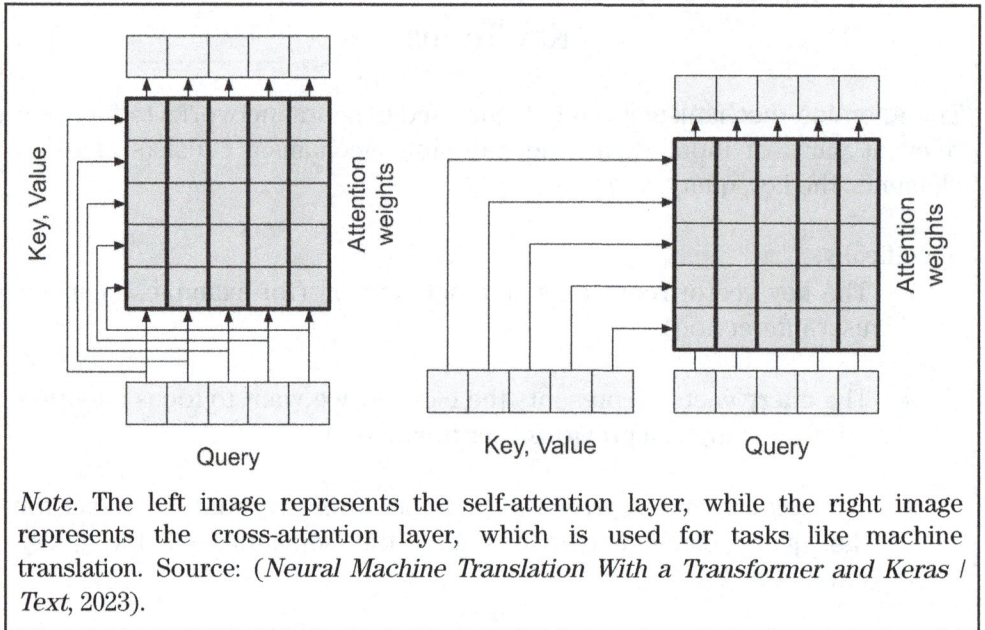

Note. The left image represents the self-attention layer, while the right image represents the cross-attention layer, which is used for tasks like machine translation. Source: (*Neural Machine Translation With a Transformer and Keras / Text*, 2023).

As a result, modern pointwise LTR models typically have the following architecture components, starting at the base of the model:

1. Input feature representations, such as embeddings.

2. Attention networks to capture sequential information, such as a user's past behavior.

3. Feature interactions, which can take the form of deep crossing (DCN, DCN v2) or embedding crossing (DeepFM, xDeepFM, DLRM).

4. Concatenation of embeddings.

5. In multi-task learning, the network divides into several branches, often utilizing an MMoE or PLE layer to share parameters across objectives.

6. A deep component, typically an MLP of 2 to 3 hidden layers with hidden units ranging in size from 64 to 1024.

7. Loss, typically sigmoid cross-entropy loss, although this is not always the case.

Not all ranking models will include all components; however, models should have (1), (4), (6), and (7). The inclusion of attention, crossing, and branching for multi-task learning is at the discretion of the ML practitioner and will depend on the specific problem being addressed.

Here is a summary of some choices made by specific industry ranking models:

Company	Product	Architecture	Source
YouTube	Video recos	Multi-task with MMoE	Recommending What Video to Watch Next: A Multitask Ranking System (Zhao et al., 2019)
LinkedIn	Homepage feed	Multi-task learning	Homepage feed multi-task learning using TensorFlow (Ackerman & Kataria, 2021)
Tencent	Kandian feed	Multi-task with contrastive sharing network	A Contrastive Sharing Model for Multi-Task Recommendation (Bai et al., 2022)
Spotify	Music recos	Multi-task learning	Multi-Task Learning of Graph-based Inductive Representations of Music Content (Saravanou et al., 2021)
Snapchat	Ad ranking	Deep crossing; Multi-task with PLE	Machine Learning for Snapchat Ad Ranking (*Machine Learning for Snapchat Ad*

			Ranking, 2022)
Bytedance	BytePlus Recommend	Embedding crossing (factorization machine)	Monolith: Real Time Recommendation System With Collisionless Embedding Table (Liu et al., 2022)
Alibaba	Taobao product recos	Attention network; Multi-task learning	Multi-Objective Personalized Product Retrieval in Taobao Search (Zheng et al., 2022)
Huawei	News recos	Attention network; Multi-task learning	Multi-Task Learning over BERT for News Recommendation (Bi et al., 2022)
Home Depot	Product recos	Transformer; Multi-task learning	Metadata-aware Multi-task Transformer for Large-scale and Cold-start free Session-based Recommendations (Shalaby et al., 2022)
Kuaishou	Video recos	Attention network; Multi-task with MMoE	Real-time Short Video Recommendation on Mobile Devices (Gong et al., 2022)
Microsoft	News recos	Attention network	Empowering News Recommendation with Pre-trained Language Models (Wu et al., 2021)

Solution 4.33: What if the model predictions need to be calibrated?

In consumer recommendation or search ranking problems, predicted scores of the model are typically used to determine the relative ranking of the items.

In online advertising, however, ad platforms might charge advertisers for the number of times their ads are displayed, also known as ad impressions, or for ad clicks. Advertisers may have different objectives in mind, such as driving a specific conversion event (*Understanding Bidding Basics - Google Ads Help*, n.d.). For example, an advertiser may want users to install a mobile app or make a purchase on their website.

This creates a potential mismatch between the billing method used by the ad platform and the advertiser's objectives. The advertiser may be bidding on a per-conversion event basis, but is being charged on a per-impression basis. This can lead to situations where an advertiser is paying for impressions that do not lead to the desired conversion event, resulting in wasted ad spend and lower ROI.

It is essential to have calibrated predictions, since they directly impact the cost for the advertisers and the revenue for the platform. This means that the total number of engagements predicted by the model should closely match the total number of true engagements across all the ad products.

Even though ranking models may be theoretically well-calibrated on training data, this does not necessarily ensure that the models will be well-calibrated in production for several reasons:

- Calibration guarantees provided by cross-entropy loss are limited to the data distribution seen during training. When a model is deployed in the real world, it may encounter new and different types of data that were not seen during training. This can lead to issues with calibration and poor performance on unseen data.

- The model may have been trained using loss functions besides cross-entropy loss. Other types of loss functions may not have the same theoretical calibration guarantees, making it even more challenging to ensure calibration in production.

- In ad marketplaces, when multiple advertisers bid for the same ad placement, the auction winner is typically the ad with the best combination of bid and relevance score. However, from the perspective of the ranking model, the auction winner's predicted score is likely to be significantly higher than the scores of the other candidates. The presence of outlier scores in selected candidates can cause the model to become over-calibrated.

To ensure that the ranking models used in the ad platform are well-calibrated in production, a calibration layer may be applied. The purpose of this layer is to adjust the predicted scores of the models so that they are better aligned with the expected number of engagements, which is the ultimate goal of the advertising system.

The calibration correction layer is typically a simple approach, such as Platt scaling or isotonic regression. This layer takes the predicted scores from the ranking models and produces a calibrated output that is used for ad serving.

- **Platt scaling:** The basic idea behind Platt scaling is to fit a logistic regression model to the predicted scores produced by the ranking model.

- **Isotonic regression:** Unlike Platt scaling, which assumes a logistic distribution, isotonic regression fits a non-parametric, piecewise-constant function to the predicted scores. The height of each interval is chosen to minimize the sum of squared differences between the predicted scores and the true values in the calibration set.

In production, a calibration loss metric can be used to track the performance of the model. This metric represents the difference between the expected and realized engagements after applying the calibration layer. The goal is to keep this metric below a certain threshold, whether it's in deployed models or in A/B testing.

Solution 4.34: What are some appropriate evaluation metrics and why?

Evaluation metrics play a crucial role in assessing the performance of ranking models in recommender systems. Evaluation metrics can be categorized into four main types: pointwise metrics, ranking metrics, infrastructure metrics, and product metrics collected via A/B testing.

Pointwise metrics:

Pointwise metrics evaluate the accuracy of individual predictions made by the model. These are simple to calculate since they do not require grouping by the query or request. Common pointwise metrics used in recommender systems include:

- **Area Under the Precision-Recall Curve (PR AUC):** Most popular offline evaluation metric for ranking models. It calculates the area under the PR curve that shows the precision versus the recall. Useful in cases where the number of positives is few.

- **Average** and **Squared Error:** Measures the difference between the prediction and actual value for each item. It calculates the mean or square of the difference to evaluate the performance of the model.

- **Relative Cross Entropy (RCE):** Evaluation metric used by Twitter for ranking, see (Belli et al., 2020). Indication of the improvement of a model compared to baseline or naive predictions by the difference between their cross-entropy measures. RCE can be likened to KL Divergence that is normalized by the baseline entropy.

Ranking metrics:

Ranking metrics evaluate the performance of the model based on the overall ranking of the candidates for a given query or request. Common ranking metrics used in recommender systems include:

- **Normalized Discounted Cumulative Gain (nDCG):** Measures the relevance of the recommended items by rank. It considers the position of each candidate and calculates the sum of discounted relevance scores, which is then normalized by the reference discounted relevance scores.

- **Recall @k:** Measures the proportion of relevant items that are recommended among the top k candidates. It evaluates the completeness of the recommendation at various thresholds.

- **Mean Average Precision (MAP):** Measures the average precision of the recommended items and calculates the mean across all queries or requests.

- **Mean Reciprocal Rank (MRR):** Measures the reciprocal rank of the first relevant item for each query or request. It evaluates the ability of the model to rank relevant items higher than irrelevant items.

- **Ordered pair accuracy:** Measures the proportion of correctly ordered candidate pairs. It evaluates the pairwise ranking accuracy of the model. This metric is relatively less expensive to calculate by sampling candidates from a given query or request.

Infrastructure metrics:

Infrastructure metrics evaluate the performance of the ranking model from an operational perspective. Common infrastructure metrics used in recommender systems include:

- **Latency:** Measures the response time of the model. It evaluates the efficiency of the model in generating predictions.

- **Success rate:** Measures the proportion of recommendations successfully delivered to users, indicating the model's compatibility with the system infrastructure.

- **Computational cost:** Measures the cost of training and serving the model. It evaluates the efficiency of the model in terms of computational resources.

Product metrics (collected via A/B testing):

Product metrics evaluate the performance of the recommendation algorithm in terms of user engagement and business impact. Common product metrics used in recommender systems include:

- For consumer:

  - **Positive engagements:** Measures the proportion of users who interact positively with the recommended items, or the total count of positive interactions. It evaluates user satisfaction and engagement.

o **Negative engagements:** Measures the proportion of users who interact negatively with the recommended items, or the total count of negative interactions. It evaluates the user dissatisfaction and disengagement.

o **Retention:** Measures the proportion of users who continue to use the recommendation system over time. It evaluates long-term user engagement and loyalty.

- For revenue:

    o **Revenue:** Measures the total revenue generated by the recommended ads. It evaluates the business impact of the recommendation algorithm.

    o **Conversion rate:** Measures the proportion of users who perform a conversion event – whether that is a click, a purchase, or some other action – or the aggregate rate of conversions per impressions. It evaluates the effectiveness of the recommendation algorithm in generating sales.

    o **Advertiser cost:** Measures the cost incurred by the advertisers for displaying their ads on the recommendation system. Changes in this value should be commensurate with the conversion rate.

Solution 4.35: How to balance multiple objectives, e.g., Likes versus Subscribes?

There are several approaches to building a ranking model that takes into account multiple objectives, at a high level:

1. **Train a multi-task model:** One way to build a ranking model that takes into account multiple objectives is to use a single multi-task model. Multi-Task Learning (MTL) involves training a single model to perform multiple related tasks simultaneously. One approach for building such a model is to use the Multi-gate Mixture-of-Experts (MMoE) architecture. The MMoE architecture features a bottom layer that is shared across all experts and deep per-objective towers. At the top of

each tower, there is a gate that takes inputs from both the shared bottom layer and other towers. In effect, the experts are shared across all tasks, but they are also trained to optimize each task. This allows the MMoE architecture to learn to model the relationships between tasks, which can improve the performance of the model.

2. **Train separate models:** Another approach to building a ranking model that takes into account multiple objectives is to train separate models for each objective and then combining their predictions by weighting them. The weights can be learned using various techniques, such as:

   ○ Perturb model weights and conduct online experiments with many treatments.
   ○ Perform random exploration by adjusting weights in batches.
   ○ Bayesian optimization techniques through trial and error online.
   ○ Pairwise prediction on historical data and connecting results to online metrics, a form of surrogate modeling.

3. **Learn from weighted labels:** Train a model from a composite label that combines the multiple objectives, which is a weighted sum of each individual label. There are several approaches to determining weights for the composite label. These include learning them through linear regression against a "north star" metric like daily active users, or performing correlation analysis from historical A/B tests. Online trial and error can also be used to tune the weights.

Solution 4.36: Should we build one multi-task model or combine multiple smaller models?

The decision to build a single model or multiple separate models depends on the team's goals and infrastructure characteristics.

- **Knowledge sharing:** A multi-task model can share knowledge across different objectives, which can improve performance on all objectives compared to separate models.
  ○ Advantage: multi-task model.

- **Per-objective performance:** When there are multiple objectives, a single model may overfit to one objective at the expense of the others, leading to undesirable performance characteristics. Separating models can make it easier to optimize for each individual objective.
    - Advantage: separate models.

- **Relationships between objectives:** If the objectives are interdependent, a multi-task model can better capture these dependencies compared to separate models.
    - Advantage: multi-task model.

- **Flexibility:** A single multi-task model may be less flexible than separate models in terms of modification and tuning. Separate models can allow for more control over the model architecture and learning procedure.
    - Advantage: separate models.

- **Complexity:** A single multi-task model can be more complex and difficult to design and train compared to separate models. The increased complexity can make it harder to interpret and debug the model. On the other hand, debugging multiple separate models demands greater domain expertise, necessitating a steeper learning curve.
    - Advantage: it depends.

- **Redundancy:** A multi-task model can reduce redundancy in the model architecture and parameters, leading to more efficient use of resources, better generalization to new data, and less code to maintain.
    - Advantage: multi-task model.

- **Deployment:** A single model can be easier to deploy, serve, and maintain compared to multiple separate models.
    - Advantage: multi-task model.

- **Resource constraints:** If there are significant resource constraints such as limited computing power or memory, a single multi-task model may not be feasible, whereas separate models can be designed to fit the available resources. However, training multiple models collectively may require more resources.
    - Advantage: it depends.

Deployment & Serving

Solution 4.37: How to enable the model to serve real-time requests?

Models are typically hosted in a model serving system to handle real-time requests. A model serving system includes components for:

- **Loading models** from the model repository.
- **Serving model requests** and returning predictions, including tasks such as input preprocessing and output postprocessing.
- Switching between **different versions of the model**, such as via hotswapping.
- **Management interface** for deployment, rollback, and debugging.

This is on top of **core functionalities** such as monitoring, logging, load balancing, and other related features.

Additionally, there is a need to manage state for multi-stage prediction requests, hydrate and cache features and predictions, convert features to the appropriate format, handle request batching and failures, and scribe requests and predictions for analysis. These requirements can be addressed by either the model server or a separate service fronting it.

Insider Tip

Read more about the components of the model server and various optimization strategies in the ML Infrastructure Design: Online section.

Solution 4.38: What can we cache in the serving system and where?

Caching can be employed in various ways in a recommender system to improve its performance and efficiency. Some of the places where caching can be employed in a recommender system include:

1. **Caching the top-k items for each user:** In this approach, the top-k items for each user are cached to avoid the need to trigger the full candidate fetch and ranking flow. Meta uses FeedState (Khandelwal et al., 2021) to keep cached recommendations fresh by adjusting the ranking score prior to serving.

2. **Caching embeddings:** Embeddings are low-dimensional vectors that represent users and items (and other entities, such as topics) in a recommender system. These embeddings can be cached for use in approximate nearest neighbors (ANN), which is a popular approach to candidate generation. Microsoft's SPANN (Chen et al., 2021) is an efficient method to implement caching for a very large-scale candidate space.

3. **Caching features:** Candidate features, which are more likely to be reused between calls, can be cached at multiple levels: e.g., locally in-memory and at the datacenter level. This technique ensures that the system does not need to fetch features with network calls every time a recommendation is requested, thereby improving the system's performance.

4. **Caching prediction scores:** Pairwise prediction scores are used to compute the relevance of candidates for users. These scores can be cached with a short time-to-live (TTL) to avoid the need to recalculate them every time the user issues a request. This technique can improve the system's performance and reduce the load on the model server.

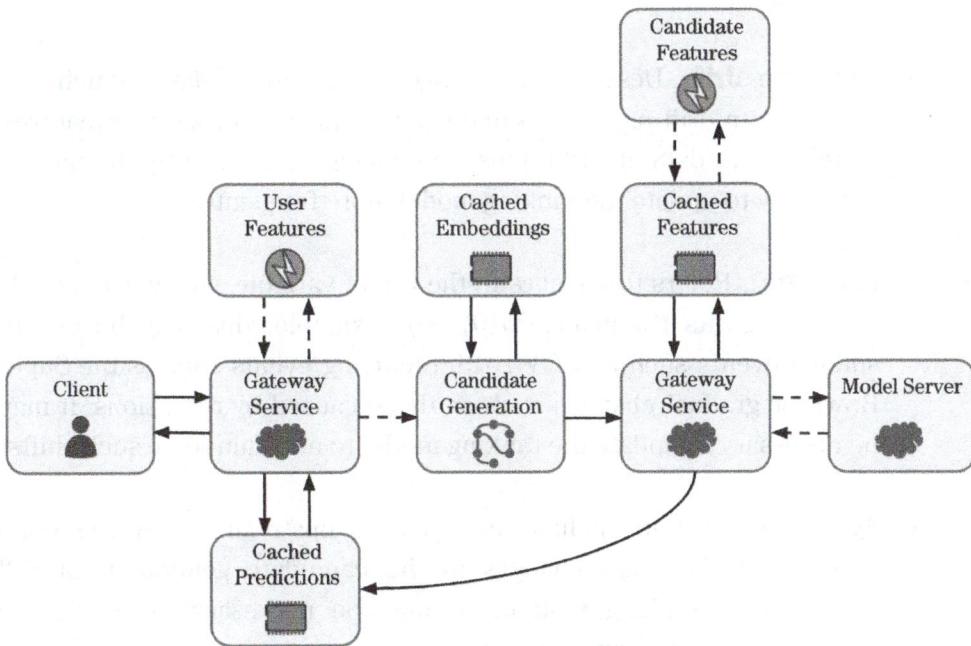

Note. Online ranking request flow. The pre-ranking stage has been omitted for simplicity. The dashed arrows are conditional connections. For example, in cases where candidate features cannot be retrieved from the cache, they can be asynchronously fetched from the feature store. If using a Two Tower model architecture, the model server doesn't have to be invoked on the critical path since the gateway service is capable of computing the similarity metric independently.

Solution 4.39: How often to update the model?

The frequency at which a ranking model needs to be updated in a recommender system depends on various factors such as concept drift, covariate drift, label drift, and system drift.

- **Concept drift:** Refers to the relationship between the features and the predicted values. If the model relies heavily on id-based or keyword-based features, it may need to be updated frequently as these features force the model to memorize more (many ad prediction models fall in this camp, see (*Machine Learning for Snapchat Ad Ranking*, 2022)). In contrast, if the model uses interaction-based counting features that enable it to be more generalized, it may require less frequent updates so long as the features themselves are rapidly updated.

- **Covariate drift:** Describes a change in the input data, which can include data drift or changes in the data collection process or features. If the input data distributions can change significantly, it may be necessary to update the ranking model more frequently.

- **Label drift:** Refers to changes in the target variable, which can include temporal shifts (Žliobaitė, 2010). For example, this may be due to sudden events such as COVID-19, recurring events such as the Super Bowl, or gradual changes such as those caused by recessions. It may be necessary to update the ranking model to accommodate such shifts.

- **System drift:** Can include changes in upstream or downstream systems. If there are changes in the candidate generation or full ranking or reranking systems, it may be necessary to update the ranking model to ensure that it remains accurate.

Solution 4.40: How does online experimentation (A/B testing) work?

A/B testing is a technique used to compare two or more versions of a system or design to determine which one performs better. In the context of a recommender system, A/B testing can be used to evaluate the effectiveness of different algorithms or models in generating recommendations for users.

At a high-level, there are two types of A/B tests, user-binned and cluster-binned.

- **User-binned:** Users are assigned to one of two (or more) groups, and the groups are compared based on their behavior or outcomes. Experiments that use user binning are better suited for observing changes in user behaviors over time, such as per-user engagement and retention metrics.

- **Cluster-binned:** Requests are randomly assigned to one of two (or more) clusters of servers, and the clusters are compared based on aggregate behavior or outcomes. Experiments that use cluster binning allow for improved monitoring of system impact, including factors such as latency.

To set up an A/B test for a recommender system, the first step is to define the experiment ID and bucket ID. The experiment ID identifies the specific experiment being conducted, while the bucket ID identifies the group to which the request belongs. The bucket ID can be randomly assigned to users or can be based on some predetermined criteria, such as geographic location or the cluster ID.

After the experiment has run for a sufficient period of time, the data can be analyzed to determine which version of the system performed better.

Interference:

When multiple A/B experiments are running simultaneously, there is a potential for experiment interference, where the results of one experiment are influenced by the presence of another experiment. This is also known as "conflict" or "collision". One simple example is where multiple experiments attempt to apply treatments to the same model or sets of parameters. There are more nuanced forms of interference in social networks (Saveski et al., 2017).

Some techniques can be used to mitigate this risk:

- **Sequential experimentation:** In this approach, experiments are run one after the other, rather than concurrently.

- **Merging experiments:** It's possible to include treatments from several experiments into a single experiment, provided that each bucket receives a sufficient number of users or requests to ensure statistical significance.

- **Mutual exclusion:** In mutual exclusion, groups of users are randomly assigned to different experiments orthogonally, in a way that ensures no overlap across the experiments.

- **Multivariate testing:** Multivariate testing involves combining treatments of otherwise separate experiments (*A/B Tests Vs Multivariate Tests*, 2019). By conducting multivariate testing, it is possible – though more challenging than traditional A/B testing – to determine which elements have the most significant effects on metrics.

Solution 4.41: How should the server support model experimentation?

To support model experimentation, a model server should be able to load models from a repository where various versions of the models are stored. This allows ML practitioners to test and deploy different models, or multiple versions of a model.

Two common approaches for loading models for experimentation into a model server are:

1. **Rolling deployment:** This involves restarting the server with the models to be tested. This approach is straightforward and ensures that the model server is always running the correct version of each model. However, it may result in increased latency or reduced availability while the server is restarted. Additionally, this approach can create

obstacles and additional work for ML practitioners who must oversee the deployment process.

2. **Hotswapping:** With this approach, model snapshots can be swapped in and out of production through a model configuration, without the need for a full server restart. This approach allows for more flexibility in experimentation, as models can be rapidly swapped in and out without interrupting service. However, hotswapping may require more sophisticated configuration and setup, and can introduce issues with compatibility or stability.

Once experiment and bucket IDs have been defined, the recommendation system can set switches that trigger different parts of the code to execute. For example, the code might use one algorithm to generate recommendations in one bucket (such as a specific model and/or version) and a different algorithm to generate recommendations in another bucket. The experimentation framework tracks interactions with the recommendations and collects data on how users respond to each version of the system.

Solution 4.42: Describe some ideas for model experiments.

There are numerous ideas for conducting modeling experiments in recommender systems. Here are some potential experiments to consider:

- **Objective:** Ranking models can be trained to optimize different objectives. For instance, in knowledge distillation, instead of training on the predictions of the teacher model, the ranking model can be trained on a different set of labels, such as whether a candidate was the top candidate or in the top-k.

    - Multi-task: Experiment with incorporating multiple objectives into the model learning procedure, such as optimizing for both user engagement and revenue (ads).

    - Composite: Another common technique is to use a composite label that combines multiple objectives using a weighted sum or more complex function. For example, for revenue (ads) try incorporating marketplace-related components into the objective, such as bid optimization factors.

  ○ Transform: Another way is to transform the label itself, which can be useful when the original label distribution has certain properties that may affect the model's performance. This transformation can involve clipping the label to remove outliers, or applying a log-transform, which can help balance the loss function in some situations. Once the label has been transformed, the model can use a different loss function that is appropriate for the transformed label distribution.

- **Features:** Experiment with different feature sets, or incorporating features from different sources.

- **Preprocessing:** Try various input preprocessing techniques such as normalization, discretization, or the use of embeddings.

- **Algorithms:** Train the model using alternative algorithms besides DNNs, such as logistic regression or gradient boosting.

- **Model architecture:** Try different variations of the model topology, such as implementing wide & deep, factorization machines, or attention mechanisms.

- **Training dataset:** Experiment with different training datasets, such as varying the size or composition of the dataset, to see how it affects model performance.

- **Retraining:** Experiment with different model update frequencies or procedures, such as batch versus online training, to see how they affect model performance.

Also, experiment with:
- Loss functions
- Activation functions
- Regularization methods
- Hyperparameters

Solution 4.43: Suppose we would like to predict which offline evaluation metrics improve online metrics (e.g., engagement). How to go about this?

One way to predict which offline evaluation metrics can improve online metrics in a recommender system is by running experiments using **A/B testing** and **measuring the correlation** between differences in offline metrics and online metrics.

First, select a handful of offline evaluation metrics such as PR AUC, nDCG, or Ordered Pair Accuracy. Then, the recommender system can be modified by changing some aspects of the model, such as:

- Model architecture
- Training dataset
- Features
- Hyperparameters

Modifying these components should result in dozens of model variations. Each of these variations can be evaluated using the chosen offline metrics.

Subsequently, the model variations can be deployed into an A/B testing environment, where users are assigned randomly to either the control model or one of several treatment models. In case there are too many treatments, running these experiments sequentially may be necessary. Online metrics, like engagement, can then be measured for all groups.

Lastly, by computing the correlation between differences in offline and online metrics, we can identify which **offline metrics exhibit the highest correlation** with the online metrics of interest.

Solution 4.44: How to debug if online experiment performance drops over time?

Debugging a drop over time in performance of an online experiment can be challenging, but there are several steps you can take to identify potential issues and find solutions. Here are five possible steps to take:

1. **Ensure metrics are statistically significant:** If a decrease in non-statistically significant metrics is observed, it is advisable not to jump to conclusions. Wait for more data to accumulate, to allow

metrics to become statistically significant. This reduces the likelihood of drawing incorrect conclusions based on incomplete data.

2. **Verify the experiment's health:** Ensure that users are being allocated properly and that the experiment is running smoothly. Check the server logs, experiment configurations, and any other relevant data to make sure that there are no technical issues, such as errors in user allocation, or data loss.

3. **Verify the data:** Ensure that the experiment data being collected is accurate and complete, and that there have been no changes to the way it is being collected.

4. **Look for changes in recent deployments:** Review recent code deployments, feature releases, or bug fixes that could have impacted the experiment's performance. Check for any changes in the codebase that may have inadvertently affected the experiment. Monitor whether infrastructure metrics have been affected.

5. **Check for interference from other experiments:** Check if there are any other concurrent experiments or launches that could be interfering with the current experiment. Ensure that the size of the control and treatments remains consistent throughout the experiment.

6. **Check secondary metrics:** Corroborate any observed decline in experimental results with secondary metrics, such as other forms of engagement. These metrics can provide additional insights into how users are interacting and help identify any underlying trends or patterns that may be contributing to the decline.

7. **Changes in user behavior:** Sometimes user behavior changes over time, particularly if there is an increase in negative engagements. Users may adapt to treatments and develop new patterns of behavior, leading to changes in the experiment's performance. Some experiments are also more vulnerable to seasonality or unexpected events.

If the reasons behind the decline in experiment results are unclear or difficult to understand, consider re-running the experiment.

5. ML System Design: Part 2

In the previous chapter, we introduced a framework for addressing ML System Design questions, and provided a detailed walkthrough of a design interview for recommender systems (RecSys).

ML System Design: Part 2 builds upon that foundation by (a) demonstrating how the approach for RecSys can be modified to suit almost any retrieval and ranking-related design problem, and then (b) guiding you through other frequently encountered types of ML System Design questions.

Retrieval and Ranking

The underlying techniques used in RecSys – which were covered in detail in ML System Design: Part 1 – such as candidate generation, pre-ranking, and heavy ranking, have many applications beyond the scope of recommender systems.

These techniques can be successfully applied to address other related problems that follow the **information retrieval (IR)** two-stage approach: candidate generation and ranking.

The main differences among such problems lie in the candidate generation procedure and features used in the models. Here are some examples:

- **Search problems** involve finding relevant results for a given query. In contrast to recommender systems, the candidate generation process for search involves matching the query terms with the content of the documents or items being searched. However, the embedding approaches used in RecSys, which involve mapping users and items to a low-dimensional space, can still be applied to generate representations of documents or entities for search purposes.

- **Finding similar entities** involves identifying users or items that have similar characteristics or behaviors. This problem is similar to collaborative filtering approaches used in recommender systems, which identifies users who have similar preferences and recommends items that are preferred by those users. The same techniques can be applied to identify similar items or entities based on their attributes and behaviors.

- **Identifying near duplicates** involves detecting items or entities that are very similar to each other, but not identical. This problem is similar to content-based filtering approaches used in recommender systems, which recommends items based on their similarity to previously liked items. The same techniques can be applied to identify near duplicates by comparing the attributes or features of the items.

- **Entity resolution** involves mapping different representations of an entity to a common taxonomy. For example, mapping company names to their corresponding ticker symbols, which are unique identifiers used in financial markets. One approach is to cast the problem as a search problem, which can be based on exact or approximate matching of the query terms with the canonical representations of the entities. Another approach to entity resolution is to learn latent representations in the form of embeddings. In the case of company names and ticker symbols, the embeddings could be learned from historical data or external sources such as news articles, social media, or financial reports.

- **Question answering (QA)** involves answering a question posed in natural language by retrieving the relevant information from a large corpus of documents. Traditionally, QA has involved five main steps:

  1. Query decomposition: Reformulate the query into smaller units, such as phrases or keywords, that can be used to retrieve relevant documents or passages from a large corpus.

  2. Hypothesis generation: Generate a set of candidate answers or hypotheses based on the queries and the retrieved documents. This step is similar to the candidate generation process in RecSys.

  3. Evidence retrieval: Retrieve and rank the evidence or supporting passages that provide the relevant information to

answer the question. This is equivalent to a separate fetch and ranking flow in RecSys.

4. Synthesis: Generate a coherent and natural language answer to the question. This requires additional processing steps, such as natural language generation or summarization, which are not present in RecSys.

5. Answer ranking: Rank the candidate answers based on their relevance and coherence with the evidence and present the most likely answer to the user. This step is similar to the heavy ranking process in RecSys.

More Design Questions

While retrieval and ranking problems are two of the most common applications of ML, there are many other problems that are prevalent in the field. They include:

- **Classification**: Classification is a type of supervised learning where the goal is to predict a categorical label for a given input. For example, a spam filter could be trained to classify emails as "spam" or "not spam" based on the email's contents. Another example is image recognition, where an algorithm might classify images of animals as "cat", "dog", or "bird" based on their features.

- **Regression**: Regression is a type of supervised learning where the goal is to predict a continuous numerical value for a given input. For example, regression could be used to predict the price of a house based on its features such as size, location, and number of bedrooms. Another example is predicting a person's age based on their demographic and socioeconomic characteristics. Regression models can be used for a wide range of applications, including forecasting, risk management, and performance optimization.

- **Extraction**: Information extraction (IE) is a subfield of natural language processing (NLP) that involves automatically extracting structured information from unstructured text data. For example, an

IE algorithm might extract the names of people, places, and organizations mentioned in a news article, or identify the key events described in a text. IE can be used for a wide range of applications, including natural language understanding (NLU), resume screening, and news parsing.

- **Clustering**: Clustering is an unsupervised learning technique where the goal is to group similar items together in a dataset. Unlike classification, clustering doesn't involve predicting a label for each item. Instead, the algorithm tries to find natural groupings in the data based on the similarity of their features. For example, clustering might be used to segment customers based on their purchasing behavior, or to group similar news articles together based on their content.

- **Generative modeling**: Generative models are a type of machine learning model that can be used to create new data that is similar to the training data. Historically, generative models were mainly used for speech recognition (ASR), text-to-speech (TTS), optical character recognition (OCR), and machine translation (MT). However, more recently, natural language generation (NLG) has become increasingly popular thanks to advancements in large language models (LLMs) such as ChatGPT.

Let's take a closer look at how we can use these problem types to effectively solve system design questions using the **ML System Design framework**: High-Level Design, Data Collection, Feature Engineering, Modeling & Evaluation, and Deployment & Serving.

Practice Interview

The following set of practice interview questions cover a range of potential ML System Design interviews. Unlike the practice interviews from earlier, it is not recommended to go through all of the questions one-by-one in a linear fashion.

Instead, begin with a High-Level Design question and then move on to specific, relevant questions from the other sections.

For example, if you are asked a High-Level Design question about natural language understanding (NLU), this should prompt a series of related questions:

1. *Develop an ML system that understands natural language commands.*
2. *How does one collect data and prepare a dataset for training?*
3. *What are some challenges when it comes to collecting labels?*
4. *How to perform feature engineering for supervised classification?*
5. *Build a model that performs classification.*
6. *How to evaluate the classifier model?*
7. *Build a model that performs information extraction.*
8. *What are some evaluation metrics for information extraction?*
9. *What are the steps to prepare a model to serve predictions?*
10. *How to enable the model to serve real-time requests?*

High-Level Design

5.1: Develop a ML system to extract information from financial reports.

5.2: Design a ML system that can gauge the positivity or negativity of a given text.

5.3: Build a ML system that can identify the prevalence of topics within a news article.

5.4: Design a ML system that condenses a body of text into a single paragraph.

5.5: Develop a ML system that understands commands like, *"Play the top songs by the Beatles"*.

Data Collection

2.1: How does one collect data and prepare a dataset for training?

> **Note:** *Find the solution to this question under* <u>ML Fundamentals – Datasets</u>.

5.6: What are some challenges when it comes to collecting labels?

5.7: How to prepare data for clustering algorithms?

Feature Engineering

5.8: How to perform feature engineering for supervised classification or regression?

5.9: What are features used by generative models?

Modeling & Evaluation

5.10: Build a model that performs information extraction, e.g., from financial reports.

5.11: What are some evaluation metrics for information extraction?

5.12: Build a model that performs classification, e.g., for sentiment analysis.

2.28: How to evaluate a classifier model?

> **Note:** *Find the answer to this under* <u>ML Fundamentals – Evaluation</u>.

5.13: Build a model that performs regression, e.g., for demand forecasting.

2.29: How to evaluate the quality of a regression model?

> **Note:** *Find the answer to this under* <u>ML Fundamentals – Evaluation</u>.

5.14: What are some techniques for matching identified topics with a taxonomy?

5.15: How to evaluate the performance of a topic modeling algorithm?

5.16: Build a model that performs clustering, e.g., to group similar news articles.

5.17: What are metrics for evaluating the performance of clustering algorithms?

5.18: Build a model that can generate text, e.g., to summarize a document.

5.19: What are some metrics used for assessing quality in generative tasks?

Deployment & Serving

5.20: What are the steps to prepare a model to serve predictions?

4.37: How to enable the model to serve real-time requests?

> **Note:** *Find the answer to this question and related real-time serving questions under* <u>ML System Design: Part 1 – Deployment & Serving</u>.

5.21: How to make offline predictions, such as inferring topics from a collection of text?

High-Level Design

When it comes to designing ML systems, it's important to remember that these systems are rarely composed of just one component. Instead, they consist of a series of interconnected parts, and it's necessary to think about the system as a whole in order to create an effective and cohesive product.

One approach to tackling these complex problems is to start with the desired output and work backwards, filling in the dependencies as needed.

As an example, let's take the case of a **voice assistant** that can answer questions about the weather. If a user asks *"What's the weather in Austin tomorrow?"* the assistant needs to be able to speak the answer back to the user.

To do this, we need some kind of **text-to-speech (TTS)** technology. But in order to generate the right response, the assistant also needs to understand the user's intent (which in this case is to know about the weather), so it needs to perform **intent classification (IC)**. To extract the relevant information from the user query, it needs to do **information extraction (IE)** or **named entity recognition (NER)** to identify the location (in this case, Austin) and the time.

Once it has identified these entities, the assistant needs to resolve the location to a zip code using **entity resolution (ER)**, which is essentially a retrieval and ranking problem. Finally, working all the way back, the assistant needs to convert the user's spoken words to text using **automatic speech recognition (ASR)** technology. Only then can you piece together the entire sequence of components: ASR → IC → NER → ER → (logic to look up and compose the answer) –> TTS.

It's a valid question to ask why we need so many components in a ML system, especially considering that each component can potentially add some error to the system, causing errors to cascade and accumulate. In fact, this kind of thinking can be helpful, as it can lead us to consider alternate, more direct solutions that might be able to reduce the number of components in the system.

For example, could we skip the text representation and use a speech encoder-decoder network with latent encodings directly? This approach might seem more straightforward, as it would allow us to go straight from input to output. However, this approach also presents its own challenges: Without a textual representation of the user's question, how can we determine what information to provide to the weather API in order to retrieve the weather data?

The design of a ML system is a balancing act between accuracy, efficiency, and complexity. By thinking through the dependencies and weighing the trade-offs, we can arrive at a system that strikes the right balance for our needs.

Let's now examine some common ML systems that arise in industry, and take a closer look at the various components that make up each of them. As we go through these examples, it's worth considering how the thinking-backwards approach we mentioned earlier could have been utilized to arrive at the solutions for each system.

Document Parsing

Context: In certain regions of the world, it is common to come across financial reports that are handwritten in a foreign language (e.g., Arabic), subsequently scanned, and published on a company's website.

Solution 5.1: Develop a ML system to extract information from such financial reports, such as "Total Cash and Cash Equivalents" and corresponding amounts.

In order to accurately extract specific line items from handwritten financial reports in a foreign language like Arabic, a multi-step process is necessary.

Firstly, we identify the desired output, which in this case is to extract the *"Total Cash and Cash Equivalents"* line item and its corresponding values from the document. To achieve this, we can employ **tabular information extraction (IE)** to extract the relevant information. However, because there may be different variations of this line item, we also need to use **entity resolution (ER)** to match canonical terms in our taxonomy.

Since the document is in a foreign language like Arabic, we convert it to a common language (e.g., English) in order to perform such operations. This requires **neural machine translation (NMT)** from Arabic to English, a generative model. Additionally, since the document is handwritten, we need to perform **optical character recognition (OCR)** to extract the text.

One important consideration is that while in the US, financial reports are available via the SEC, in other countries they may simply be posted to a company's Investor Relations website. Therefore, we would want to build a web crawler to check for changes to the website and **classify** whether the posted content is a financial report like a balance sheet. To avoid triggering the entire ML flow, we can examine the headline first to determine whether the content is relevant.

In summary, the ML system requires: Web Crawler → Classifier → OCR → NMT → tabular IE → ER to successfully extract the desired components from a handwritten financial report in a foreign language. Generative models are used for the OCR and NMT components in this flow.

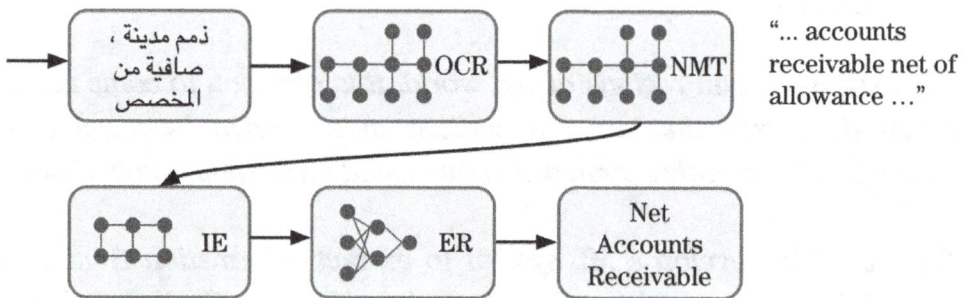

Note. A representation of the flow for parsing the document after a foreign language balance sheet has been received by the system.

Insider Tip

It is crucial that the ML system accurately extracts the relevant components from the financial report, as investment professionals make significant decisions based on this information. Additionally, it is important to ensure that the process is fast, so that investors can gain an edge over others in the market.

To achieve accuracy and efficiency, it is important to incorporate human oversight into the process. One way to do this is by using ML to quickly parse the document and alert the user that the content has been automatically extracted. The parsed results can then be reviewed by a human, who can double-check the entries and make any necessary corrections. Another approach is to have humans review the parsed outputs before publishing them into the financial database, to ensure that the data is accurate and reliable. By incorporating human review into the process, we can strike a balance between speed and accuracy, while also maintaining the integrity of the financial data.

Sentiment Analysis

Solution 5.2: Design a ML system that can gauge the positivity or negativity of a given text.

Sentiment analysis is a popular field in natural language processing (NLP) that involves analyzing text to determine the emotional tone or attitude of the author. Sentiment analysis presents several challenges, including:

- Negation: *"I did not like this dish at all."*
- Sarcasm: *"The weather is nice and warm – for a polar bear."*
- Comparisons: *"The movie is better than the book, though both are just ok."*
- Inversions: *"This phone has a pretty UI, but that's about it."*
- Negatives that are positives: *"Lebron James is one bad man!"*

There are several approaches to sentiment analysis, some of which are listed below:

- **Rule-based:** In this approach, a set of rules are defined to assign sentiment to text. For example, a rule might be to assign a positive sentiment to any text containing the word "happy" or "excited" and a negative sentiment to any text containing the word "sad" or "disappointed". One can also add rules for negations (Das & Chen, 2001), for example adding NOT_ to every word between the negation and the following punctuation. Similar rules can be devised for other challenging scenarios.

- Pros: Simple to implement, easily customized, can be effective for identifying nuances such as sarcasm or irony.

- Cons: Time consuming, requires domain expertise, brittle, may not generalize well.

- **Lexicon-based:** Involves using a pre-defined lexicon of words that are associated with positive or negative sentiment. The sentiment score of a text is calculated by adding up the scores of the words in the text that are present in the lexicon. Words that possess a higher degree of ambiguity in terms of their polarity may be assigned lower weights. Other relevant methods involve calculating the pointwise mutual information between observed words and unambiguous affect words, such as "excellent" or "poor" (Turney, 2002).

  - Pros: Fast, can be effective when the text input is large (like an article).

  - Cons: Difficult to handle challenging cases like negation or irony, limited by the scope and quality of the lexicon.

- **Non-neural models:** Involves training a machine learning model on a labeled dataset of texts and their corresponding sentiment. The model learns to recognize patterns in the data and can then be used to predict the sentiment of new texts. There are numerous non-neural ML methods for sentiment analysis, including SVMs, logistic regression, even topic models (Blei & McAuliffe, 2007). The majority of non-neural approaches represent the input text as a bag-of-words.

  - Pros: Can identify sentiment without rule or lexicon creation, generalizes well.

  - Cons: Still challenging to handle nuances such as sarcasm, requires a large amount of labeled training data.

- **Neural networks:** The most effective machine learning models for sentiment analysis are those that can capture the context and relationships between words, including **LSTMs** (Long Short-Term Memory) and **Transformer encoders**. These models can take into account the sequence of words and their dependencies, which is especially useful for sentiment analysis because the sentiment of a word may depend on the context in which it is used.

One example of a state-of-the-art sentiment analysis model is based on **RoBERTa** (Robustly Optimized BERT pre-training Approach) (Liu et al., 2019), which is a variant of the BERT (Bidirectional Encoder Representations from Transformers) model (Devlin et al., 2019). RoBERTa was trained for longer and on more data as compared to BERT. RoBERTa also removes the next sentence prediction task, supposedly to focus on modeling the relationship between individual words. RoBERTa also applies dynamic masking during training, which randomly masks out different tokens in each batch, to help with generalization. The model is pre-trained on large amounts of unlabeled text and fine-tuned on smaller sentiment analysis datasets. This approach has achieved state-of-the-art performance on benchmark datasets for sentiment analysis (Hartmann et al., 2023, *AllenNLP - Demo*, n.d.).

- o Pros: Can handle complex and nuanced expressions such as sarcasm and irony, doesn't require a large amount of training data for fine-tuning.

- o Cons: Can be computationally expensive, limited interpretability.

Insider Tip

Check out this notebook for fine-tuning RoBERTa for sentiment analysis in Colab (*Sentiment-Analysis-Using-Roberta.ipynb - Colaboratory*, n.d.).

Topic Modeling

Solution 5.3: Build a ML system that can identify the prevalence of topics within a news article.

At a high level, there are several different ways to perform topic modeling, including:

- **Word-based techniques:** This approach involves using word embeddings or word frequency-based methods to identify topics from the presence of words associated with those topics. This approach is simple to implement and fast, but doesn't capture the complex relationships between topics (Meddeb & Romdhane, 2022). One way that this could be implemented:

  1. Keyword extraction: The first step would be to extract the most salient keywords from each document. This could be done using a variety of techniques, such as TF-IDF, chunking, or topic words.

  2. Word embeddings: The next step would be to represent each of the extracted keywords or phrases (Wu et al., 2020) as a low-dimensional vector using word embeddings, such as GloVe (Pennington et al., 2014).

  3. Embedding similarity: Once the keywords have been represented as embeddings, the embeddings can be matched to seed words of topics by comparing the distance between the keyword embeddings and the embeddings of the seed words. Alternatively, It is possible to directly match keyword embeddings with topic embeddings by training a shared embedding space using techniques such as matrix factorization.

- **Matrix factorization:** This approach involves factorizing a matrix of word co-occurrences or term-document counts into a lower-dimensional matrix of latent topics and their corresponding weights. Latent Semantic Analysis (LSA) (*Latent Semantic Analysis*, n.d.) is a popular matrix factorization method used for topic modeling. Non-negative Matrix Factorization (NMF) (Arora et al., 2012) is another approach to topic modeling that imposes a constraint that the matrix factors must be non-negative, resulting in more interpretable results; the non-negative factors can be interpreted as additive components of documents.

- **Probabilistic topic modeling:** This approach involves modeling each document as a mixture of topics and each topic as a distribution over words. Latent Dirichlet Allocation (LDA) (Blei et al., 2003) is a popular probabilistic topic modeling method. To estimate the topic distributions, LDA uses Bayesian inference. It assumes that each document is generated by a two-step process: first, a set of topic probabilities is drawn from a Dirichlet distribution, and then a set of words is drawn from the corresponding topics. The model then infers the most likely topic distribution for each document over a number of iterations to maximize the likelihood of the observed data.

Hierarchical Dirichlet Process (HDP) (Teh et al., 2006) is an extension of LDA that allows for an unbounded number of topics to be inferred from the data, and Correlated Topic Models (CTM) (Blei & Lafferty, 2005) is an extension of LDA by allowing the topics to be correlated. CTM assumes that the topics are generated from a multivariate Gaussian distribution with a shared covariance matrix.

- **Neural topic models (NTM):** NTMs use neural networks to discover latent topics and represent documents as topic distributions. This approach presents several improvements over probabilistic topic modeling methods: (1) it allows the representation of topic and word distributions as probability vectors or embeddings; (2) it is efficient to scale to large corpora and take advantage of GPUs; (3) it is straightforward to combine with other neural network structures for joint training purposes, such as for text generation (Wang et al., 2019a) and summarization (Cui et al., 2020).

The most popular form of NTMs are based on variational autoencoders (VAE). In a VAE, the encoder maps the input data to a latent space, and the decoder maps the latent representation back to the input space. In the context of NTMs, VAEs can be used to learn either an implicit representation of the document without directly modeling topics, or they can explicitly model topic assignments and the distribution of words within those topics. When using VAEs for NTM, the Dirichlet distribution is replaced with other distributions (such as Guassian (Miao et al., 2017)) to make the optimization process easier. NTMs have outperformed probabilistic topic models like LDA in various settings (Miao et al., 2016).

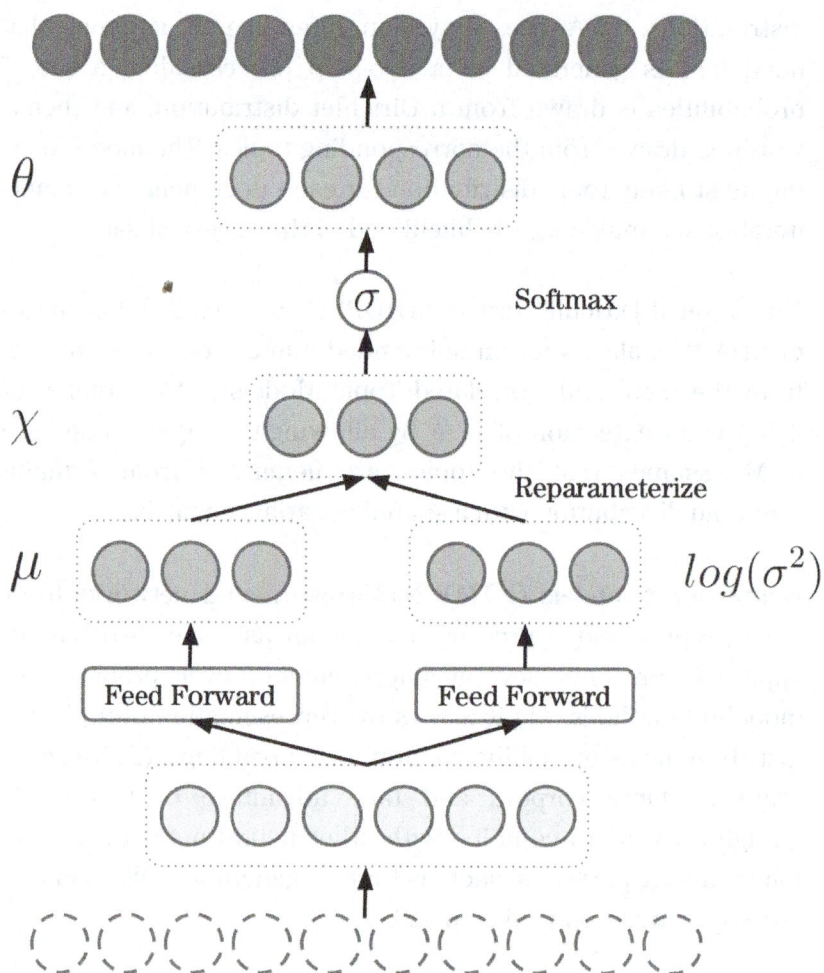

Note. Illustration of NTM using VAE. The input words are converted to embeddings, followed by a feed forward network to compute the mean μ and log-variance σ^2 vectors. A reparameterization trick – which enables gradient descent optimization – is employed to produce a sampled latent representation χ. A softmax function is applied to generate the topic proportions θ, from which the reconstructed input can be generated.

Insider Tip

Read more about the various types of NTMs in (Zhao et al., 2021).

Text Summarization

Solution 5.4: Design a ML system that condenses a body of text into a single paragraph.

There are two primary approaches for text summarization: extractive and abstractive.

- **Extractive summarization** involves selecting important sentences or phrases from the original text and arranging them in a coherent summary. This technique typically involves identifying and ranking important sentences using various features such as the terms, position, and topic representation.

  o Pros: Generally easier to implement and can be more reliable, as the generated summary consists of sentences that are directly taken from the original text.

  o Cons: Can sometimes result in summaries that are disjointed or less readable.

Extractive summarization typically involves several steps. Here is an overview of the most common steps involved in extractive summarization:

1. **Feature extraction:** To extract features from the input text for use in summarization, the first step is to clean the text through sentence splitting, tokenization, stemming, and stopword removal. Once the text has been simplified, various features can be extracted, including term features, embeddings, topics, and sentential features such as position and length.

2. **Sentence selection:** In this step, the most important sentences in the text are identified and selected for the summary. This can be done using various techniques such as scoring individual sentences based on their relevance and importance to the overall topic of the document, or by treating the document as a graph of topics and selecting the most relevant subgraphs.

3. **Redundancy removal:** This step involves removing redundant sentences that convey the same or similar information as other sentences in the summary. This can be done by comparing the similarity of each sentence to other sentences in the summary and removing those that are too similar.

4. **Sentence ordering:** Once the most important sentences have been selected, they need to be arranged in a coherent and readable order. This can be done using various techniques, such as ordering them based on their position in the document, their salience to the content, or by identifying sentence relationships and dependencies.

5. **Coreference resolution:** In this step, any anaphoric references (e.g., "he", "she") in the summary are resolved to ensure consistency of entities across sentences. This can be done using various techniques, such as using coreference resolution models to identify pronouns and their antecedents.

6. **Summary:** Finally, the selected and ordered sentences are combined into a single coherent summary. This summary may be limited to a specific length or number of words, depending on the application.

- **Abstractive summarization**, on the other hand, involves generating a summary that is not a simple extraction of text, but rather a new text that conveys the most important information from the original document in a more concise form. Abstractive summarization is typically done using **encoder-decoder networks** trained on large datasets of text, for example (Liu & Zhao, 2020). These models can generate summaries by predicting the most likely words and phrases to appear in a summary given the input text.

Modern encoder-decoder networks, such as **Transformers** (Vaswani et al., 2017), are well-suited to abstractive summarization tasks for several reasons. Attention mechanisms enable the network to selectively attend to different parts of the input text, allowing it to capture relationships between words and phrases across the entire document. Transformers have a large capacity, enabling them to capture a mixture of latent concepts with great precision. Using a beam search approach, the decoder leverages a combination of self-attention, cross-attention, and positional encodings to produce summaries that are both fluent and coherent.

- Pros: Can generate more coherent and concise summaries by creating new sentences and phrases that capture the most important information from the original text.

- Cons: Relies on generating new sentences that capture the essence of the input text, rather than simply selecting and rearranging existing sentences. This can introduce the risk that the generated text may contain errors or inaccuracies that are not present in the source text.

Natural Language Understanding

Solution 5.5: Develop a ML system that understands commands like, "Play the top songs by the Beatles".

To design a ML system that understands a command like *"Play the top songs by the Beatles"* we can follow the three key components of Natural Language Understanding (NLU): intent classification (IC), information extraction (IE), and entity resolution (ER) (Tyagi et al., 2020).

1. **Intent classification (IC):** Intent classification is the process of identifying the underlying intention or action that a user wants to perform through a command or statement. In this case, the intent is to "play music". To accomplish this, we can use a model that classifies the user's input into different predefined categories. There exist various approaches, ranging from rule-based systems (which are still effective for many use cases) to supervised models, including multinomial logistic regression and neural networks.

2. **Information extraction (IE):** Once we have identified the intent, we need to extract the relevant information from the input command. In this case, we need to extract the type of music and the artist. The type of music is specified as "top songs", which can be considered a slot. The artist, in this case, is "the Beatles". To extract this, we can apply Named Entity Recognition (NER) techniques.

3. **Entity resolution (ER):** Entity Resolution is the process of mapping the extracted entities to a specific representation in the system. In this case, we need to understand that "top songs" refer to the most listened to songs and map "the Beatles" to an artist in the system's database. We can use a knowledge graph or lookup table that maps each entity to its unique identifier in the system. In this case, we can then use a music library API to retrieve a list of top songs by the Beatles and then play them.

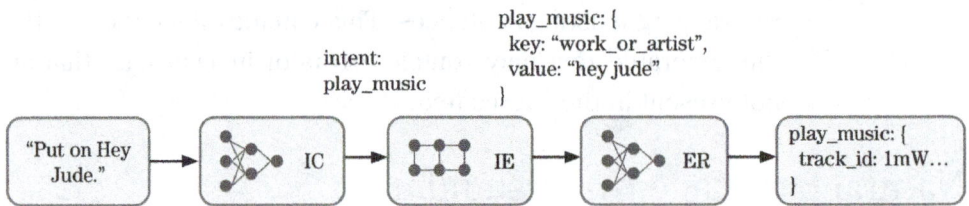

Note. To achieve high recall, production NLU systems often rely on the use of multiple models. Some models can jointly classify intent and extract entities. NLU systems may implement a fallback mechanism, such as a prioritized list of models, or model ensemble.

Recently, **Large Language Models (LLMs)** have been increasingly applied to NLU tasks such as intent classification (IC) and information extraction (IE) (Kalyan et al., 2021). One of the strengths of LLMs is that they can perform IC and IE in a single step (Chen et al., 2019b) through **fine-tuning** approaches. Fine-tuning is a process of re-training a pre-trained language model on a specific task with a small amount of task-specific data.

Insider Tip

In Appendix – Generative Models, we go over different fine-tuning approaches for LLMs.

Data Collection

Supervised

Solution 5.6: What are some challenges when it comes to collecting labels?

In supervised machine learning, there are typically two types of labels that are used to train models: logged labels and human-labeled labels.

Logged labels come from observed behaviors, such as clicks, transactions, or other interactions that a user has with a system.

- One major challenge with using logged labels is that they can be **subject to various biases**, such as position bias or presentation bias. For instance, a recommendation system may display items higher up on the page, leading to more clicks, even if those items are not necessarily the best recommendations for the user. These biases can make it difficult to train accurate models, as the labels themselves may not accurately reflect the true preferences of the users.

Insider Tip

Read more about addressing the challenges of logged labels in ML System Design: Part 1 – Data Collection under *"4.10: What sorts of biases might be found in the dataset?"*.

Human-annotated labels are generated by human annotators who complete specific tasks, such as labeling images or text. Although human-annotated labels are relatively less prone to bias, **mislabeled data** presents a significant obstacle.

Mislabeled data can arise from a variety of reasons, such as annotators misunderstanding the instructions, making errors, or even intentionally mislabeling data in some cases – for instance, due to incentives of platforms like Amazon Mechanical Turk which may prioritize fast and cheap labeling.

There are many approaches for quality assurance for human-annotated labeling, including:

1. **Clear instructions:** It is crucial to have clear and concise instructions for annotators to follow when labeling data. These instructions should be reviewed by other experts as well as annotators, and should be treated as an iterative process, where the annotators try labeling a bit, then refine based on mistakes and misunderstandings, and so on.

2. **Screening:** Another approach is to aim for higher quality annotators, although this means paying more. Some platforms have tiers for annotator quality. One way to do this is to have the annotators complete a test. If they pass, then they can be added to the roster. If they fail, consider having them iterate and take another test as it's possible they misunderstood the instructions.

3. **Tracking:** Sprinkle in golden data with real annotation data to sample and track annotator performance over time. Golden data is pre-labeled data that is used as a benchmark for evaluating the quality of annotations. By comparing the annotator's labels to the pre-labeled golden data, it is possible to identify potential issues and areas for improvement.

4. **Voting:** This method involves obtaining multiple responses from different annotators and combining them to form a final answer. The combination can be done through a majority answer, where the most commonly chosen answer is used, or through weighted voting, where the answers of high-quality annotators are given more weight.

5. **Validation:** An expert or a known quality annotator verifies the annotations before considering them submitted. Validation can be especially valuable when working with a large team of annotators who may have different levels of expertise or understanding of the task at hand. This provides a fast and simple way to catch errors or inaccuracies in the annotations.

6. **Adding "captchas":** In the context of human-annotated labeling, captchas can be used to verify that the annotator is paying attention. For example, you might insert a question asking a simple math problem. By making it clear that workers will not be paid if they don't

answer the captchas correctly, you can incentivize them to take the task seriously.

7. **Adding a simple task:** This technique is similar to adding captchas, but instead of inserting a separate question, you can add a simple task to the annotation process itself. For example, you might ask annotators to type in the last word of the passage while assigning a label. This helps ensure that annotators are reading the content and not just clicking through the task without paying attention.

8. **Checking for patterns:** Patterns in annotator behavior can be a red flag for low-quality data. For example, if an annotator is spending very little time on each task, it may indicate that they are not taking the task seriously or are using automated tools to generate responses. You can filter out these responses by setting minimum time limits for each task.

Insider Tip

(Mason & Suri, 2012) provides a valuable reference for annotating data, particularly when using platforms like MTurk.

Unsupervised

Solution 5.7: How to prepare data for clustering algorithms?

Clustering is a type of unsupervised learning that groups similar samples together based on their features. Unlike supervised learning, clustering does not require labeled data. However, to achieve reliable clustering results, it is important to carry out some data preprocessing steps.

Categorical features:

Most traditional clustering algorithms do not natively accept **categorical features**. This is because the similarity or distance metrics used in these algorithms are typically designed for continuous numerical data, and categorical features need to be converted into numerical representations before they can be used. However, there are some clustering algorithms that can handle categorical features natively or have been adapted to do so, such as k-prototypes (Huang, 1997), or neural network-based algorithms such as Deep Embedding Clustering (DEC) (Xie et al., 2016).

When working with clustering algorithms that do not natively accept categorical features, it is necessary to convert these features to a continuous format.

- One way to achieve this is through **one-hot encoding**, which involves creating a new binary feature for each unique value in the categorical feature. The new features represent the presence or absence of the value in the original feature. However, one-hot encoding can lead to a high-dimensional feature space, which can be more computationally expensive.

- Another method is **label encoding**, which involves assigning a unique integer to each category in the feature. This approach works well when there is a relationship between categories that can be represented with integers, such as the relative size of values.

- **Ordinal encoding** is similar to label encoding but represents the order of the categories. This method assigns each unique category in the feature a unique integer based on its rank order. However, ordinal encoding can introduce a false sense of ordinality if there is no actual order between categories.

Continuous features:

Clustering algorithms involve assessing the similarity between samples, but not all continuous features have the same scale or distribution. For example, some features may have very large or small values, while others may have a skewed or non-normal distribution. To address these issues, we can apply some transformations to the features:

- **Log transformation:** Reduces the skewness and spread of a feature that follows a power law distribution. For example, the count of views may follow a power law distribution. A log transformation can make such a feature more evenly distributed by taking either the natural logarithm or the logarithm of one plus the feature value (log1p). This transformation does not require any additional data, but it does not handle negative values.

- **Z-score scaling ("normalization"):** Standardizes a feature that follows a normal (Gaussian) distribution, by subtracting from the mean and dividing by the standard deviation. For example, item ratings might conform to a normal distribution. This transformation requires more data than log transformation to calculate the mean and standard deviation.

- **Bucketing e.g., quantiles:** Can be applied to features of any distribution by creating bins of equal size relative to the feature values. For example, user age may be discretized into ranges. After quantile discretization, the distance of two samples is proportional to the number of samples between them. This transformation requires the most data (rule of thumb: 10X the number of buckets (*Prepare Data / Machine Learning*, 2022)) and results in some information loss, but it can effectively handle irregular distributions.

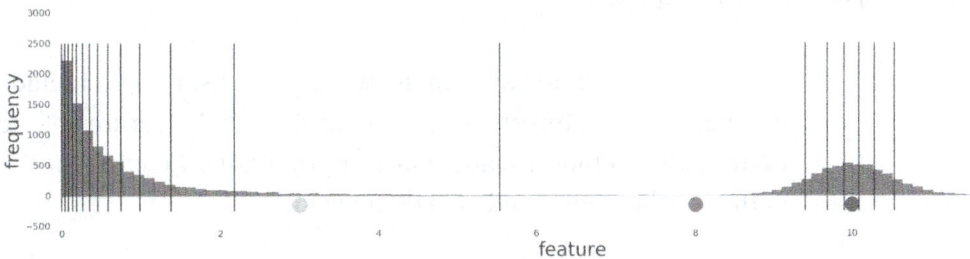

Note. Quantile discretization can be useful for nonparametric distributions. Source: (*Prepare Data / Machine Learning*, 2022).

Missing features:

To perform clustering, it is important to have values for all the columns as it relies on similarity measures. In cases where there are **missing features**, you have a few options: remove the samples (if missing data is minimal), remove the feature entirely, or impute missing feature values.

Insider Tip

See ML Fundamentals – Features under *"2.9: How would you deal with missing feature values?"* for a range of imputation techniques.

Feature Engineering

Discriminative

Solution 5.8: How to perform feature engineering for supervised classification or regression?

Below we propose a mental model for feature engineering for discriminative problems. While the specific features will vary significantly depending on the problem domain, there are some general categories that can be helpful to consider:

- **Features of the entities** involved, whether it be words, images, users, items, or something else entirely. These provide information about the properties and characteristics of the entities being analyzed or classified. For example:

  - In a recommendation system, features of the user might include demographics, interests, or past behavior, while features of the item might include its attributes or popularity. Features of the author of the item could also be relevant.

  - For detecting bot traffic, these features might include the IP address of the traffic and the user agent. Additionally, the content and structure of the request can also be analyzed to detect bot traffic. This might include looking for patterns in the request URL or the HTTP headers that are commonly associated with bots.

  - In natural language processing (NLP) tasks, the features may comprise various forms of the input text, encompassing n-grams, stems, lemmas, lowercase, word embeddings, POS tags, prefixes, suffixes, and more.

  - In the case of computer vision (CV), the input features may consist of the raw pixel values, which can be represented in various color spaces such as RGB or HSV. However, it is also common to apply transformations to the images, such as equalization, filtering, blurring, and other techniques, which can produce different representations of the same image.

These features can be either **static or dynamic**, depending on whether they change over time or not. In some cases, they might be collected at the time of the user's registration and never change (e.g., demographics), while in other cases, they might be collected and updated regularly (e.g., past behavior).

Static and dynamic features can also be applicable to other domains, as seen in the example of hotel pricing, where static features may describe the attributes of the room, while dynamic features may include factors like recent views, bookings, and reviews.

- **Contextual features** are another important type of input feature to consider. These features capture information about the broader context in which the problem is occurring. For instance:

    - In a NLP task like named entity recognition (NER), contextual features might refer to the surrounding text or the document.

    - In a recommendation system, contextual features might include information about the originating request, such as the time of day, the device type, or location.

    - In pricing models, these may involve various aspects of the market, including the competitive environment such as nearby listings, their reviews, and number of views. Additionally, the location and neighborhood may also contribute to the prediction and form a part of the feature set.

- **Sequential features** are another type of input feature that can be useful in many discriminative problems. These features capture information about the order in which events are occurring. For example, in a time-series prediction task, sequential features might include historical data on some variable of interest. In a recommendation system, sequential features might include a user's past behavior or interactions with the system. In NLP tasks, the text is inherently sequential.

- **Crossing features** are a type of feature that capture the interactions between two or more input features. These interactions can be either interaction-based or engineered crossings. Interaction-based crossings refer to the features that are created based on the interactions between the existing input features, whereas engineered crossings refer to features that are engineered or created by combining two or more input features.

  In the case of recommender systems, **interaction-based crossing** features can refer to the interactions between users and items, users and authors, or users and advertisers. For example, a crossing feature between users and items might capture how frequently a particular user interacts with a particular item. This type of feature can be useful in identifying the preferences of the user.

  On the other hand, **engineered crossing** features are features that are created by combining two or more input features. For instance, in text processing, n-grams can be combined with frequency information to capture the idiomatic usage of words. Combining words with their POS tags can provide useful disambiguation, as the same word can have different meanings depending on its context.

  Another type of crossing is done at the modeling level to **capture feature interactions**. For instance, if the input features are transformed into an embedding space, the embeddings can be crossed with each other. One example of this is DeepFM (Guo et al., 2017a).

- **Derived features** are another type of input feature created by using existing features. This is not a feature group in itself, but rather a way to generate new features from the current ones.

  One such example is **binarization** of features, which involves converting is_a and has_a features. For instance, in NLP tasks, features like IsUpper, IsAcronym, and IsNumber can be created through binarization.

  Using **windowed** or decaying mechanisms are another popular way of creating derived features. For example, interaction features can be counted and then windowed into 1 day, 3 days, or 1 week granularities.

In addition, older interactions can be decayed to give more weight to more recent interactions. **Ratios** between features are also commonly used as derived features.

Generative

Solution 5.9: What are features used by generative models?

Generative models learn to generate new data that resembles the training data. In most cases, generative models just take the raw data as input, which usually undergo some transformations.

For example:

- In natural language processing (NLP), **language models (LMs)** take tokenized text as input, which is a process of breaking down a text into individual words or tokens.

- **Machine translation (MT)** models rely on large amounts of parallel data, which consists of pairs of sentences in the source language and their translations in the target language. These sentence pairs are known as sentence-aligned translations and are typically obtained through manual or automatic alignment methods.

- The training data for **optical character recognition (OCR)** typically consists of a vast collection of scanned images or documents that contain printed or handwritten text. To train an OCR system, these images are labeled with their corresponding ground truth text. In the model training process, the images undergo various transformations, including normalization, skew adjustment, scaling, and other preprocessing techniques.

- In **speech recognition (ASR)**, the input features are typically either filter banks or Mel-frequency cepstral coefficients (MFCCs), which are derived from the filter banks. The filter banks are used to decompose the audio signal into frequency components, while the MFCCs are obtained by applying additional transformations on top of the filter bank outputs.

- **Text-to-Speech (TTS)** systems use the raw text as the input feature, which needs to undergo normalization (e.g., digits spelled out), and converted into phonemes (example: (*Kyubyong/g2p: G2p: English Grapheme To Phoneme Conversion*, n.d.)), which are used as the input features for the acoustic model. The output of the TTS system is in the form of waveforms or waveform blocks.

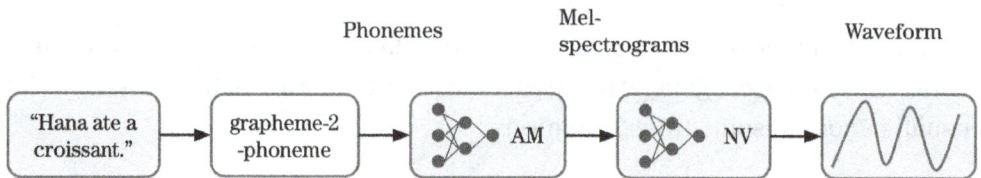

Note. TTS system that includes an acoustic model (AM) and neural vocoder (NV). The AM produces mel-spectrograms as output, which contain information about the spectral characteristics of the speech signal over time. The NV then takes the mel-spectrograms and generates the final waveform that corresponds to the synthesized speech. Some recent TTS systems use a different approach where they generate the waveform blocks directly from the phonemes without an intermediate mel-spectrogram representation.

There are cases where ML practitioners provide additional types of input features into generative models, notably the "conditional" variant of generative models, such as conditional variational autoencoder (CVAE) (Sohn et al., 2015) and the conditional generative adversarial network (CGAN) (Mirza & Osindero, 2014). In such instances, typically, the models are applied to classification and regression tasks rather than generating outputs that resemble training inputs, e.g., (Madireddy et al., 2018).

Modeling & Evaluation

Information Extraction

Solution 5.10: Build a model that performs information extraction, e.g., from financial reports.

To achieve effective information extraction (IE), multiple approaches are often combined as there are numerous methods to perform this task.

- **Rule-based systems:** This approach involves creating a set of rules and patterns to identify and extract specific information from a given text. These rules are often handcrafted by domain experts and can be applied to a wide range of texts.

  Despite the availability of more advanced techniques, rule-based systems continue to play a vital role in many IE systems! They can help practitioners address specific gaps in the performance of ML models by adding high-precision rules. This combination of approaches can significantly improve the overall recall of the system.

- **Rule-based hybrid approaches:** These approaches combine rule-based and statistical models to improve accuracy and coverage. For example, a rule-based system can be used to extract candidates, such as noun phrases and proper nouns, and a trained classifier can be used to classify those entities.

  Hybrid systems provide increased flexibility and interpretability compared to fully statistical approaches, but they may also be more expensive to develop and maintain due to the need for domain expertise.

- **Statistical models:** In the earlier days of IE and named entity recognition (NER), the most popular classifiers were Hidden Markov Models (HMMs), Maximum Entropy Markov Models (MEMMs), and Conditional Random Fields (CRFs).

  - **HMMs** were one of the earliest statistical models applied to information extraction, and they modeled the probability of a sequence of tags given a sequence of input tokens using joint probability. They relied solely on the observed tokens and didn't consider any additional features.

  - **MEMMs** were an extension of HMMs that allowed for the conditional modeling of the emission probability distribution via logistic regression. This enabled the incorporation of additional features into the sequential labeling task, which was not possible in HMMs.

○ **CRFs** are an extension of MEMMs that solve the "label bias" problem, which occurs when states with low-entropy label transitions effectively ignore their other features. To address this, CRFs model the dependencies between the input and output sequences using feature functions. A feature function is responsible for encoding a particular aspect of the input-output sequence, such as the relationship between neighboring labels and features of the input.

• **Neural models:** In recent years, the conventional statistical models have been gradually supplanted by neural models. Among these, the CNN and BiLSTM have become highly popular choices for IE tasks.

○ **Convolutional Neural Networks (CNNs)** can be used for IE by applying the convolution operation to the input text. In the context of IE, CNNs use a sliding window approach, where the CNN applies a convolution operation to a fixed-sized window of tokens (e.g., 3 tokens) at a time, producing a feature map for each window. The feature maps are then passed through a max-pooling layer to extract the most relevant features, and the resulting feature vector is fed into a fully connected layer that outputs a probability distribution over the possible labels for the center token in the window.

Insider Tip

Read more about convolution operations under Modeling & Evaluation -- Classification.

○ **Bidirectional Long Short-Term Memory (BiLSTM)** networks are a type of neural network that are designed to process sequential data, such as natural language text. It consists of two LSTM layers, one that reads the input sequence from left to right, and another that reads it from right to left. The outputs of both LSTM layers are concatenated to form a representation of each token in the sequence.

To facilitate long-distance memory, LSTM incorporates gates which regulate the amount of information to forget or to pass along to the next state. This way, a BiLSTM can capture both the forward and backward context of a token, taking into account long-range dependencies in the sequence.

Although these models have been used for IE independently, the real power lies in their combination. One popular approach, called BiLSTM-CNN-CRF (Ma & Hovy, 2016) involves combining three different components: a CNN, a BiLSTM, and a CRF.

1. The first component is a CNN that processes the characters in each word to capture morphological information such as prefixes. This information is then used to generate a character-level word representation.

2. The second component is a BiLSTM that concatenates the character-level word representations with the word embeddings, and processes them in both forward and backward directions to capture long-distance relationships between words in the input sequence.

3. Finally, the CRF layer takes the contextualized word representations from the BiLSTM and considers the dependencies between adjacent output labels to produce a final output label sequence.

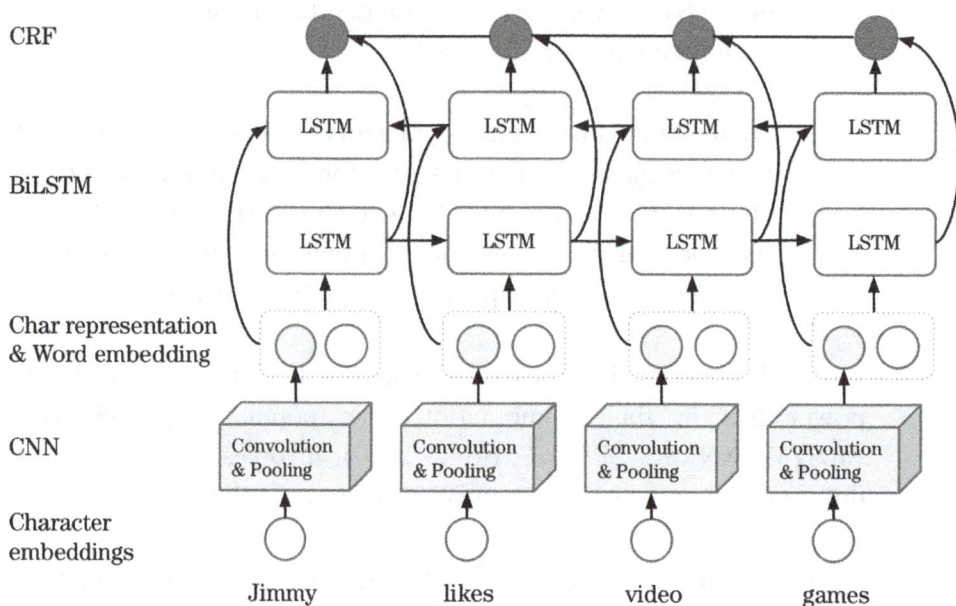

Note. Graphical depiction of the BiLSTM-CNN-CRF.

Other variants of the architecture use different combinations of components or different ways of combining the outputs of the BiLSTM and CNN.

For example, one variant extracts features in parallel from the BiLSTM and CNN and concatenates them before passing them through the CRF layer. Other variants use only the BiLSTM and CRF, without the CNN component.

Yet another variant is to replace the CNN component with a pre-trained language model such as BERT (Bidirectional Encoder Representations from Transformers) (Devlin et al., 2019). By using a pre-trained BERT encoder as the input to the BiLSTM-CRF architecture, the model may be particularly effective at capturing contextual information in the input text (Liu et al., 2021).

Insider Tip

A useful survey on the various neural approaches for IE and NER can be found in (He et al., 2020).

Solution 5.11: What are some evaluation metrics for information extraction?

Most IE tasks – including named entity recognition (NER), relation extraction (RE), coreference resolution, chunking, and tabular IE – use the following metrics:

- **Precision:** Proportion of instances predicted by the model that are correct. It is calculated by dividing the number of correctly predicted instances by the total number of instances predicted by the model.

- **Recall:** Proportion of instances in the text that are correctly identified by the model. It is calculated by dividing the number of correctly predicted instances by the total number of instances in the text.

- **F1 Score:** Harmonic mean of Precision and Recall, and provides a balance between the two metrics.

Part-of-speech (POS) tagging uses **accuracy**, which is the proportion of all tokens in the text that are correctly labeled by the model.

Classification

Solution 5.12: Build a model that performs classification, e.g., for sentiment analysis.

Specific sentiment analysis models are discussed earlier and can be found in High-Level Design – Sentiment Analysis.

Presented below is a sequential framework of models that may be taken into account for solving classification problems in general:

- **Rule-based models:** Rule-based models use a set of pre-defined rules to classify data. These rules could be based on domain knowledge or heuristic reasoning. While rule-based models are useful for quickly getting started and can be effective for simple problems, they may not be scalable or robust enough for complex tasks.

- **Logistic regression:** Popular statistical method used for binary or multinomial classification. It estimates the probability of events occurring based on the values of the input features. Logistic regression models can be easily interpreted and provide a good balance between accuracy and computational complexity. However, the algorithm assumes that the relationship between input features and the outcome is linear, which may not always be the case.

- **Gradient boosting:** Gradient boosting is an ensemble learning technique that combines multiple weak learners to create a strong classifier. In gradient boosted trees, decision trees are used as weak learners, and each subsequent tree is trained to correct the errors made by the previous tree. Gradient boosted trees are highly effective and can handle a wide range of input data types. However, they have limitations in their ability to handle categorical features, sensitivity to outliers, and integration with other model types such as DNNs.

- **Deep neural networks (DNNs):** There are many kinds of DNNs, including feedforward networks, convolutional neural networks, recurrent neural networks, and transformers. DNNs are regarded as state-of-the-art for a wide range of problems. They benefit from numerous open source tools and optimization techniques, such as distributed and GPU training, that enhance their performance and speed up their training process. However, they can be computationally expensive to train and may require large amounts of data.

The key to employing DNNs effectively is to consider **feature interactions**. For example:

  o **Factorization machines (FM)** enable feature crossings, which can help capture complex interactions between features. FMs are well-suited for recommender systems that involve diverse and large numbers of input features, as well as interactions between the entities.

  o **Attention-based mechanisms**, such as Transformer encoders, attend to all positions in the input sequence, enabling them to capture long-range dependencies effectively. Attention mechanisms are well-suited for sequential data, such as time-series, language modeling, and alignment tasks such as machine translation.

Insider Tip

Read more details of attention mechanisms in ML System Design: Part 1 – Modeling & Evaluation under *"4.32: Describe what your model architecture might look like."*

- ○ **Convolutions** are used for processing spatial data where there are often strong local correlations between adjacent regions of the input. The output of the convolutional layer is passed through a pooling layer, which compresses the output by reducing its spatial dimensions. Capsules are an alternative to pooling, where each capsule models a different property of the input region. This makes CNNs effective for tasks such as image classification, graph representation, and capturing speech signals.

Key Terms

A **convolution** is an operation that involves sliding a filter, also known as a **kernel**, over an input (e.g., image) to produce a **feature map**. The filter is designed to detect certain features in an input, such as edges, corners, or textures of an image.

The sliding window refers to the process of moving the filter over the input, one small step at a time, and performing the convolution operation at each location. Specifically, the filter is placed at each location in the input, and the element-wise multiplication is performed between the filter and the corresponding input values within the region covered by the filter, also known as the **receptive field**. The resulting values are then summed up to produce a single output value, which is assigned to the corresponding location in the feature map.

By sliding the filter over the entire input in this way, a model is able to extract various features from the input at different locations and scales. Additionally, by combining the outputs of multiple filters, the model is able to capture complex patterns and higher-level features in the input.

Note. Illustration of the receptive fields in a Convolutional Neural Network (CNN). Input locations can be processed in parallel, but receptive fields are limited in size. Convolution layers need to be stacked to capture far-ranging dependencies. Source: (*Neural Machine Translation With a Transformer and Keras / Text*, 2023).

Support Vector Machines (SVMs) were once popular in the industry, but are not commonly used today. One reason for this is that SVMs do not typically perform as well as gradient boosting or DNNs on larger and more complex datasets. SVMs also do not natively handle multiclass problems. Additionally, SVMs do not transition easily to DNNs as logistic regression models do, which can limit their longevity.

Insider Tip

Read more in-depth about logistic regression, gradient boosting, and DNNs in ML Fundamentals – Modeling under *"2.10: What are some common modeling algorithms?"*.

Regression

Solution 5.13: Build a model that performs regression, e.g., for demand forecasting.

Similar to classification models, a systematic approach can be taken when determining which regression models are best suited for a specific problem:

- **Linear regression:** Linear regression is a common starting point for regression problems. It assumes a linear relationship between the dependent variable and the independent variables.

- **Polynomial regression:** Uses a polynomial function to approximate the relationship between the independent variable and the dependent variable. Polynomial regression can be prone to overfitting if the degree of the polynomial is too high.

  Polynomial regression models are susceptible to outliers and noise, but can be useful in certain applications such as predicting solar panel energy output, where noise levels are relatively low.

- **Support Vector Regression (SVR):** In SVR, the loss function is a margin-based loss known as the ε-insensitive loss. This loss function allows for a certain degree of deviation from the true value, as long as the error falls within a threshold known as ε. The goal of SVR is to find the hyperplane that best fits the data, while minimizing the number of data points that fall outside of the ε threshold. This makes SVR less sensitive to outliers and noise.

  SVR is commonly used in price modeling – which can be noisy – where underlying relationships between the features and target variable are complex and nonlinear.

- **Tree-based approaches:** Ensemble learning techniques that involve combining multiple decision trees to make a prediction. **Random Forest Regression** is a bagging approach that trains each decision tree on random subsets of the data and features. **Boosted Tree Regression** is a boosting approach that trains decision trees sequentially and focuses on correcting the errors or residuals of the previous trees.

  Tree-based approaches are suitable when dealing with datasets that have large numbers of features that can be either continuous or categorical. They also have the ability to deal with missing features and capture feature interactions.

- **Deep neural networks (DNNs):** DNNs have gained immense popularity for a wide range of regression problems. One of the advantages of DNNs for regression is that they can model complex and high-order interactions among the input features, which may be difficult or impossible for traditional methods such as support vector regression (SVR) or boosted trees.

Like in classification models, designing DNNs for regression tasks requires considering how to model **feature interactions**. Factorization Machines (FMs), attention mechanisms, convolutions, and other techniques can be used to achieve this.

Insider Tip

Check out <u>ML System Design: Part 1 – Modeling & Evaluation</u> under *"4.32: Describe what your model architecture might look like."* for a detailed analysis of the DNNs that are employed in industry for regression.

Topic Modeling

In <u>High-Level Design – Topic Modeling</u>, we covered modeling techniques for topic modeling, such as probabilistic topic modeling (e.g., LDA) and neural topic modeling (NTM). Below, we will explore some further aspects of topic modeling.

Solution 5.14: What are some techniques for matching identified topics with a taxonomy?

Topic modeling is typically an unsupervised machine learning technique, which means that it does not require any labeled data to learn from. Instead, it relies on patterns and structures within the data to identify topics.

There might already be a pre-existing taxonomy of topics, which can serve as a reference for the matching process. For instance, if the topic modeling is being done on a dataset of medical records, the taxonomy could include categories such as "cardiology", "neurology", "oncology", etc.

When it comes to matching topics with a taxonomy, there are several techniques that can be used. Here are a few:

- **Top-down approach:** A pre-existing taxonomy is used to guide the topic modeling process. One method involves using a set of prior words or phrases that are known to be relevant to each category in the taxonomy (Jagarlamudi et al., 2012). These priors are incorporated into the topic model through a process called topic seeding, where each prior word or phrase is associated with a particular topic. The topic model is then trained using this seeded approach, which encourages the model to generate topics that are consistent with the predefined vocabulary.

Another method, called supervised LDA (sLDA) (Mcauliffe & Blei, 2007) tries to infer latent topics that are predictive of the response variables (e.g., categories in a taxonomy) at the document level. In other words, sLDA attempts to identify the topic mixture distributions that are most closely associated with particular categories. However, this method restricts documents to being associated with only one category.

A third method, Labeled LDA (L-LDA) (Ramage et al., 2009) overcomes this constraint by modeling each document as a combination of latent topics, while simultaneously constraining the model to generate only the topics that correspond to the pre-existing taxonomy. This is done by modifying the Dirichlet distribution that governs the topic mixture distribution. Specifically, the Dirichlet is restricted to only the topics that correspond to the document's topic labels.

- **Bottom-up approach:** Topics are first identified through topic modeling, and then the most representative words or phrases for each topic are extracted. These words or phrases are then compared to the categories in the taxonomy to determine the best match. This can be done using various methods, such as keyword matching, string matching, or cosine similarity.

- **Human-in-the-loop approach:** This is similar to the bottom-up approach, except that human experts are involved in the process of matching topics with a taxonomy. This can be done by having the experts review the topics, words, and/or phrases identified through topic modeling and manually mapping them to the appropriate categories in the taxonomy.

Solution 5.15: How to evaluate the performance of a topic modeling algorithm?

The evaluation metrics for topic modeling are not universally agreed upon, and there is quite a variety of metrics used. Here are a few:

- **Perplexity** evaluates a topic model by measuring the log-likelihood of a test set, which is the probability of observing words in the test set given the trained model:

$$perplexity = \exp \left\{ -\frac{\sum_{d=1}^{M} log(p(w_d))}{N} \right\}$$

  where $p(w_d)$ is the probability of observing words w_d given the topic distribution for each document and word distribution for each topic, and N is the total number of words in the test set.

  Although perplexity is a commonly used metric, it has been observed that its correlation with human evaluation of topic quality is often weak (Chang et al., 2009).

- **Topic coherence** is a metric that is more closely aligned with human evaluation of topic interpretability (Lau et al., 2014). Topic coherence measures how well the top words in a topic are related to each other, and higher coherence scores generally indicate more coherent and interpretable topics. There are several different methods for calculating topic coherence, but a common approach is to use pointwise mutual information (PMI), which captures the co-occurrence probability of two words. For a given topic, the coherence score is calculated as the average PMI between top words in the topic.

- **Topic diversity** is a complementary metric that is used to evaluate the breadth of topics generated by a model. It measures the percentage of unique words among the top 25 words of all topics. A higher diversity score indicates that the model is capturing a wider range of topics.

- **Downstream performance** can also be used to evaluate the quality of topic models. For example, the topic distributions generated by a model can be used as features for document classification, or in document retrieval and ranking. By examining how well the downstream model performs, we can assess how well the topic model captured the relevant topics within the data.

Clustering

Solution 5.16: Build a model that performs clustering, e.g., to group similar news articles.

Document clustering aims to group similar documents together based on their content. Over the years, several methods have been developed for document clustering, with significant advancements in **document representation** and **cluster assignment** techniques.

Document representation:

The earliest methods for document clustering relied on a **bag-of-words (BoW)** representation, where each document was represented as a vector of word frequencies. However, BoW fails to capture the semantic meaning of words, resulting in poor clustering performance. To address this limitation, **Term Frequency-Inverse Document Frequency (TF-IDF)** was introduced. TF-IDF takes into account the importance of each word in the document and across the corpus, resulting in better clustering performance.

With the rise of deep learning, **word embeddings**, such as Word2Vec and GloVe, became popular. Word embeddings encode words into dense, continuous vectors, capturing the semantic meaning of words. Word embeddings can be used for document representation in a variety of ways: one approach is to compute the average of the word embeddings for all words in a document, creating a single vector that represents the document. Alternatively, word embeddings can be fed into a recurrent neural network (RNN) or long short-term memory (LSTM) model, which can learn to capture the sequential dependencies between words in a document. The final hidden state of the RNN or LSTM can then be used as a fixed-length representation of the document.

More recently, **attention-based mechanisms and Transformer models** like BERT have been used to generate document embeddings by attending to relevant parts of the document. These models can capture long-range dependencies and context, resulting in more accurate and meaningful document representations that can be used for clustering tasks. Furthermore, BERT can also handle out-of-vocabulary (OOV) words through the use of subword tokenization. This process involves splitting words into smaller subword units based on their frequency of occurrence in a large corpus of text. This allows BERT to represent OOV words as a combination of subword units that it has seen before, rather than treating them as completely unknown.

Cluster assignment:

The earliest method for cluster assignment was **k-means**, which partitions the data into a fixed number of clusters based on the distance between data points. However, k-means has several limitations, including sensitivity to initialization, the need for the number of clusters to be specified, and the inability to handle non-spherical clusters.

To address these limitations, **hierarchical clustering** was introduced, which groups similar documents together recursively, resulting in a tree-like structure of clusters. Another approach is **density-based clustering**, such as DBSCAN, which identifies clusters based on regions of high density in the data space.

Gaussian Mixture Models (GMMs) are probabilistic models that aim to find a mixture of multiple Gaussian distributions (clusters) that best fit a given dataset. The training process involves estimating the parameters (mean, covariance, and mixing coefficients) for each Gaussian distribution in the mixture, where popular methods include Expectation Maximization (EM) and variational inference. A GMM assigns a cluster to a new document based on the likelihood of that document belonging to each of the Gaussian distributions (clusters) in the mixture, selecting the cluster with the highest likelihood.

Recent advances in deep learning have led to the development of neural methods for document clustering. **Deep Embedding Clustering (DEC)** (Xie et al., 2016) casts the clustering problem in the form of an autoencoder, where the network is trained to minimize reconstruction error. In the context of clustering, DEC uses an autoencoder structure to learn the underlying clusters. DEC has an alternating two-step procedure. The first step is assigning documents using a probability distribution over clusters; initial cluster centroids are identified with k-means. In the second step, DEC updates the clusters using a KL-divergence loss between the soft assignments and a target distribution, which is computed based on high confidence assignments. A related approach is Deep Convolutional Embedding Clustering (DCEC) (Guo et al., 2017b).

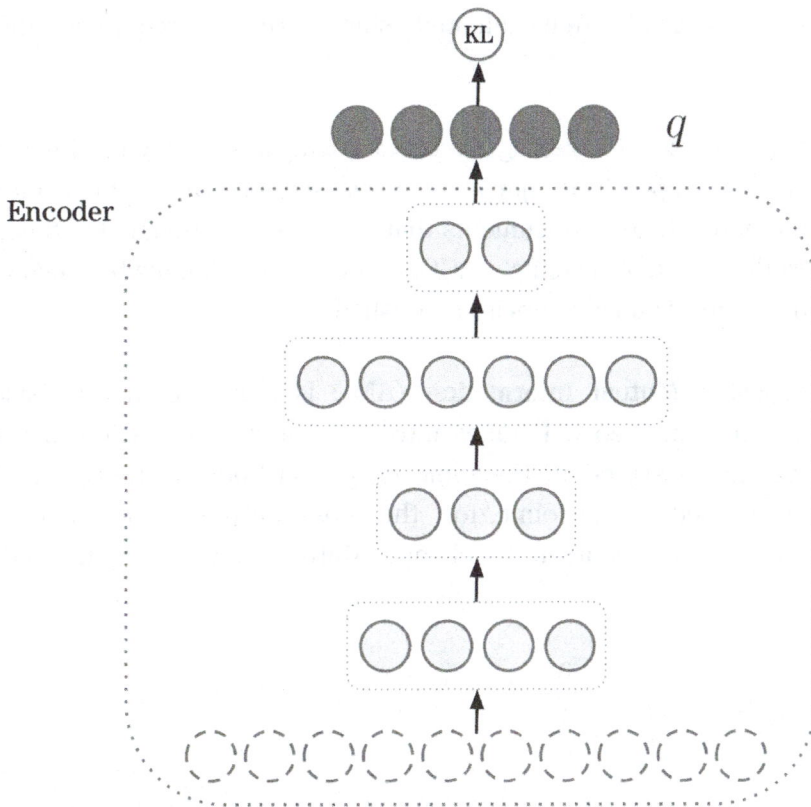

Note. Network structure for DEC. The network is initialized with a stacked autoencoder using least squares loss (not pictured). After this, the decoder is discarded, resulting in the encoder-only structure above. q represents the soft assignment of each data point. The learning process of DEC involves minimizing the KL-divergence loss between the soft assignments q and a target distribution, computed based on high confidence assignments.

It should be noted that the neural methods have the capability to jointly learn both document representation and cluster assignments.

Insider Tip

See this blog (Dahal, n.d.) on DeepNotes for a comparison of recent deep clustering approaches.

Solution 5.17: What are metrics for evaluating the performance of clustering algorithms?

Document clustering is often evaluated using metrics that require ground truth labels.

- **Unsupervised Clustering Accuracy (ACC)** is a widely used metric and is the unsupervised equivalent of classification accuracy. It measures the percentage of documents that are correctly assigned to the ground truth cluster. To calculate ACC, a one-to-one mapping between ground truth labels and clusters is established.

- **Adjusted Mutual Information (AMI)** is a metric that is based on information theory. It takes into account the proportion of samples that are assigned to the same cluster in both clusterings, and then normalized to account for the possibility of the same cluster assignments occurring by chance. Mutual information (MI) is defined as:

$$MI(U, V) = \sum_{i=1}^{|U|} \sum_{j=1}^{|V|} \frac{|U_i \cap V_j|}{N} \log \frac{N|U_i \cap V_j|}{|U_i||V_j|}$$

  where U and V are the two clusterings.

- **Adjusted Rand Index (ARI)** measures the similarity between two clusterings. To be more specific, it considers all pairs of samples and tallies the ones that are assigned to the same cluster in both clusterings, as well as those assigned to different clusters. This metric is adjusted to account for the possibility of chance grouping of elements.

AMI and ARI share similarities. ARI is usually preferred when the reference clustering has a balanced distribution, while AMI is recommended for more unbalanced distributions (Romano et al., 2016).

Generative Modeling

Solution 5.18: Build a model that can generate text, e.g., to summarize a document.

In <u>High-Level Design – Text Summarization</u>, two methods were introduced for text summarization: the extractive approach, which is a cascade of classifiers, and the abstractive approach, which uses generative modeling.

The **extractive method** is already covered above, so we will only provide a brief overview here. The extractive summarization method involves a cascade of classifiers. The process starts with a classifier that (1) identifies relevant sentences, where (2) duplicates can be removed by clustering redundant sentences based on a measure of similarity (e.g., latent representation). Next, sentences are (3) ordered based on their importance or other criteria, such as their position in the text. Finally, (4) coreference resolution can be performed using pairwise classification to group together mentions of the same entity in the text.

Abstractive summarization:

Early approaches to abstractive summarization were grounded in the **noisy channel approach**, inspired by Statistical Machine Translation (SMT) (Banko et al., 2000, Wubben et al., 2012). The noisy channel approach consists of two components, content selection and surface realization, which bear similarity to the Translation Model and Language Model used in SMT. Content selection is focused on the probability of specific tokens appearing in the summary, while surface realization is focused on the arrangement of selected tokens in a meaningful manner.

In recent years, abstractive summarization has become significantly more developed with the advent of **neural approaches**. These approaches use Deep Neural Networks (DNNs) to map the input text to a summary. There are several types of neural approaches that were used for abstractive summarization:

- **Recurrent Neural Networks (RNNs)** are able to model arbitrarily long contexts by leveraging their ability to store previous context information in the network's hidden state. As the network processes each new input token, it updates its hidden state to include information from both the current input and the previous hidden state. An example of an RNN-based text summarizer is (Nallapati et al., 2016).

- **Long Short-Term Memory (LSTMs)** are a variant of RNNs that are designed to better handle long-term dependencies. They do this by incorporating memory cells, which are connected to a series of gates that regulate the flow of information into and out of the cells. These gates are designed to selectively forget or retain information from previous timesteps in the sequence. An example of an LSTM-based text summarizer is (Chopra et al., 2016).

- **Convolutional Neural Networks (CNNs)** were less frequently used for sequence modeling, but offer several advantages. One of the key benefits of CNNs is that they generate fixed-size contextual representations while RNNs store information from the entire past. This enables CNNs to more precisely control the range of dependencies to be modeled. Additionally, CNNs have the ability to build hierarchical representations over input sequences. This hierarchical structure allows them to capture long-range dependencies in the input sequence through a shorter path. An example of a CNN-based text summarizer is ConvS2S (Gehring et al., 2017).

The latest advancements in abstractive summarization are focused on utilizing pre-trained **Large Language Models (LLMs)**. Unlike earlier neural approaches, these models are based on the Transformer architecture and are pre-trained on vast amounts of raw text data before being fine-tuned on the summarization task. Transformer-based models use the attention mechanism to focus on the most relevant parts of the input text when generating the summary.

Insider Tip

See the Appendix – Generative Modeling for a more thorough exploration of Transformers and LLMs.

Some popular approaches leverage the pre-trained LLMs T5, BART, and PEGASUS, for example (Gupta et al., 2021). Unlike the GPT family of LLMs, which are decoder-only models, all three of the aforementioned LLMs are based on the encoder-decoder Transformer architecture.

- **T5 (Text-to-Text Transfer Transformer)** is a LLM developed by Google (Raffel et al., 2020). T5 is trained on a large and varied set of tasks such as machine translation, text classification, and question answering. The unique feature of T5 is that it converts all language problems into a unified text-to-text format. This pre-training approach makes T5 highly flexible for a wide range of natural language processing tasks. T5 is pre-trained using randomly masked text spans of varying sizes and mask ratios.

- **BART (Bidirectional and Auto-Regressive Transformer)** is a LLM that was introduced by Facebook AI Research in 2020 (Lewis et al., 2020). BART is trained using a denoising autoencoder approach, where the model is trained to reconstruct the original input text from a corrupted version of it. BART utilizes a variety of corruption functions during its pre-training phase, which includes masking tokens, deleting tokens, and shuffling sentences randomly.

- **PEGASUS** is an LLM designed specifically for abstractive summarization and shares the same model architecture with BART (Zhang et al., 2020). The pre-training task for PEGASUS is Gap Sentences Generation (GSG), which differs from that of BART. The approach involves masking entire sentences from a document and then training the language model to generate those masked sentences based on the remaining document context. To select which sentences to mask, PEGASUS employs different strategies, such as randomly selecting a set number of sentences, or selecting the first few sentences.

Insider Tip

Read more about neural abstractive summarization techniques in (Cao, 2022).

Solution 5.19: What are some metrics used for assessing quality in generative tasks?

Evaluation metrics for generative tasks share a common objective of measuring the **similarity between machine-generated text and reference text(s)**. To achieve this, two types of metrics are used: co-occurrence-based and edit distance-based.

Co-occurrence metrics:

- Text summarization primarily uses **ROUGE** (Recall-Oriented Understudy for Gisting Evaluation). ROUGE measures the overlap between the generated summary and the reference summary(ies) in terms of n-gram co-occurrence. ROUGE-1, ROUGE-2, and ROUGE-L – using longest common subsequence – are variants of ROUGE.

- Machine Translation uses the **BLEU** (Bilingual Evaluation Understudy) score. Like ROUGE, BLEU also measures the degree of n-gram co-occurrence. The main difference lies in their orientation towards either precision or recall. BLEU is precision-oriented, measuring the percentage of n-grams in the machine-generated text matching those in the reference text. In contrast, ROUGE is recall-oriented, measured by the percentage of n-grams in the reference text matching the machine-generated text.

Edit distance metrics:

- ASR systems are evaluated using the **WER (word error rate)**. WER measures the difference between the machine-generated transcript and the reference transcript(s) in terms of the number of word substitutions, deletions, and insertions.

- OCR systems are evaluated using two metrics - **word accuracy** and **character accuracy**. This is analogous to how ASR systems are assessed. To compute accuracy in OCR, either WER or CER (Character Error Rate) is used. Accuracy is derived by subtracting the value of WER or CER from 1.

Deployment & Serving

Since online prediction is addressed in other sections of this guide (see ML System Design: Part 1 – Deployment & Serving and ML Infrastructure Design – Online, below we will concentrate on offline predictions.

Solution 5.20: What are the steps to prepare a model to serve predictions?

The typical ML modeling workflow includes components for:

1. **Data preparation, analysis, and transformation:** This step involves collecting, cleaning, and transforming data into a format that is suitable for training ML models. During this phase, data may undergo analysis and/or visualization to identify patterns and relationships that could be leveraged to develop the model, or any anomalies or irregularities that could potentially impair the model's predictive capabilities.

2. **Training, tuning, and evaluating:** In this step, the model is developed and trained using the prepared data. The model is then evaluated using various metrics to assess its performance. One may choose to tune the hyperparameters of the model during the training phase by conducting a hyperparameter search based on various factors such as a defined search space and objective. Upon completing the hyperparameter tuning process, the model trainer can be fed with the optimized hyperparameters.

3. **Deploying to production:** Before deploying the model to production, it is important to ensure that it is accurate and reliable. This is typically achieved through a **model blessing** step, where the model is validated against a set of predefined criteria to ensure that it meets the desired level of performance.

    Once the model has been blessed, it can be deployed to the production environment. This involves uploading the model to the **model repository**, which serves as a centralized location for storing and managing trained models and associated metadata, such as versions. The model repository allows developers to easily manage, store, and retrieve models, facilitating the sharing of models across teams and projects.

Before deploying the model, it can be helpful to perform a model **infrastructure check** to ensure that the model can be successfully integrated into the production environment. This may involve loading the model into a sandbox environment and testing its performance by serving a few predictions. This helps to identify any potential issues that may arise when the model is deployed in a production setting.

Insider Tip

Libraries like TFX Pipelines (*Understanding TFX Pipelines*, 2023) are frequently used to define production workflows and are executed within an orchestration system like Kubeflow Pipelines (*Introduction / Kubeflow*, 2022).

Solution 5.21: How to make offline predictions, such as inferring topics from a collection of text?

Context:

Offline prediction refers to the use of ML models in batch scoring jobs for a large number of data points, where predictions are not required in real-time serving. This approach is typically used in scenarios where it is not necessary to generate predictions immediately or in real-time, but instead, the focus is on processing a large number of data points in an efficient manner.

Use cases for batch prediction include:

- **Email and push notifications**, such as retention campaigns and promotion campaigns, which do not require real-time serving.

- Building **datasets that feed into other systems**. One example of this is inferring demographics for users, which can then be used for ad targeting. Another example is extracting key aspects or features from customer reviews, which can be used for filtering purposes.

- Performing **data analysis**, such as sentiment analysis, which involves reviewing customer feedback, capturing trending topics in a given market, and identifying emergent customer behaviors, such as shifts in customer preferences.

- **Demand and price modeling** is another area where offline predictions can be used to adjust pricing strategies and optimize inventory levels to ensure that products are priced competitively while still meeting demand.

Approach:

Unlike online prediction, batch prediction involves the collection of data in a data warehouse or cloud storage, followed by a scheduled processing of that data. Here are the steps involved:

1. If the data is stored in a data warehouse, it can be exported to **cloud storage**, such as Google Cloud Storage. Data stored in a data warehouse is typically structured and optimized for querying, but not necessarily optimized for batch processing with ML models.

2. To prepare the data for batch prediction, it can be preprocessed by filtering, aggregation, or transformation. A **data processing pipeline** like Dataflow can be used to perform these preprocessing steps as a scheduled job or via a trigger.

3. A **batch prediction job** is executed which uses the trained model from the model repository to generate predictions for all relevant data points, such as all the data within a specific time window. The model is loaded into memory, and the predictions are produced in parallel using distributed computing resources. One method is with Hadoop MapReduce, which can parallelize the prediction process across multiple nodes.

4. After the batch prediction job is finished, the resulting predictions are **written back to cloud storage** in a suitable format, such as CSV or Parquet. Along with the actual predictions, the output also includes any related metadata or information, such as row identifiers or confidence scores.

5. Finally, the predictions can be **exported into a data warehouse or other system** for further analysis or use. For example, they could be loaded into BigQuery for data analysis, or used to populate a feature store that other models can employ in online predictions.

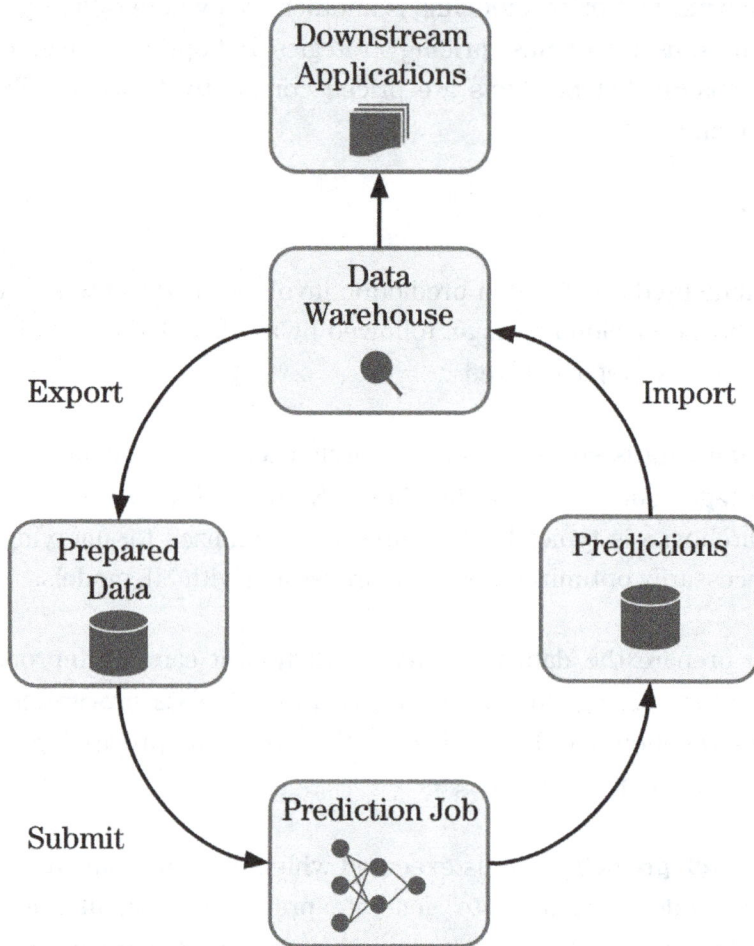

Note. Example pipeline for offline predictions. There are many different approaches that can be taken. One variation is the absence of the data warehouse component in certain pipelines. Another variation is the use of a separate job to prepare the data for scoring. Finally, downstream dependencies can be updated from distributed storage via batch job, or receive updates directly via pub/sub.

Insider Tip

> Read more about offline and online predictions in the Google Cloud Architecture blog (*Minimizing Real-Time Prediction Serving Latency in Machine Learning | Cloud Architecture Center*, 2023).

A Note about LLMs

This chapter discussed the prevalence of neural components, such as DNNs, in modern ML systems. Over the years, these neural components have improved at modeling feature interactions through approaches such as deep factorization machines, convolutions, and attention-based mechanisms.

A recent development in the field is the use of pre-trained Large Language Models (LLMs) for traditionally discriminative tasks through fine-tuning techniques. For instance, **BloombergGPT** (Wu et al., 2023b) is a LLM that was evaluated on sentiment analysis, text classification, and NER tasks, achieving impressive results – although it was not directly compared to other state-of-art systems like the BiLSTM-CNN-CRF for NER (Vajjala & Balasubramaniam, 2022).

Additionally, LLMs have even been explored for **retrieval and ranking purposes**. Baidu, for instance, experimented with using ChatGPT for relevance ranking (Sun et al., 2023).

These developments are still new and are not required knowledge for ML interviews. However, it is always a good idea to stay up-to-date with significant advances in the field, as they could have implications for major changes in the industry.

Insider Tip

For a more comprehensive exploration of LLMs and fine-tuning, please refer to the Appendix – Generative Models.

---

6. ML Infrastructure Design

If you are a Senior+ ML candidate, interviewers may want to evaluate your proficiency in implementing ML solutions at scale. Applying ML to real-world problems poses unique challenges, such as handling large amounts of data and traffic, balancing accuracy and performance, optimizing training and serving processes, and crafting resilient systems for feature and model management. In this chapter, we will explore the questions that arise in such interviews.

In the preceding chapters of ML System Design, specifically in the Deployment & Serving sections, we examined various components of ML infrastructure. In the subsequent discussion, we will delve into additional subjects related to ML infrastructure, including more advanced topics.

In practice, these interview questions are often incorporated in the ML System Design interview session itself. Occasionally, the interviewer may shorten or skip the Serving segment of the ML System Design interview to allocate more time for questions about ML at scale.

Practice Interview

Once again, we list common questions for this interview session below.

Read through each question, write down an answer, before consulting the Interview Solutions section.

Offline

6.1: Do you have some ideas for accelerating the model development process?

6.2: How to speed up model training (on a single instance)?

6.3: How to train a model on distributed instances?

6.4: What are key criteria when evaluating model training pipelines (orchestration)?

6.5: What happens if one or more instances fail during training?

6.6: What are some approaches for keeping the model up-to-date?

6.7: Describe some ways to optimize the model you trained for ultra low-latency.

Online

6.8: What are components of the model serving system?

6.9: What are some things that can break? If I'm on-call, what to check for?

6.10: How to speed up feature hydration and processing at serving time?

6.11: What are some ways to improve serving latency?

6.12: How to enable the server to handle a large number of requests?

6.13: Describe the process to update the model in the model server.

6.14: How to deploy and roll-back a model?

6.15: What metrics should the server monitor?

6.16: How to troubleshoot inferior online model performance compared to offline metrics?

Interview Solutions

Offline

Solution 6.1: Do you have some ideas for accelerating the model development process?

There are several approaches to speed up the model development process:

- **Experiment with smaller datasets:** Training on smaller datasets can reduce training time and allow for quicker iteration. Prototyping with Pandas for data loading and transformation is faster compared to using TFX Pipeline. Models built with Pandas can be easily carried over to TFX.

- **Start with simpler models:** Similarly, if your goal is to prove a product thesis by building a model from the ground up, it is advisable to start with a basic model architecture, like a multilayer perceptron (MLP), employing straightforward feature preprocessing techniques – see (*Training Using the Built-In Wide and Deep Algorithm | AI Platform Training*, 2023) for some ideas. Using smaller models can also help mitigate the risk of overfitting on smaller datasets.

- **Leverage rapid prototyping frameworks:** BigQuery ML (BQML) and AutoML facilitate rapid testing of hypotheses, from data loading to model training, with minimal coding effort. They are capable of efficiently training on large datasets. The main drawbacks are the limits on customization (e.g., model size limits, feature preprocessing, missing value imputation) and therefore model performance. However, to achieve additional customization, one would need to rewrite the model, such as with Keras.

- **Perform feature selection:** While having more features can generally improve a model's performance, with careful feature selection, there are diminishing returns compared to improvements in development speed. A model with 2,000 features may only modestly outperform a model with the top 200 most important ones. When selecting features, consider not only their importance but also incorporation into the model. Take into account the costs of hydrating the features. Additionally, certain types of features, such as sparse, variable-length, sequential, and hierarchical features, require more development effort to set up model training.

- **Select efficient algorithms:** Consider algorithms that are easily parallelized and known for training speed and efficiency, such as XGBoost and LightGBM. One drawback of this approach is reduced compatibility with Tensorflow and PyTorch, which can make it more difficult to transition from one to the other.

- **Use transfer learning:** In certain situations, using pre-trained models – or at least reusing existing embeddings – can save time. However, if your task is domain-specific and requires knowledge that is not captured in the pre-trained model, it may not be appropriate to use it.

- **Hyperparameter tuning:** Automate the process of hyperparameter tuning to save time and improve model performance. Many platforms support automatic hyperparameter tuning out-of-box, such as Tensorflow (*Introduction to the Keras Tuner*, 2022) and SageMaker (*Perform Automatic Model Tuning With SageMaker - Amazon SageMaker*, n.d.).

Solution 6.2: How to speed up model training (on a single instance)?

Assuming no changes to the model architecture or additional feature engineering, to speed up model training on a single instance, you can consider the following approaches:

- **Minimize data loading time:** When dealing with larger datasets, be wary of using some Tensorflow extract, transform, and load (ETL) components out-of-box. For example, TFX BigQueryExampleGen may be convenient, but it may be more efficient to persist the dataset as TFRecords on disk and directly read the data. Additionally, TF Transform has been known to operate slowly on large datasets – particularly for normalization – and it may be faster to instead sample the dataset and adapt a Keras Normalization layer on the sampled data.

- **Larger batch sizes:** Larger batch sizes reduce the number of times the parameters are updated, which can speed up training by reducing the time spent updating the parameters. Larger batch sizes may converge faster, but they may also require more epochs to achieve the same level of accuracy as smaller batch sizes.

- **Optimize learning rate schedules:** Fine-tune the learning rate schedule to balance the speed of convergence and the stability of the optimization process.

- **Cheaper gradients:** Consider using activation functions with a low cost of gradient computation, such as ReLU or PReLU.

- **Use optimized implementations:** Use libraries and frameworks that have optimized implementations of popular algorithms, such as TensorFlow and PyTorch.

- **Single-instance parallelism:** Methods such as Hogwild! (Niu et al., 2011) enable batch-level parallelization of stochastic gradient descent (SGD) on a single instance. Matrix multiplication and other linear algebraic operations can also be parallelized.

- **Utilize GPU acceleration:** GPUs are optimized for parallel processing, have large memory bandwidth, and are designed specifically for matrix calculations, which can significantly speed up training time.

- **Smart initialization:** Providing good starting values for the model parameters can lead to faster convergence and better performance. For example, weights can be initialized with values drawn from a normal distribution with zero mean and a target variance (e.g., Glorot, or Xavier initializer). Another approach is to use parameters from a previously trained version of the model to initialize parameters in the new model.

- **Batch normalization:** This technique normalizes the inputs to each layer of a DNN, which helps to prevent the activations from becoming too large or too small. This can improve the stability of the training process and lead to faster convergence.

- **Downsampling:** In some cases, training data can be reduced without significant penalty to model performance. For example, when dealing with a dataset that has imbalanced classes, downsampling the negative class may lead to improved model performance in addition to faster training.

Solution 6.3: How to train a model on distributed instances?

There are several ways to distribute model training:

1. **Data parallelism:** In this approach, each worker node has a copy of the entire model, and the data is split among the nodes. Each node computes gradients on its portion of the data, and the gradients are aggregated to update the model parameters. This approach can be further divided into two sub-approaches:

   - Synchronous data parallelism: All worker nodes compute gradients at the same time and then aggregate the gradients before updating the model. Copies of the updated gradients are sent to all the workers. This ensures workers will always have the same model parameters, but can slow down training.

   - Asynchronous data parallelism: Each worker node computes gradients independently, and the model parameters are updated whenever a node completes its computation. This approach enables workers to operate independently, which is beneficial when workers have varying computational capacities, at the expense of working on slightly stale versions of the model.

2. **Model parallelism:** In this approach, different parts of the model are assigned to different worker nodes. This approach is most suitable for models that are too large to fit in the memory of a single device or node. Models can be partitioned horizontally (split inside layers) or vertically (split between layers) (Langer et al., 2020). Each node computes gradients on its portion of the model, and the nodes communicate with one another to exchange shared parameters in the forward and backward passes.

There are two methods for implementing data parallelism:

1. **Centralized:** In this approach, parameter servers store the model parameters. During training, worker nodes communicate with parameter servers to (1) fetch model parameters, and (2) send gradient updates. This method decouples the tasks of gradient computation and model updates, simplifying model state management, but it has the disadvantage of making the parameter servers a communication bottleneck.

2. **Decentralized:** In a decentralized architecture, worker nodes communicate with other worker nodes to update the model parameters. One way to do this is Ring AllReduce (Patarasuk & Yuan, 2009), where a worker node communicates with its neighbors in a ring topology to aggregate gradients. Gradients are transmitted clockwise around the ring, and at each step, each node combines the gradients it has received with its own gradients. This process continues until all nodes have combined their gradients, and the resulting aggregated gradient is sent back around the ring to each node. The nodes then use this aggregated gradient to update their copies of the model.

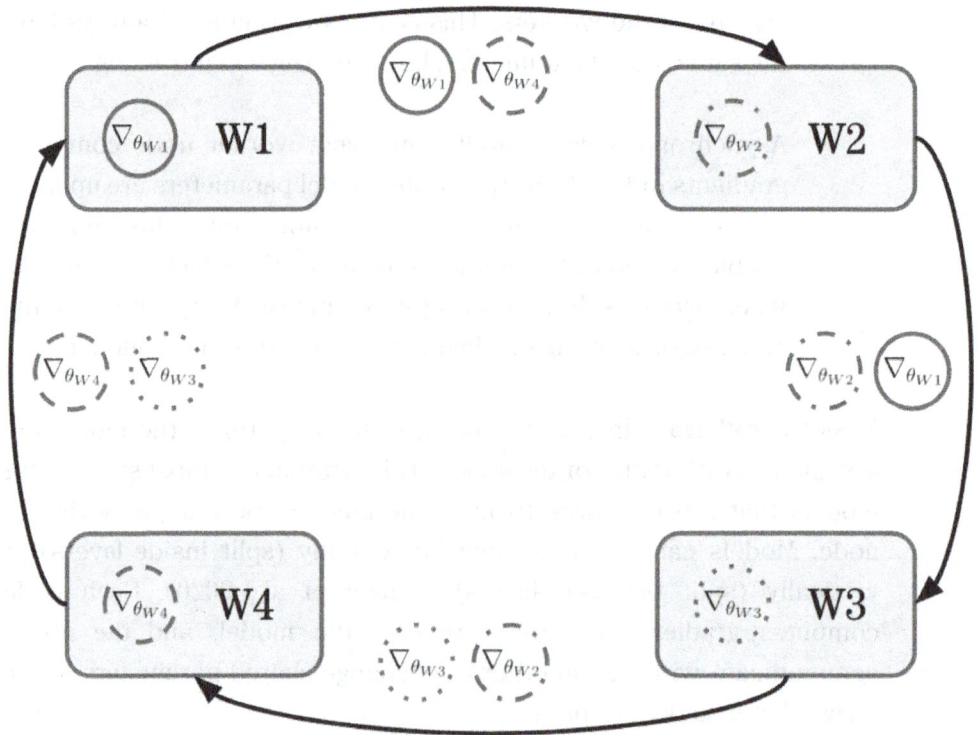

Note. In Ring AllReduce, each worker transmits its partial gradient to the next worker, which accumulates the partial gradient with its own partial gradient. Once all the partial gradients have been accumulated, the full gradient is circulated without further accumulation.

Insider Tip

Read Twitter's blog for practical considerations in distributed model training (Bean, 2020).

Solution 6.4: What are key criteria when evaluating model training pipelines (orchestration)?

When evaluating model training pipelines, there are several key criteria that should be considered to ensure that the pipeline is efficient, robust, and reliable. Some of the most important criteria include:

1. **Ease of retraining:** The ability to retrain the model easily is important, especially when new data becomes available or when the model needs to be updated. The pipeline should have the capability to handle warm starting, where training is resumed from a previously trained model, without losing previous training progress. Other factors to consider include the time and resources required to retrain the model, and the ability to schedule and automate the process.

2. **Fault tolerance:** Modeling pipelines can fail due to various reasons, such as data corruption or network issues. Therefore, it's essential to have a fault-tolerant pipeline that can handle retries, resume training from the last successful checkpoint, and continue training from the last good state, should training fail.

3. **State management:** State management is crucial when it comes to modeling pipelines. The pipeline should be able to handle different training dates and scenarios such as skipping ahead if data got corrupted or if the model is delayed. It should be easy to roll back to a previous state, revert to a checkpoint or change the pipeline configuration.

4. **Observability:** Observability is the ability to monitor model training progress, identify issues, and obtain actionable insights. The pipeline should provide real-time monitoring and logging of training events, with the ability to track metrics and visualizations over time. The logs should be easily accessible and queryable for debugging purposes. Alerts should be set up to notify the team of any unusual activity in the pipeline.

Other factors to consider when evaluating model training pipelines include scalability, cost, and ease of deployment.

Solution 6.5: What happens if one or more instances fail during training?

If one or more instances fail during model training in a distributed setting, it can have several impacts:

- **Training time increase:** If an instance fails, the training process will slow down as the remaining instances pick up the slack.

- **Data loss:** If an instance fails while processing data, some data may not be processed. If the instance that fails was responsible for processing a particular subset of the training data, the resulting model may be biased towards the data that was processed by the remaining instances.

- **Performance degradation:** If an instance fails while updating model parameters, the model parameters may become inconsistent, reducing the performance of the model.

To mitigate the impact of instance failures, it is important to have a robust mechanism in place for monitoring and controlling the training process. This can include strategies for:

- Checkpointing model parameters.
- Replicating instances.
- Automatically restarting failed instances.

Additionally, it may be beneficial to use fault-tolerant algorithms and protocols that can handle failures and maintain consistency in the presence of faults.

Solution 6.6: What are some approaches for keeping the model up-to-date?

Model updates are important to ensure that the model continues to produce accurate and relevant predictions over time. Models can get stale due to changes in data over time, such as changes in the features, the labels, or the relationship between the features and the labels.

Models can be updated upon a number of triggers, including (1) **time-based periodic refresh**, (2) **performance-based refresh**, such as when model performance degrades beyond a threshold, (3) or when **data changes**, such as when features are added, fixed, or deprecated.

There are several approaches to update a model, including:

- **Batch:** A new model is trained from scratch on the latest data and then redeployed to prediction. This offers the advantage of reduced susceptibility to underlying issues that might have been present in the previous model. However, a disadvantage is that this approach may lead to underperformance since the new model is not trained on all of the available data.

- **Online:** Utilize existing parameters as the basis for the new model (aka. "warm start") and then fine-tune it using the latest data. This approach should lead to a gradual improvement in the model's performance, unless the new data significantly deviates from the old data.

    When deploying the new model to a model server, the server can (1) simply be restarted to incorporate the latest version of the model, (2) or model snapshots can be swapped in and out of production through a model configuration (aka. "hotswapping"). Hotswapping can help reduce downtime and allow for more flexible and adaptive deployment of models, such as when model servers host a large number of models.

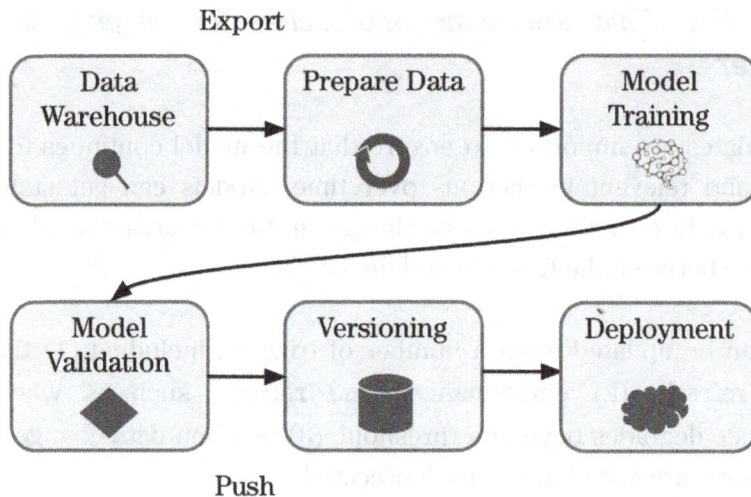

Export

Data Warehouse → Prepare Data → Model Training

Model Validation ← Versioning → Deployment

Push

Note. A training and deployment pipeline for batch and online workflows.

- **Continuous:** This approach involves incrementally updating the model as new data streams in, allowing the model to continuously adapt to changing data distributions. This may be required in cases where models can become stale faster than the time it takes for the model to fully retrain, e.g., in ads click prediction (Ktena et al., 2019). In continuous training, a training server which hosts the model subscribes to a stream of training data. The training server computes gradients and updates model parameters (e.g., online gradient descent (Hazan et al., 2007)), publishing those updates to the model server. The setup of such systems is complex, and the models that can be supported are limited.

Solution 6.7: Describe some ways to optimize the model you trained for ultra low-latency.

Suppose that conventional methods such as feature selection, reducing the number of layers, and decreasing layer size have already been implemented.

Here are several techniques to further optimize the model for serving:

- **Clean up the model:** First, it is important to remove any unnecessary components that may exist in the model's prediction path. These may include unused nodes, redundant nodes, or other components that were necessary for training but are no longer needed for prediction.

Another step is to look for sub-graphs within the model that always evaluate to constant expressions. These sub-graphs can be replaced with their corresponding constant values. In addition, it may help to fold multiplications from batch normalization into weight multiplications of the previous layer.

Insider Tip

Read about these techniques and more in the Google blog on optimizing TensorFlow models (Ramsey, 2018).

- **Input compression:** Production ranking models often use thousands if not tens of thousands of input features. However, this can result in significant latency during inference because the features must be hydrated from various sources and sent over the network to the model server. Additionally, the model must ingest and preprocess the features. To address this issue, store dense embeddings for target and candidate features during training and fetch only the embeddings at inference time. The embeddings can be fed into the inner layer of the model. It is also important to consider how features are passed into the model, as the tf.Example format can be quite verbose. To reduce space, densify the inputs by combining features, such as through concatenation, and obfuscating feature names. The drawback of this approach is that it becomes more challenging to modify features and model architecture once deployed.

- **Efficient caching strategies:** Caching can have a significant impact on the latency of production systems, and there are multiple points where caching can be implemented. For instance, caching of target and candidate features can occur at both the instance (in memory) and datacenter level (e.g., memcache) to optimize latency and hit rate. Additionally, optimization of crossing feature hydration can be achieved by fetching the crossing features in parallel with target features, often early in the ranking request. Pairwise model scores can even be cached with a short time-to-live (TTL). As mentioned above, rather than caching individual features, embeddings can be cached to densify the feature space and improve latency.

- **Batch inference:** One common challenge in ranking problems is the network throughput to the model server, particularly when the number of candidates is high. Adjust the batch size of each request in order to achieve a balance between network traffic and per-instance computational load.

- **Two Tower:** Also known as SplitNet or vector-product DNNs, the Two Tower approach partitions the existing DNN into two parallel sub neural networks. Target features are fed into one network, and candidate features are fed into the other. At the end of each network is a fixed size vector which represents the target embedding and candidate embedding respectively. The final prediction score can be computed many ways, for example, a dot product with sigmoid activation. This can significantly speed up inference at serving time by fetching the target and candidate embeddings (e.g., from a cache) and performing a dot product. This approach is adopted by a number of companies for ranking models, such as Twitter (Dilipkumar & Chen, 2019). On the flip side, DNN architectures that rely on crossing target and candidate features are not compatible.

- **Quantization:** Quantize the model to reduce the precision of weights and activations from float32 to int8 or even binary, which can reduce computation time.

Insider Tip

Read more about various quantization strategies in the Tensorflow documentation (*Model Optimization*, 2021).

- **Efficient neural network families**, such as ShuffleNet (Zhang et al., 2018) which groups convolutional layers, MobileNet (Howard et al., 2017), and EfficientNet (Tan & Le, 2019).

- **Model compression:** There are numerous recent advances in model compression techniques. Here are some examples:

  - Knowledge distillation (Cho & Hariharan, 2019).
  - Low-rank approximations of weight matrices (Ma et al., 2019).
  - Compressing the input layer of DNNs (Nakkiran et al., 2015).

- Pruning weights and connections that contribute least to model performance (Han et al., 2015).
- Sharing weights by clustering each layer (*Weight Clustering | TensorFlow Model Optimization*, 2022).
- Dynamic DNNs that activate sub-regions of the DNN based on the input (Han et al., 2021).

Online

Solution 6.8: What are components of the model serving system?

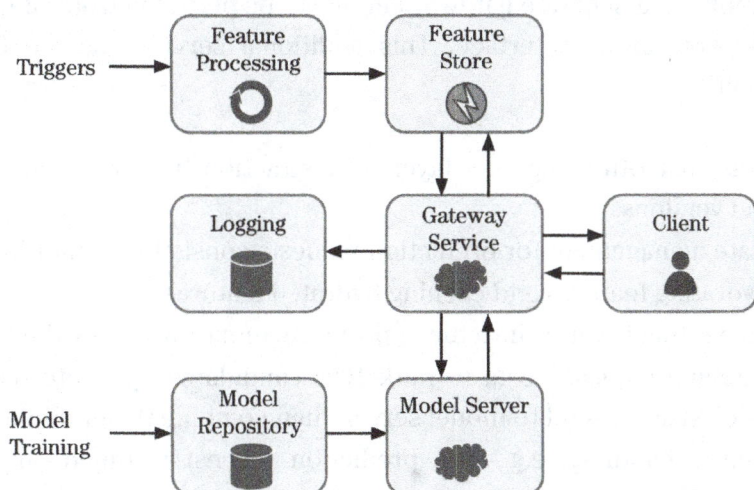

Besides typical functions of web servers like monitoring & logging, load balancing, and authorization, a model serving system typically consists of the following components:

1. **Model loading and management:** Functionality for loading models of varying formats and from different repositories, and organizing models for efficient access.

2. **Model serving:** Handle model requests and return model predictions to the client.

3. **Model versioning and hotswapping:** Manage model versions, poll for model updates, and support hotswapping of models without

downtime. This allows for seamless updates of models without interrupting the service.

4. **Model repository:** This component stores the trained models, metadata, and version history, allowing the model server to switch between different versions of the model as needed.

5. **Management interface:** A web-based or command-line interface for managing and deploying models, as well as monitoring and possibly debugging the model output.

It is common for a separate gateway service to be placed in front of the model server to serve as an interface. This additional service has the following responsibilities:

- APIs that offer clients a layer of abstraction from raw model names and versions.
- State management for prediction requests consisting of multiple calls.
- Hydrating features and caching hydrated features.
- Converting features into the appropriate input format for the models.
- Batching requests: e.g., to rank 1000 candidates, split into requests of batch size 32, send to model server, then combine the predictions.
- Failure handling: e.g., if a prediction request is timed out, apply a backoff strategy.
- Scribing the request and predictions for data analysis and model training.
- Publishing predictions to a store for other systems to consume.

Solution 6.9: What are some things that can break? If I'm on-call, what to check for?

As an on-call engineer for a model server, there are a variety of things that can potentially break and require your attention. Here are some common issues that you may encounter:

- **Model failure:** The model can fail to load, fail to predict or produce incorrect outputs, or produce inconsistent results over time. This can happen due to a variety of reasons such as a corrupted model file, issues with the model code, or changes in the input format.

- **Infrastructure issues:** The model server infrastructure may encounter issues such as network failures, hardware failures, disk space issues, or other problems that can impact the availability and performance of the server. It is possible for the failure of a few problematic instances – "bad actors" – to trigger alarms, as thresholds may be set at high percentiles (such as p99) or based on the count of failures.

- **Resource constraints:** The model server may encounter resource constraints such as running out of memory, CPU, or GPU resources, which can impact the performance and availability of the server. Such scenarios occur particularly during instances of high traffic, data center failovers, or the deployment of a new service.

- **Code issues:** The model server code may have bugs or errors that can impact its functionality and performance, or it may not be optimized for efficiency and scalability. This occurs particularly when deploying code changes.

- **Data issues:** The input features to the model may contain errors or missing values, which can impact the model's performance and produce incorrect outputs.

- **Dependency issues:** The model server may have dependencies on other software components, such as database servers, data catalogs, or external APIs, that can fail or have performance issues that impact the model server.

As an on-call engineer, it's important to have a plan in place for triaging issues quickly and escalating them as appropriate to ensure the availability and reliability of the model server.

Solution 6.10: How to speed up feature hydration and processing at serving time?

There are several ways to speed up feature hydration and feature processing at serving time:

- **Optimize lookup:** Improving feature storage and retrieval is a way to improve feature hydration, which generally involves two types of features: static reference features (e.g., demographics) and dynamic real-time features (e.g., windowed counts). To handle static features, an offline process reads entity data from a data warehouse and performs feature engineering before storing the features in a low-latency lookup. For dynamic features, a streaming pipeline can be used to capture and aggregate events in real time. The real-time aggregates are then stored in a low-latency lookup.

Insider Tip

Examples of low-latency lookup data stores include Google's Datastore for reads and Bigtable for read/writes. Consider using a feature store such as Feast to manage features for serving (Sell & Pienaar, 2019).

- **Caching:** Caching extracted features, frequently referenced feature values (e.g., for crossing features), and even prediction scores can greatly reduce latency. Caching can occur at both the individual instance and datacenter levels, and can even be performed preemptively for warm start situations.

- **Multi-stage hydration:** Feature hydration may occur at different times in the request lifecycle. For a recommendation request, target features (and even some crossing features) can be hydrated at the start of the request in parallel with candidate generation.

- **Densifying:** Storing features (which may be natively in a format like JSON) in a format that is more suitable for input to the model can greatly reduce the fetch latency.

- **Precomputing:** Extracted features are often used to derive other features, such as rates and ratios, windowed features, binary features, etc. Precompute derivative features in advance and keep them in storage to reduce the processing time.

- **Grouping features:** Organizing features into logical groups (e.g., candidate features of a particular interaction type) and storing them together reduces network congestion.

- **Parallel processing:** Use parallel processing techniques to hydrate features and process them concurrently. For example, retrieve features in parallel from multiple sources, such as different data stores, and combine them prior to prediction.

- **Same-instance:** Feature extraction and prediction can take place on the same instance to save the hop to the model server. However, in certain situations this is not practical, such as when a ranking request needs to be batched to multiple model servers for prediction.

Solution 6.11: What are some ways to improve serving latency?

Here are some ways to improve serving latency in a model server:

- **Feature hydration:** Improving feature hydration can speed up prediction and optimize overall system performance. One way to speed up feature hydration is by using a low-latency data store optimized for fast read operations. Densifying features by encoding them in a more compact format can further reduce the amount of time required. Another approach to improving feature hydration is to be creative in the hydration logic itself, such as adjusting the ordering of network calls.

Insider Tip

See the above question *"6.10: How to speed up feature hydration and processing at serving time?"* for more details on how these can be achieved.

- **Caching:** With caching, the server can avoid re-computing or fetching results repeatedly for the same inputs, which can help to reduce the overall latency of the server. Caching can be used to cache different types of data, such as features, predictions, or even the output of intermediate layers of the model. However, it is important to note that caching also increases the complexity of the system and associated maintenance effort. Another challenge of caching is that it can lead to stale data.

- **Model optimization:** Optimizing the model can significantly improve the performance of your model server. The model can be sped up by reducing its size or complexity, pruning unnecessary features, and optimizing its computations.

- **Precomputing predictions:** Precompute predictions in an offline batch scoring job and store them in a low read-latency lookup data store. This eliminates the need for the client to call the model for online prediction. Instead, the client fetches the precomputed predictions from the data store using a unique key. The process involves ingesting and processing data, running a batch prediction job to produce predictions, exporting the predictions to the low-latency lookup, and finally, having the client send a prediction request to the data store (sometimes via a gateway service).

Precomputing predictions for all entities or items may not be feasible due to the high computational cost and time required. One solution is to use a hybrid approach, where predictions are precomputed only for the top entities by some criteria such as activity. For the remaining entities, rely on the model server for online prediction.

Another technique involves mapping high cardinality entities to a smaller number of hash buckets with lower resolution. This can significantly reduce the number of unique entities that need to be precomputed, thus decreasing the precomputation time and storage space required. However, this approach comes with the downside of reduced prediction accuracy.

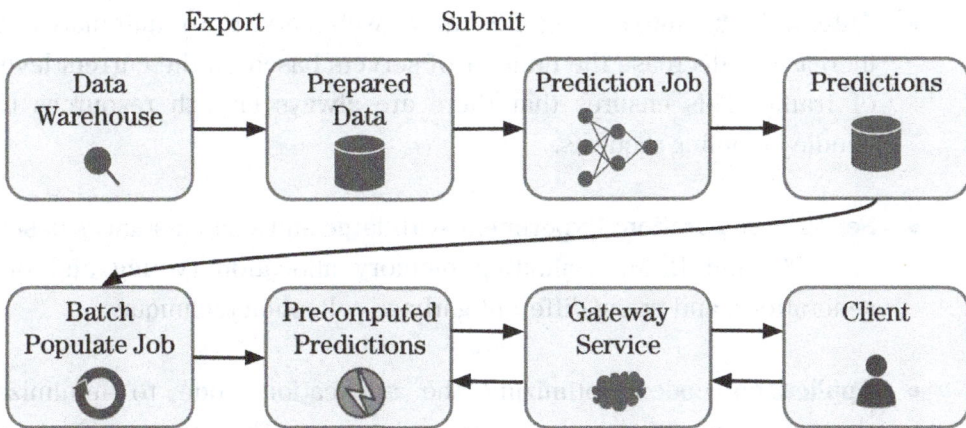

Note. Workflow for precomputing and caching predictions for online serving.

- **Scaling resources:** Make sure your model server is well scaled and close to the client: Deploying your model server closer to the users can significantly reduce the network latency and improve the overall serving latency. Scale the model server horizontally by adding more instances, or vertically by adding more hardware resources, to handle load.

- **Inspecting the model server:** Identifying and fixing bottlenecks in the model server can help to improve the overall serving latency. Bottlenecks can be caused by a variety of issues, such as inefficient garbage collection, slow I/O operations, or network congestion.

Solution 6.12: How to enable the server to handle a large number of requests?

In general, a web service can be scaled to handle a large number of requests using various techniques:

- **Load balancing:** Load balancing is a technique used to distribute incoming traffic across multiple servers to prevent any single server from becoming overwhelmed. Round robin is a simple method that cycles through a list of servers, distributing incoming requests equally among them. Other techniques include least connections, IP hash, and weighted round robin.

- **Auto-scaling:** Auto-scaling allows a web service to automatically increase or decrease the number of servers based on the current level of traffic. This ensures that there are always enough resources to handle incoming requests.

- **Server configuration:** Experiment with large and small instances based on CPU and RAM, evaluating memory allocation (young and old generation), and trying different garbage collection techniques.

- **Application code:** Optimizing the application code to minimize response times and reduce resource usage. This can also include effective use of timeouts and fallback strategies, and quality factor to dynamically adjust compute based on traffic (*Resilient Ad Serving at Twitter-Scale*, 2016).

- **Dependency optimization:** Dependencies are often a bottleneck in web services. For example, optimize database dependencies by using appropriate indexing, partitioning, and caching techniques can significantly improve the performance of the web service. Reuse established database connections instead of creating a new connection for each request.

- **Microservices:** Microservices are small, independently deployable services that can be used to break down a monolithic web service into smaller, more manageable components. This can make it easier to scale individual components based on the level of traffic they receive.

In addition to these, serving ML models benefit heavily from caching:

- **Cache features, embeddings, and even model predictions.** Caching may occur at multiple levels: instance-level caching and datacenter-level caching (e.g., memcache) involve a trade-off between latency and hit rate.

- For exceptionally high throughput requirements, consider **precomputing** offline the embeddings (e.g., for Two Tower approach) and/or model scores.

Solution 6.13: Describe the process to update the model in the model server.

At a high-level, there are two approaches to updating a model in general:

1. **Separate the hardware** used for model training and model serving. By dedicating distinct resources to each task, hardware can be optimized for the specific demands of either training or serving, resulting in faster training times and lower latency during serving. Additionally, keeping training and serving separate can make it easier to scale the system, as each component can be scaled independently to accommodate changing demand. To support this there are several techniques:

   o When deploying the trained model to a model server, the server can (1) simply be **restarted** to incorporate the latest version of the model, (2) or model snapshots can be swapped in and out of production through a model configuration (aka. "**hotswapping**"). Hotswapping can help reduce downtime and allow for more flexible and adaptive deployment of models, such as when model servers host a large number of models.

   o An alternative technique, referred to as **continuous training**, involves incrementally updating the model as new data streams in. In continuous training, the training server which hosts the model subscribes to a stream of training data. The training server computes gradients and updates model parameters, publishing those updates to the model server in real-time.

2. Train and serve the model on the **same instance**. Although training and serving the model on the same hardware instance may simplify the model update process, this approach is generally avoided due to several drawbacks. These include inefficient allocation of compute resources, lack of resilience to failure, and redundant work. Consequently, this approach is not widely adopted.

Updating a model in a model server typically involves the following steps:

1. **Training the updated model:** Train a new version of the model using updated data and/or a different architecture.

2. **Evaluating the model:** Test the updated model to ensure that it's working as expected, ensuring sufficient performance to be pushed to production.

3. **Packaging the model:** Package the updated model in a format that can be easily loaded by the model server, such as a TensorFlow SavedModel.

4. **Uploading the model:** Push the packaged model to the model repository, which stores all the trained models and associated metadata, like version history.

5. **Activating the model:** Enable the model server to use the updated model for incoming requests. This may involve updating a configuration file, sending a request to the model server, or setting a "live" flag in the model repository. Alternatively, the model server may be configured to automatically poll for the latest model version.

6. **Monitoring the model:** Monitor the performance of the updated model in production to ensure that it's working as expected.

It's important to have a well-documented process for updating models in a model server to minimize downtime and ensure that the model server is always running the latest version of the model. Additionally, having a rollback plan in place can help to quickly revert to a previous version of the model in case of any issues with the updated model.

Solution 6.14: How to deploy and roll-back a model?

Deploying a model involves the same steps as described in the previous answer – packaging, uploading, and activating the model – with a few additional considerations:

- **Staged deployment:** Deploying models in stages can be beneficial in certain cases, especially when dealing with new models that show significant differences in quality or latency. Deploying models that may have backwards incompatibility issues – such as models trained on different platforms or expecting different inputs or outputs – may also require a staged deployment process.

- ○ In **Staging**, the model can be tested in a non-production environment to ensure it is functional and meets quality standards.

- ○ In **Canary**, a small percentage of live requests are exposed to the new model to monitor its performance.

- ○ Once the model is deemed stable, it is finally deployed to **Production**. A rolling deployment to Production involves gradually updating the model server by deploying the new model to a subset of instances while keeping the remaining instances running the old model until the update is complete.

- **Rolling back the model:** If the new model isn't performing as expected, it can be rolled back to a previous version via hotswapping: this may involve updating the model server configuration to use an earlier version of the model, sending a request to the model server, or pointing the "live" version in the model repository to an earlier model. If the model server doesn't support hotswapping, it may need to be redeployed.

Solution 6.15: What metrics should the server monitor?

Metrics that are important to monitor in a model server can be grouped into categories:

- **Model quality metrics:** Periodic evaluation of a production model using scribed data can detect changes in model quality. This can also serve as a trigger to train and deploy a model update.

- **Data quality metrics:** Data is subject to change over time, including changes in features (such as new or deprecated features, missing values, as well as bugs and outliers), changes in labels, and changes in the relationship between features and labels. Data can also become stale, improperly sampled, or the schema itself can change, so it's important to monitor it for these issues.

- **Request metrics:** Metrics such as latency, throughput (number of requests per second), success and error rates, and errors by type. Latency can be further decomposed into request stages (e.g., feature hydration latency, prediction latency), and can be measured from different vantage points (e.g., client-side or model server-side) to identify issues like network congestion.

- **Prediction metrics:** Metrics involved in a prediction should be tracked, such as model size and memory footprint. Monitoring throughput and latency for individual models can be useful in ensuring that experiments are running smoothly. The current model version can be used to monitor the progress of model updates. For feature hydration, monitor cache hit rates.

- **Hardware metrics:** Amount of CPU, memory, disk I/O, and network bandwidth being consumed.

In addition to infrastructure metrics, user metrics, such as positive and negative interactions, should be monitored.

Solution 6.16: How to troubleshoot inferior online model performance compared to offline metrics?

There are a few ways to identify diminished model performance following deployment:

1. As the served data is logged, the model predictions are also scribed. This information can be used along with the ground truth label to **evaluate the served model offline** and identify significant deviations from metrics observed during training.

2. Transform the test data into a suitable format that can be sent as **requests to the model server.** Then compare disparities in model predictions, and the overall evaluation metrics, with the offline results obtained using the same test data.

To troubleshoot when a served model is underperforming training results:

- **Check the data:** Make sure that the data used in training and serving is the same or at least very similar. To do this, scribe the hydrated features in addition to the model predictions in order to validate performance offline. Check for data leakage (missing values) or data drift in the hydrated features compared to the training data. Evaluate the model offline using the hydrated features to rule out issues with the model server.

- **Log model metadata:** Check the model names and versions being served – or save model snapshots if models are continuously updated – to differentiate models, particularly in scenarios where multiple models are being served to clients during experiments.

- **Add monitoring:** Adding metrics related to cache staleness, cache misses, and prediction errors (e.g., timeouts) can be particularly useful in identifying issues that arise during serving. If the cache becomes stale, it can negatively impact the model's performance by returning outdated data. High cache miss rates can lead to longer response times or more timeouts and therefore missing feature values.

- **Add unit tests:** Ensure that the inputs are correctly formatted and that any necessary feature hydration is applied correctly by adding unit tests for corner cases. Ensure that any input processing techniques applied are also well tested.

- **Add debuggers:** Developing a debugger, whether in the form of a command-line or web-based tool, can aid in troubleshooting issues in model serving. The debugger should be capable of dumping intermediate formats when sending a request, displaying the hydrated features, which helps to identify missing values or problems with the caching policy. Additionally, the debugger can dump the raw input, such as tf.Example, to identify discrepancies in feature names and values. It can also check whether the model generates predictions within expected bounds and whether the prediction is correctly packaged, particularly when request batching is applied.

- **Disable caching and timeouts** (in Staging): Functionalities such as feature hydration logic, caching behavior, and timeouts (hydration timeouts, dependency timeouts, model prediction timeouts, etc.) can significantly affect model performance. As prescribed earlier, logging hydrated features can aid in debugging. Identifying caching issues can be challenging. In such cases, one possible solution is to disable caching in Staging, and increase or disable timeouts, to isolate the problem.

- **Check the evaluation metrics:** Verify that the evaluation metrics used during training and when assessing the model server are the same and appropriate for the given problem. Apply one of the above-mentioned approaches to evaluate the served model. Differences in feature hydration processes and evaluation metric computation between online and offline can have significant effects on the performance metrics. Additionally, it's important to recognize that some gap between offline and online model performance may naturally exist due to model staleness, so it's necessary to account for this and monitor for deviations.

7. Advanced ML Questions

There are some particularly challenging problems in machine learning that can arise in industry settings. One of the primary issues is that the ground truth, or the objective truth against which a model's predictions are compared, may not be readily available or easily measurable.

These types of problems are encountered at the highest levels of ML interviews and demand both problem-solving skills and a thorough grasp of the foundational principles of machine learning. By understanding how to tackle these difficult problems, ML practitioners can extrapolate them to other similar issues, improving their ability to design and implement effective ML solutions in a variety of practical contexts.

Each of the following problems presents a critical constraint that must be taken into consideration to achieve success. Here are some general guidelines that can help you address these constraints and solve difficult ML problems:

1. **Focus on what's available.** In complex ML problems, it's often easy to fixate on the limitations of the data, which is usually constrained in some significant way. It's important to remember that there are still valuable insights that can be extracted from the remaining data.

2. **Consider restructuring the data for better signal.** If you encounter data that is noisy, imbalanced, or poorly labeled, you can try to restructure it in a way that makes it easier for the ML algorithm to extract meaningful patterns. Techniques like sampling, reweighting, and relabeling can potentially help reduce biases in the data and boost the accuracy of the model.

3. **Formulate the prediction task.** Before you can start building your ML model, clearly define what you're trying to predict. This process involves carefully choosing the appropriate label or labels that you want to incorporate. Think about how the model will piece the prediction together.

4. **Choose the right objective function.** Once you have formulated an approach, choose an objective function that can guide the optimization process. Using conventional loss functions may not be sufficient; the loss function may need to accommodate the available data and selected formulation. Consider also regularization to avoid overfitting.

5. **Optimize the objective function.** Finally, optimize the objective function to improve the performance of the model. Some variation of gradient descent is often used to update model parameters incrementally.

Steps 3 and 4 in particular require creativity and thinking outside the box to tackle challenging ML problems. Although Step 5 is often not extensively discussed in interviews, it is an important aspect to consider in practice.

Delayed Labels

Context: Ad systems commonly face the issue where conversion events (clicks, installs, etc.) are only observed after possibly long delays.

Question 7.1: How do delayed labels affect the quality of a model's training data?

One of the primary problems with delayed labels is that the **model can become stale** while waiting for conversion events to occur. If the model is not updated frequently, it may continue to make decisions based on outdated information, leading to poor prediction performance.

Another issue with delayed labels is the **risk of false negatives**. For example, if a user sees an ad but a conversion is not recorded until several days later (in the case of an app install), the delayed conversion may not be attributed correctly to the ad, resulting in a false negative. This results in more negative labels than in the actual data distribution.

Finally, it is often **unclear what the ideal window length should be** for delayed labels. If the window length is too short, it may not capture all relevant conversions, leading to inaccurate predictions. On the other hand, even if the window length is extended to capture delayed conversions, there is still a risk of false negatives for conversions that fall outside the window.

Question 7.2: How to train and update a model with delayed positive labels?

There are several solutions that can be used to mitigate these challenges and improve the quality of the model's training.

- **Use a time window that is sufficiently long** before training the model (He et al., 2014). While this approach reduces the risk of false negatives, it may result in the model becoming stale.

- Reweight or relabel the data:

    - **Importance sampling** (Bottou et al., 2013) is a technique that can be used to reweight unlabeled data based on shared traits from a separate, historical dataset. The challenge is obtaining the proper estimate of weights.

    - **Positive-unlabeled (PU) learning** (Elkan & Noto, 2008) adjusts the weights of unlabeled data based on their estimated probability of belonging to the positive class, which is typically estimated using a classifier.

    - **Inverse propensity weighting** (Austin & Stuart, 2015) is another reweighting technique that can be used to adjust the training data based on the probability that the unlabeled data has already been labeled. This, too, requires training a separate model.

- Model delay jointly:

    - Model the probability of conversion as a function of **two separate models** (Chapelle, 2014), a **delay model** that predicts the expected time until a conversion event, and a **conversion model** that predicts the probability of the event itself. These models are jointly optimized using Expectation Maximization (EM), which helps to untangle their respective contributions.

The delay modeling approach has been refined over time to estimate more complex distributions (Yoshikawa & Imai, 2018). The conversion model is used at serving time.

- ○ **Delayed bandit algorithms** (Vernade et al., 2017) have also been used to model both the probability of conversion and expected delay until the conversion is observed. In the context of ad systems, the available actions correspond to different ad candidates, and the rewards correspond to the number of conversions at time t, where the distribution of time-to-click delay is estimated using historical data. At each round the agent selects the arm with the highest expected reward, taking into account the expected delay until the reward is received.

- **Adjust the loss function:** Fake negative weighted loss (Ktena et al., 2019) is a technique that can be used to reweight the training loss for positive and negative samples in the dataset based on their estimated contribution to the bias in the dataset. Alibaba later proposed a refinement on the importance sampling technique (Gu et al., 2021). The popularity of these approaches has grown due to their compatibility with existing model architectures.

Learning Without Labels

Context: After iOS 14, Apple required explicit user consent before tracking data across apps. As a result, user-level conversion data became inaccessible for most users, and apps had to rely on delayed and aggregated campaign-level data.

Question 7.3: What are the main challenges posed by this limitation?

In the context of iOS 14, the changes to the privacy policy require users to explicitly opt-in to conversion tracking. This means that both the referring app and the installed app need to receive user consent in order to access row-level data, which includes information such as the user ID, app ID, and timestamp. Without user consent, only click data, which includes the user ID, app ID, and click ID, will be available.

Without user consent, the data provided by iOS 14 will be limited. Apple will only show **aggregated data by the SKAdNetwork (or SKAN) campaign ID**, where a campaign is a value from 1 to 100. The app ID can be part of the metadata, so advertisers will be able to see which app generated the click, but the data will be limited to the campaign ID and a timestamp range of +/- 12 hours. This means that advertisers will not have access to user-level conversion data, which can make it more difficult to build accurate prediction models.

Apart from the significantly reduced amount of user-level data, some important factors to consider when addressing this problem include:

- Since only a fraction of iOS users have opted in to tracking, any model built using the remaining iOS data will be inaccurate, since **negative labels represent either no conversion (or not yet converted) or opt-outs**, which might actually be positives.

- **Campaign design** is another important consideration. There are different approaches to campaign design. One approach aims to reduce the entropy within a user group, in order to minimize the variability of instance labels within the group, regardless of conversion probability. Another approach is to optimize for precision, which involves targeting conversions that will take place with high probability. This is useful when the primary goal of the campaign is to collect positive labels for training.

Question 7.4: How to train a prediction model when most user-level labels are missing?

Short-term solutions involve making minor adjustments and can be done without much difficulty.

- **Frozen model:** Use a pre-existing model trained before the new privacy policy was introduced. This approach assumes that the patterns of user behavior have not significantly changed over time. The model also won't be effective for new users. While it may not be the most accurate solution, it can buy some time while a new model is being developed.

- **Proxy labels:** Use the click data that is still available (userId, appId, clickId) to train a prediction model. Using click data as a proxy for installs is advantageous because it can still provide an indication of user behavior. However, click data may be unreliable as a proxy for installs, resulting in biased or noisy data, which may limit the accuracy of the model.

- **Soft labels:** Aggregate data from users who share similar characteristics into a campaign, and use the grouped data as soft labels to train the model. Grouping data from campaigns has the advantage of estimating the conversion rate for a group of users with similar characteristics, such as demographics or interests. However, the model may not be able to predict the behavior of individual users accurately, as individual users may have unique characteristics and behavior patterns not captured by the aggregated data.

Medium-term solutions require modifications to the model structure and/or the training procedure.

- **Multi-task learning:** In this approach, multiple signals are used to train the model, such as other engagements (such as clicks or dwell time) and campaign data. For example, engagement data can be combined with campaign data (such as the campaign ID and associated labels) to train a multi-task model. This approach can help improve the accuracy of the model by providing more information to work with.

- **Calibrated proxy labels:** Expanding on the proxy label approach, engagement data is used to create proxy labels, which are then used to train the model. The campaign labels are then used for calibration. For example, if a group of users (by campaign ID) are more likely to click than to install, this information can be used to improve the accuracy of the model.

- **Android model:** An alternative solution is to develop a specialized model for Android and use it to predict conversion rates for all users, including those who have opted out on iOS. The Android model can be calibrated for iOS users using campaign labels, as discussed previously. However, it is important to note that user behavior and demographics may vary between Android and iOS. Additionally,

Android is expected to implement similar privacy protections in the near future, which could affect the longevity of this solution.

Long-term solutions involve leveraging the positive labels from iOS users who have opted-in to tracking. It's important to note that the iOS dataset will be biased because negative labels may indicate either no conversion (or not yet converted) or an opt-out. Therefore, the negative labels should be considered unlabeled data.

- Train a model using the iOS data after applying **opt-in bias correction**. There are various methods to perform opt-in bias correction, such as:

  - Downsampling the negatives, reweighting the negatives, or applying cost-sensitive training. These approaches are simple but do not account for the possibility that the negatives might actually be positives.

  - **Importance sampling:** Reweight or relabel the unlabeled data based on shared characteristics with the labeled data. By identifying instances in the unlabeled data that share similar features, importance sampling can assign higher weights to these instances and use them to train a predictive model. One limitation is that it makes assumptions about the relationship between the labeled and unlabeled data.

  - **Positive-unlabeled (PU) learning:** Another way to reweight or relabel the unlabeled data is through PU learning. This is a semi-supervised approach that trains a classifier on the labeled data (opt-in users with observed conversions), and then applies it to the unlabeled data. These predictions can be used to reweight or relabel the unlabeled data based on the estimated probability of being positive.

  - **Probabilistic attribution:** Assign fractional credit (e.g., fractional weight) to the unlabeled data based on observed install counts in a campaign (Müller, 2021). Users in a campaign receive different weights based on their likelihood of converting. This method can be implemented using a probabilistic model that estimates the probability of each user converting based on their historical behavior, such as time of click, and leveraging other available data, such as labeled data from opt-in users.

- **Transduction:** Instead of inducing information about the negatives, a transductive learning approach can be used to incorporate information from the existing positives, the campaign labels, and the unlabeled data. In the paper "On Learning from Label Proportions", (Yu et al., 2015) demonstrated that it is possible to train a classifier to label individual instances using label proportions at the campaign level, leveraging the transductive properties of the unlabeled data. They achieved this by developing an algorithm (Yu et al., 2013) inspired by large-margin clustering. The algorithm leverages the proportion of labels in each campaign and the clustering of unlabeled instances in the high-dimensional space to identify a decision boundary that optimizes for both. The objective function can be adapted to accept positive labels at the instance level.

Pricing Models

Context: In contrast to conventional supervised learning, price prediction lacks a "ground-truth" optimal price label, as is the case with Airbnb listings, where it is unknown what the ideal listing price should be.

Question 7.5: How can prices be optimized when the ideal price is unknown?

Context:

When dealing with the problem of dynamic pricing, obtaining labels for price prediction can be challenging. One way to obtain labels is to use the booking history of the listing.

If the listing is booked:

- If suggested price <= list price, then optimal price must be >= suggested price.

- If suggested price > list price, we don't know the optimal price relative to suggested price.

If the listing is not booked:

- If suggested price < list price, we don't know the optimal price relative to suggested price.
- If suggested price >= list price, then optimal price must be < suggested price.

Objective:

For non-booked nights, we can set a **lower bound** of c_1 * the list price, where c_1 is a constant < 1, and an **upper bound** of the list price.

For booked nights, we can use the list price as a **lower bound** for the optimal price and set an **upper bound** of c_2 * the list price, where c_2 is a constant >= 1.

We can then construct a **loss function based on these bounds**. If the suggested price is within the bounds, we incur a loss of 0 since we don't know the optimal price relative to the suggested price. If the suggested price is outside the bounds, we incur a loss equal to the margin between the suggested price and the nearest bound. This is analogous to the ϵ-insensitive loss which is used in Support Vector Regression (*Sklearn.svm.LinearSVR*, n.d.).

Formally, the loss can be defined as

$$argmin \sum_{i=1}^{N} (\phi_L + \phi_U)$$

where ϕ_L and ϕ_U are the lower bound and upper bound functions:

$$\phi_L = max(0, L(P_i, y_i) - f_\theta(x_i))$$
$$\phi_U = max(0, f_\theta(x_i) - U(P_i, y_i))$$

and

$$L(P_i, y_i) = y_i P_i + (1 - y_i)c_1 P_i$$
$$U(P_i, y_i) = (1 - y_i)P_i + y_i c_2 P_i$$

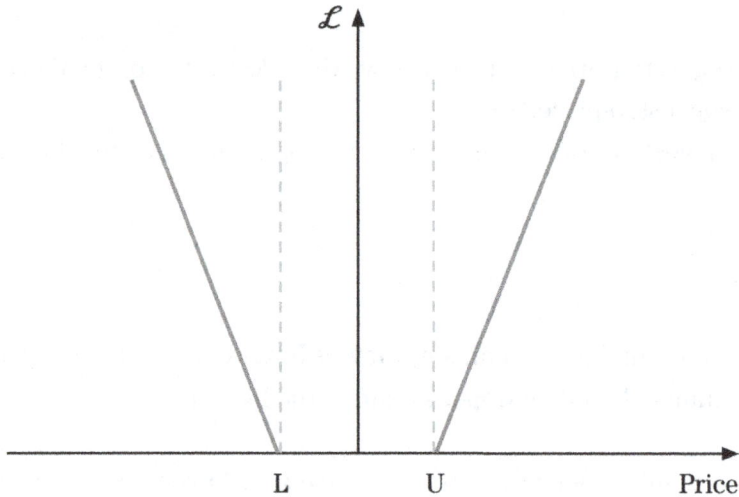

Note. Illustration of the loss function. If the suggested price falls between the lower and upper bounds, the loss is zero.

This objective has been adopted in a range of industries, including airlines (Shukla et al., 2019) and hospitality (Zhu et al., 2022).

Question 7.6: Build a model to suggest the optimal price.

With a clearer understanding of the objective, we can proceed to minimize the custom loss function. Several model types have been applied to this prediction task. AirBnb (Ye et al., 2018) implemented a **regression model** based on Support Vector Regression (SVR). Meituan (Zhang et al., 2019) – a Chinese shopping platform – employed a **DNN**, while Alibaba (Zhu et al., 2022) utilized a more complex **multi-task DNN** that captured sequential features such as the frequency of searches over time. To minimize the custom loss function, the authors utilize some variant of stochastic gradient descent (SGD).

Here are some ideas for the features of the model, using AirBnb listings as an example:

- **Listing features:** room type, capacity, reviews, location, amenities, etc.

- **Temporal features:** length of stay, day of year, events, availability in time window, etc.
- **Competitive features:** number of nearby listings, their reviews, number of views, etc.

These features can be adapted for use in other domains. For instance, when creating an airfare forecasting model, the "listing features" may consist of trip attributes (group size, booking class, number of stops, arrival and destination airport, etc.), while "competitive features" might encompass alternative flights in the same booking category.

Another issue is the tuning of hyperparameters c_1 and c_2. When these values are close to 1, the suggested prices are assumed to be more accurate. If the values are further from 1, the system is deemed less reliable. There are several approaches to tune the hyperparameters:

1. Select the values that optimize offline evaluation metrics, which are explained in the next question.

2. Perform A/B testing with different values of c_1 and c_2.

3. Constrain the lower and upper bounds based on certain business objectives, such as avoiding excessively low or high prices.

Question 7.7: How to evaluate this model offline?

Define metrics that evaluate the effectiveness of the model's price suggestions in relation to whether the listing was booked or not. The objective of these metrics is to maximize the overall revenue.

- **Price Decrease Recall (PDR):** Among non-booked nights, the percentage of suggestions < the list price.

- **Price Decrease Precision (PDP):** Where suggested price < list price, the percentage of nights that are non-booked.

- **Price Increase Recall (PIR):** Among booked nights, the percentage of suggestions >= list price.

- **Price Increase Precision (PIP):** Where suggested price >= list price, the percentage of nights that are booked.

- **Booking Regret:** The revenue that would have been lost (as a percent) if the suggested price P_{sugg} had been chosen instead of the actual list price P, across all booked nights.

$$BR = mean_{bookings}(max(0, 1 - \frac{P_{sugg}}{P}))$$

Appendix

Generative Models: Noisy Channel to LLM

The field of generative modeling has seen a remarkable surge in the past few years, with approaches like LLMs and models like ChatGPT gaining prominence. It can be overwhelming to witness their widespread adoption and the emergence of pundits left, right, and center. Even seasoned industry professionals are finding it challenging to keep up with the constant barrage of new advancements.

If you're feeling a bit lost, don't worry – you're not alone! In this passage, we'll break down the essential concepts that you need to know to catch up with the latest developments in generative modeling.

Generative models, which aim to generate data similar to the training data, have evolved significantly over the years in various domains. In order to review their progress, let's examine the key advancements in two specific applications: Automatic Speech Recognition (ASR) and Machine Translation (MT).

For Machine Translation (MT):

- **Statistical Machine Translation (SMT)** was the dominant paradigm for many years, based on the noisy channel approach. The noisy channel approach assumes that a source sentence is a noisy version of a target sentence. SMT models consist of two components: a Translation Model (TM) that estimates the probability of target phrases given source phrases, and a Language Model (LM) that estimates the probability of the target sentence. Popular methods for training TMs include Expectation Maximization (EM) or Bayesian inference techniques (Knight, 2009), which involve estimating the posterior distribution over source-target translations by learning word alignments.

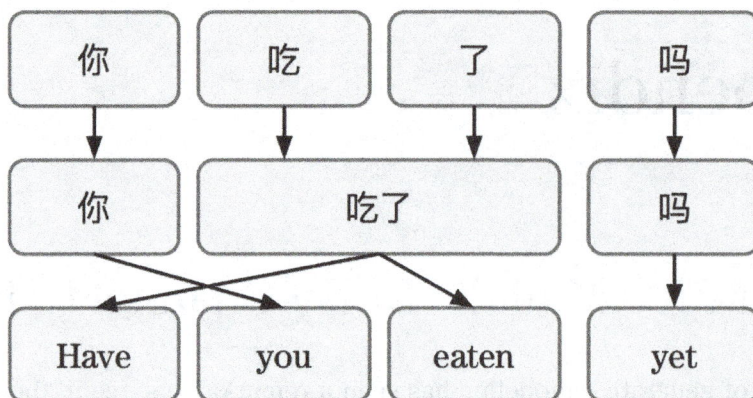

你 吃 了 吗

你 吃了 吗

Have you eaten yet

Note. In SMT, learning a phrase translation table starts with word alignment. Popular approaches include EM and Variational Bayes.

Insider Tip

If you're interested in this topic, read more about the different steps of SMT in the documentation for the Moses SMT system (*Moses - Moses/Background*, 2013).

- In the mid 2010s, **Neural Machine Translation (NMT)** supplanted SMT as the dominant approach for MT. NMT models use a neural network to directly map a source sentence to a target sentence, without explicitly modeling the noisy channel as in SMT. This makes them simpler in construction than the two-model representation of SMT models. Furthermore, DNNs enabled NMT models to better capture the context of the source sentence and generate more fluent translations in the target sentence.

  NMT models consist of an encoder and a decoder. The encoder reads in the source sentence and encodes it into a fixed-length vector representation, which captures the meaning of the sentence. The decoder then generates the target sentence word by word, conditioned on the source sentence representation produced by the encoder.

  For some years, the encoder and decoder were implemented as RNNs or Long Short-Term Memory (LSTM) networks such as seq2seq (Sutskever et al., 2014). These RNN-based models process the source sentence sequentially, one word at a time, and update the hidden state of the network at each time step.

Attention-based mechanisms have significantly improved the performance of NMT models. The key advantage of attention-based mechanisms is their ability to selectively focus on different parts of the inputs and outputs. Specifically, self-attention is a mechanism that allows the network to compute attention weights over its own sequence, while cross-attention allows the model to selectively attend to different parts of the source sentence when generating each target word.

For ASR:

- **Gaussian Mixture Models (GMMs)** were commonly used for a long time to model the probability distribution of speech features. Like SMT, ASR was implemented using the noisy channel concept, in the form of GMM-HMMs, where GMMs represented the Acoustic Model (AM) and HMMs represented the LM.

Key Terms

The features consumed by ASR models include:

Filter Banks
Filter bank features are a way to describe an audio signal by its power at different frequencies. To get filter banks, transform the audio waveform into (1) a sequence of frames, and (2) convert each frame into its corresponding frequency domain representation, then (3) group nearby frequency bins together using filters in a way that approximates the human auditory system's sensitivity to different frequency ranges.

MFCCs
To get MFCCs, further process filter banks using the discrete cosine transform (DCT). This step decorrelates the filter bank features and compresses them into a more compact representation.

MFCCs are decorrelated representations that are lossy, but better suited for use with GMMs. In contrast to GMMs, DNNs are better able to handle correlated features, so they directly work on filter bank features instead.

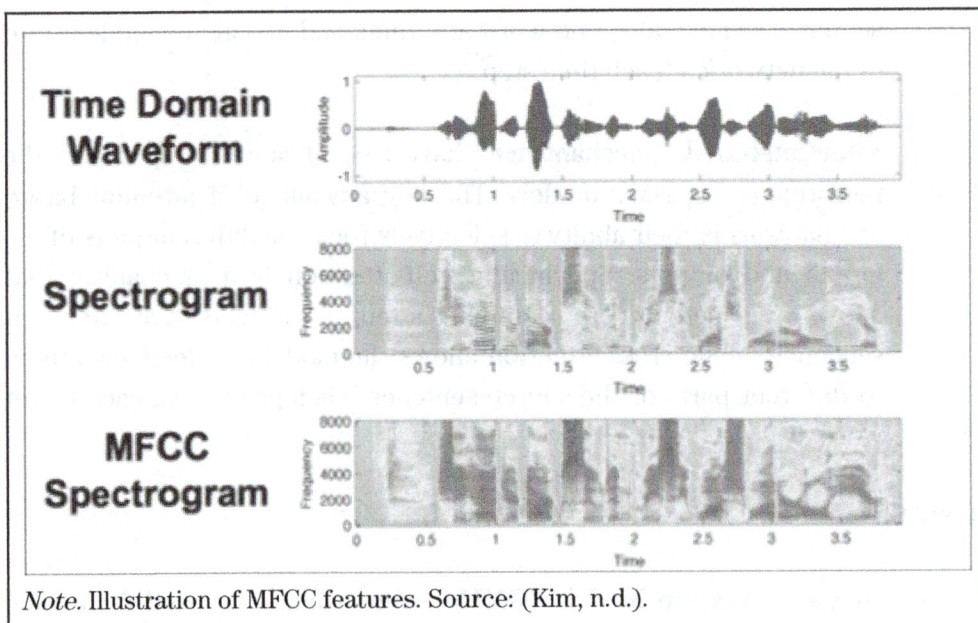

Note. Illustration of MFCC features. Source: (Kim, n.d.).

GMMs are based on the assumption that the acoustic features are generated by a mixture of Gaussian distributions, each corresponding to a different phoneme. However, GMMs had several limitations, such as difficulty in modeling complex dependencies between features, and they struggled with large datasets.

- **Deep Neural Networks (DNNs)** quickly supplanted GMMs as the go-to model for ASR. DNNs can learn complex nonlinear relationships between the input features (filter banks) and output labels, which makes them more effective for modeling ASR. Additionally, DNNs can leverage the power of parallel computing to train large models quickly.

  Recent advances in DNNs for ASR have driven home this advantage. For instance, RNNs and later **attention-based mechanisms** enable the model to selectively focus on relevant parts of the input sequence when generating each output element. This helps the model learn the soft alignment between input and output sequences.

  Additionally, **Convolutional Neural Networks (CNNs)** have also been used in ASR, where they can be used to construct 2D feature maps from the acoustic signal. Similar to images, these feature maps organize the acoustic features such as Mel-Frequency Cepstral Coefficients (MFCCs) in a 2-dimensional feature map, where one axis represents the frequency domain and the other represents time. This enables the model to capture the local patterns in the acoustic signal.

Many modern ASR models combine elements of both attention and convolutions, such as the Conformer model (Gulati et al., 2020) and the convolutional Transducer model (Mohamed et al., 2019).

Converging to Transformers:

The convergence of generative approaches towards attention-based mechanisms, particularly versions of the Transformer (Vaswani et al., 2017), has been a significant development in ML.

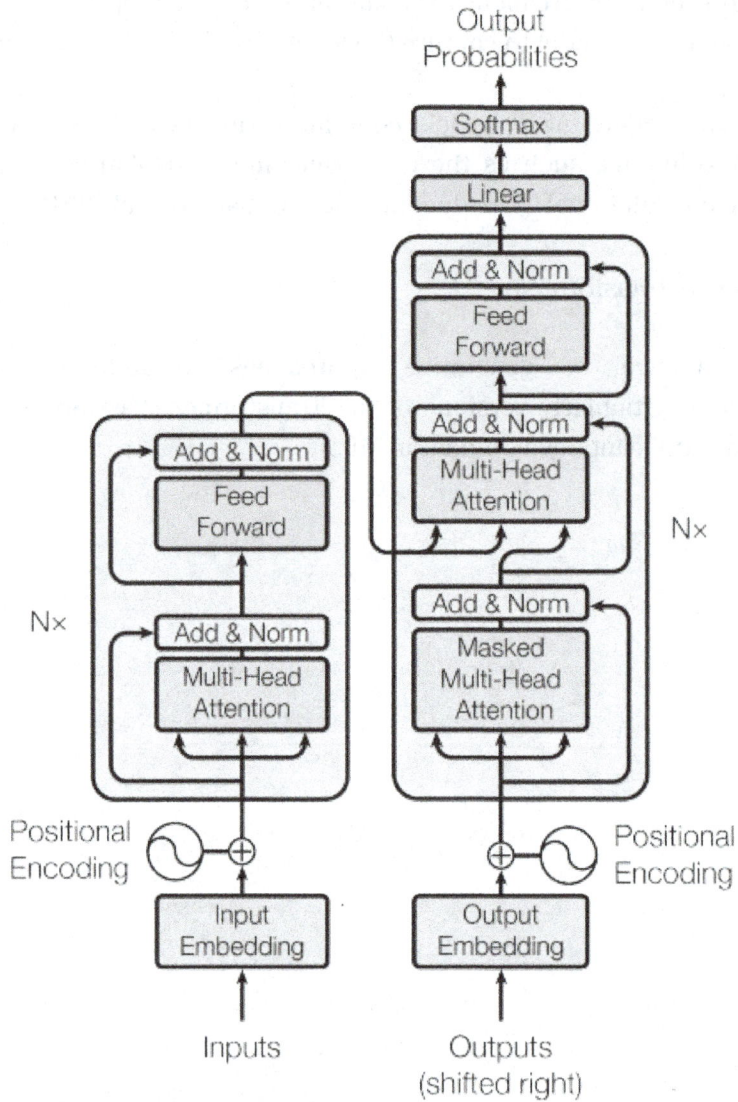

Note. The encoder-decoder network that comprises the Transformer. Source: (*Neural Machine Translation With a Transformer and Keras / Text,* 2023).

Insider Tip

Check out the outstanding Tensorflow tutorial on neural machine translation with Transformers (*Neural Machine Translation With a Transformer and Keras / Text,* 2023).

There are generally three forms of Transformer:

- The full form of the Transformer is the **encoder-decoder network**. In this architecture, the input sequence is fed through an encoder network, which produces a fixed-length vector representation of the input. This vector is then passed through a decoder network, which generates the output sequence one element at a time.

  The encoder-decoder network is widely used for canonical sequence-to-sequence modeling tasks such as NMT and text summarization.

- The **encoder-only network**, on the other hand, learns an encoded representation of the inputs by corrupting the inputs and generating the original variants. This is known as the autoencoder architecture, which can be used for a variety of unsupervised learning tasks such as dimensionality reduction.

  The encoder-only network is typically used for tasks such as classification and regression, where the encoded representation of the input is passed into a softmax, sigmoid, MLP, or other network.

- The **decoder-only network**, which is also known as an autoregressive model. In this architecture, the model generates output elements one at a time, conditioned on the previous elements it has generated. To prevent the model from "cheating" by looking ahead, the input sequence is masked so that the model can only attend to the previous tokens in the sequence.

  Many modern **Large Language Models (LLMs)**, such as the GPT family of models (Brown et al., 2020), are built on top of a decoder-only network. The GPT models use a left-to-right autoregressive decoding process, where each token is generated based on the previous tokens in the sequence.

Insider Tip

Read (Versloot, 2020), an informative article on github comparing these three encoder and decoder architectures.

On architecture choice for LLMs:

Encoder-decoder networks and decoder-only networks share a lot of similarities, and they have both been used to build LLMs. The primary difference between them is the way they process the input sequence.

One of the key benefits of using an encoder-decoder architecture over a decoder-only autoregressive model is that the encoder allows for the computation of hidden states for **all time steps** of the input sequence simultaneously, whereas the decoder-only model can only reference **previous hidden states** in a sequential manner. Decoder-only LLMs offer advantages in terms of training simplicity and memory requirements.

However, recent research has challenged the intuition that encoder-decoder models are superior to decoder-only models for LLM tasks. In a study by (Wang et al., 2022), a causal decoder, which is a left-to-right autoregressive decoder, **demonstrated better zero-shot generalization abilities** than an encoder-decoder after unsupervised pre-training.

Although the author doesn't delve into the reasons behind it, here are some points to consider:

- One possible reason is that the autoregressive nature of the decoder-only model allows it to better **capture the regularities and patterns of the language**, by conditioning each token on the previous tokens. In contrast, an encoder-decoder model may struggle to generate fluent text in novel contexts, as it may be limited by the input representation and the alignment between the input and output sequences.

- Another possible reason is that the decoder-only model may be less prone to overfitting, due to its **simpler architecture** and the fact that it does not need to align the input and output sequences. This can be particularly beneficial in zero-shot settings, where the model needs to generalize to new tasks and domains without any task-specific fine-tuning.

Tuning for real-world tasks:

As LLMs become increasingly large and sophisticated, they are capable of acquiring knowledge on their own. However, applying this knowledge effectively to solve specific real-world problems is still a challenge.

Fine-tuning is a technique that has been widely used to address this issue. Fine-tuning involves pre-training an LLM on a large amount of data and then adapting it to a downstream task. Typically, LLMs are fine-tuned on instruction templates (Bosma & Wei, 2021) in which there is a prompt, some context, and an answer. The LLM is trained to generate an answer that is similar to the one provided.

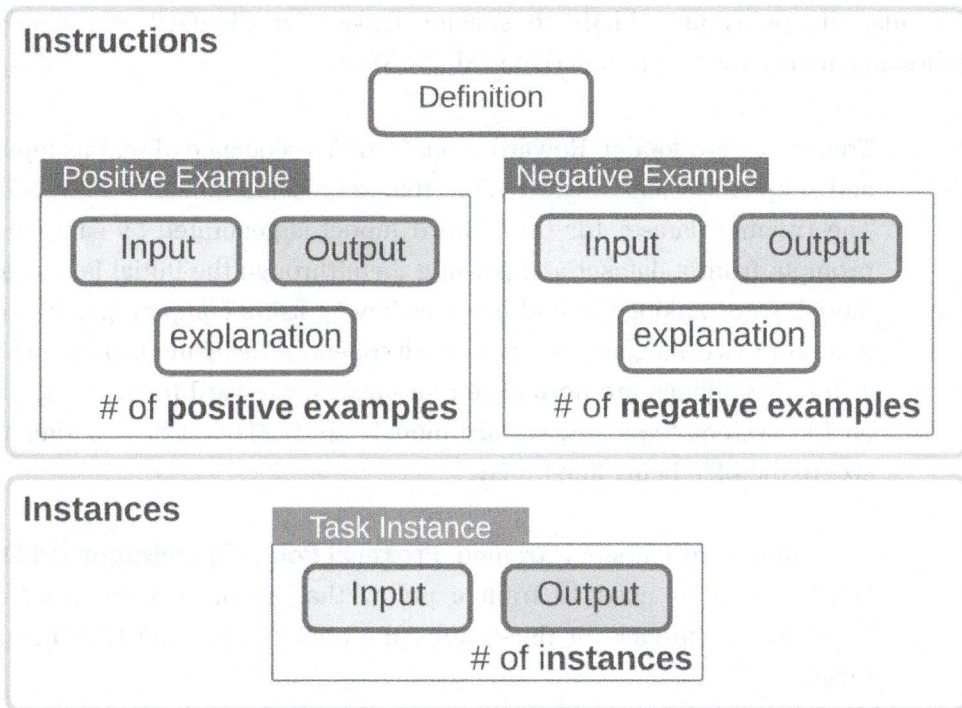

Note. Schema for the Natural Instructions dataset. Source: (*Allenai/natural-Instructions: Expanding Natural Instructions*, n.d.).

There are two main approaches to instruction fine-tuning for adapting LLMs to real-world tasks.

- **Downstream approach:** The LLM is frozen, meaning its weights are not updated during fine-tuning. Instead, the embeddings produced by the LLM for each token in the input sequence are passed through additional layers, such as a softmax, sigmoid, MLP, or other neural network, which are trained to output the desired task-specific predictions.

- **Holistic approach:** The LLM's parameters are updated directly during fine-tuning, which allows the LLM to learn more task-specific information. This approach tends to result in better performance compared to the first one, but it is more computationally expensive since the large number of LLM parameters need to be updated during fine-tuning.

Reinforcement Learning with Human Feedback (RLHF) is another technique for adapting pre-trained LLMs to specific tasks. For ChatGPT, it's a step following instruction fine-tuning (OpenAI, 2023).

1. Train a **reward model**. Reward models take a sequence of text as input and output a scalar reward value that represents human preference. The training dataset for the reward model is generated by sampling prompts from a dataset and passing them through the initial language model. One ranking method involves having users compare generated text from two language models conditioned on the same prompt. The different rankings are normalized into a scalar reward for training via an Elo system. Typically, reward models are LLMs that have a similar size to the LLM being fine-tuned.

2. Once the reward model is trained, **Proximal Policy Optimization (PPO)** is an algorithm used to train a policy that maximizes the reward function. In the case of fine-tuning, the policy is just the LLM being tuned.

   During PPO training, the current LLM is created by copying the initial LLM. The initial LLM remains frozen and is used as a reference. Meanwhile, the current LLM is optimized through the training process. The reward model evaluates the current LLM's predictions and provides feedback in the form of a scalar reward.

   The objective function of PPO encourages the current policy to stay close to the initial policy, avoiding too large updates and ensuring a stable optimization process. A penalty is introduced according to the KL divergence between the outputs of the current and initial LLMs:

$$L^{KLPEN}(\theta) = \mathbb{E}\left[\frac{\pi_\theta}{\pi_{\theta_{old}}}A - \beta KL[\pi_{\theta_{old}}, \pi_\theta]\right]$$

where A is the advantage – defined by the difference between the expected reward predicted by a value function model and the actual reward obtained from the reward model (Stiennon et al., 2020) – and β is a hyperparameter that can be constant or decayed. For a visual, see (Yuan et al., 2023).

A variant of PPO, PPO-Clip (*Proximal Policy Optimization — Spinning Up Documentation*, n.d.), applies hard constraints on gradient updates like this:

$$L^{CLIP}(\theta) = \mathbb{E}\left[min(\frac{\pi_\theta}{\pi_{\theta_{old}}}A, clip(\frac{\pi_\theta}{\pi_{\theta_{old}}}, 1 - \epsilon, 1 + \epsilon)A)\right]$$

where ϵ is a hyperparameter that sets the bounds. In this clipped version of PPO, the KL divergence term is excluded from the objective.

Insider Tip

Hugging Face has an illustrative summary of RLHF (Lambert et al., 2022).

References

A/B Tests vs Multivariate Tests. (2019, November 22). Mixpanel. Retrieved May 5, 2023, from https://mixpanel.com/blog/ab-tests-vs-multivariate- tests/

Ackerman, I., & Kataria, S. (2021, June 3). *Homepage feed multi-task learning using TensorFlow*. LinkedIn Engineering. Retrieved May 5, 2023, from https://engineering.linkedin.com/blog/2021/homepage-feed-multi-task-learning-using-tensorflow

AdSense revenue share - Google AdSense Help. (n.d.). Google AdSense Help. Retrieved May 5, 2023, from https://support.google.com/adsense/answer/180195?hl=en

Agrawal, R., Imieliński, T., & Swami, A. (1993). Mining association rules between sets of items in large databases. *ACM SIGMOD Record, 22*(2), 207-216.

Alade, O. A., Selamat, A., & Sallehuddin, R. (2020). The Effects of Missing Data Characteristics on the Choice of Imputation Techniques. *Vietnam Journal of Computer Science, 7*(2).

allenai/natural-instructions: Expanding natural instructions. (n.d.). github. Retrieved May 7, 2023, from https://github.com/allenai/natural- instructions

AllenNLP - Demo. (n.d.). AllenNLP. Retrieved May 5, 2023, from https://demo.allennlp.org/sentiment-analysis/roberta-sentiment-analysis

Arora, S., Ge, R., & Moitra, A. (2012). Learning Topic Models - Going beyond SVD. *FOCS*.

Austin, P. C., & Stuart, E. A. (2015). Moving towards best practice when using inverse probability of treatment weighting (IPTW) using the propensity score to estimate causal treatment effects in observational studies. *Stat Med, 34*(28), 3661-3679.

Automatic feature preprocessing | BigQuery. (2023, May 3). Google Cloud. Retrieved May 4, 2023, from https://cloud.google.com/bigquery/docs/reference/standard-sql/bigqueryml-auto-preprocessing

Awesome XGBoost. (n.d.). github. Retrieved May 5, 2023, from https://github.com/dmlc/xgboost/tree/master/demo#machine-learning-challenge-winning-solutions

Ba, L. J., & Caruana, R. (2014). Do Deep Nets Really Need to be Deep? *NIPS*.

Bai, T., Xiao, Y., Wu, B., Yang, G., Yu, H., & Nie, J. (2022). A Contrastive Sharing Model for Multi-Task Recommendation. *WWW*.

Banko, M., Mittal, V. O., & Witbrock, M. J. (2000). Headline Generation Based on Statistical Translation. *ACL.*

Bean, A. (2020, September 23). *Distributed training of sparse ML models — Part 1: Network bottlenecks.* Twitter Blog. Retrieved May 6, 2023, from https://blog.twitter.com/engineering/en_us/topics/insights/2020/distributed-training-of-sparse-machine-learning-models-1

Bejeck, B. (2012, November 30). *Calculating a Co-Occurrence Matrix With Hadoop.* Random Thoughts on Coding. Retrieved May 5, 2023, from http://codingjunkie.net/cooccurrence/

Belli, L., Ktena, S. I., Tejani, A., Lung-Yut-Fong, A., Portman, F., Zhu, X., Xie, Y., Gupta, A., Bronstein, M., Delić, A., Sottocornola, G., Anelli, W., Andrade, N., Smith, J., & Shi, W. (2020). Privacy-Aware Recommender Systems Challenge on Twitter's Home Timeline. *arXiv:2004.13715.*

Beutel, A., Chen, J., Zhao, Z., & Chi, E. H. (2017). Data Decisions and Theoretical Implications when Adversarially Learning Fair Representations. *Presented as a poster at the 2017 Workshop on Fairness, Accountability, and Transparency in Machine Learning.*

Bi, Q., Li, J., Shang, L., Jiang, X., Liu, Q., & Yang, H. (2022). MTRec: Multi-Task Learning over BERT for News Recommendation. *ACL.*

Bidding Strategies Overview. (n.d.). Snapchat's Business Help Center. Retrieved May 5, 2023, from https://businesshelp.snapchat.com/s/article/bidding-strategies?language=en_US

big-data-rosetta-code/TfIdf.scala. (n.d.). github. Retrieved May 5, 2023, from https://github.com/spotify/big-data-rosetta-code/blob/main/src/main/scala/com/spotify/bdrc/pipeline/TfIdf.scala

Blei, D., & McAuliffe, J. D. (2007). Supervised topic models. *NIPS.*

Blei, D. M., & Lafferty, J. D. (2005). Correlated Topic Models. *NIPS.*

Blei, D. M., Ng, A. Y., & Jordan, M. I. (2003). Latent Dirichlet Allocation. *JMLR.*

Bordes, A., Usunier, N., Garcia-Duran, A., Weston, J., & Yakhnenko, O. (2013). Translating Embeddings for Modeling Multi-relational Data. *NIPS.*

Bosma, M., & Wei, J. (2021, October 6). *Introducing FLAN: More generalizable Language Models with Instruction Fine-Tuning.* Google AI Blog. Retrieved May 7, 2023, from https://ai.googleblog.com/2021/10/introducing-flan-more-generalizable.html

Bottou, L., Peters, J., Quiñonero-Candela, J., Charles, D., Chickering, D. M., Portugaly, E., Ray, D., Simard, P., & Snelson, E. (2013). Counterfactual Reasoning and Learning Systems. *JMLR.*

Bredillet, T. (2019, May 17). *Core Modeling at Instagram. At Instagram we have many Machine… | by Thomas Bredillet.* Instagram Engineering. Retrieved

May 5, 2023, from https://instagram-engineering.com/core-modeling-at-instagram-a51e0158aa48

Broadcasting — NumPy v1.24 Manual. (n.d.). NumPy. Retrieved May 4, 2023, from https://numpy.org/doc/stable/user/basics.broadcasting.html

Brown, T., Mann, B., Ryder, N., Subbiah, M., Kaplan, J., Dhariwal, P., Neelakantan, A., Shyam, P., Sastry, G., Askell, A., Agarwal, S., Herbert-Voss, A., Krueger, G., Henighan, T., Child, R., Ramesh, A., Ziegler, D. M., Wu, J., Winter, C., … Amodei, D. (2020). Language Models are Few-Shot Learners. *NIPS.*

Cai, L., & Wang, W. Y. (2018). KBGAN: Adversarial Learning for Knowledge Graph Embeddings. *NAACL HLT.*

Callison-Burch, C. (2009). *Fast, Cheap, and Creative: Evaluating Translation Quality Using Amazon's Mechanical Turk.* EMNLP

Cao, M. (2022). A Survey on Neural Abstractive Summarization Methods and Factual Consistency of Summarization. *arXiv:2204.09519.*

Cao, S., Lu, W., & Xu, Q. (2016). Deep neural networks for learning graph representations. *AAAI.*

Cao, Z., Qing, T., Liu, T., Tsai, M., & Li, H. (2007). Learning to rank: from pairwise approach to listwise approach. *ICML.*

Categorical Data — xgboost 1.7.5 documentation. (n.d.). XGBoost Documentation. Retrieved May 4, 2023, from https://xgboost.readthedocs.io/en/stable/tutorials/categorical.html

Celebi, M. E., Kingravi, H. A., & Vela, P. A. (2013). A Comparative Study of Efficient Initialization Methods for the K-Means Clustering Algorithm. *Expert Systems with Application, 40,* 200-210.

Chang, J., Gerrish, S., Wang, C., Boyd-graber, J., & Blei, D. (2009). Reading Tea Leaves: How Humans Interpret Topic Models. *NIPS.*

Chapelle, O. (2014). Modeling delayed feedback in display advertising. *KDD.*

Chapelle, O., & Zhang, Y. (2009). A dynamic bayesian network click model for web search ranking. *WWW.*

Chen, M., Beutel, A., Covington, P., Jain, S., Belletti, F., & Chi, E. (2019a). Top-K Off-Policy Correction for a REINFORCE Recommender System. *WSDM.*

Chen, Q., Zhao, B., Wang, H., Li, M., Liu, C., Li, Z., Yang, M., & Wang, J. (2021). SPANN: Highly-efficient Billion-scale Approximate Nearest Neighbor Search. *NIPS.*

Chen, Q., Zhuo, Z., & Wang, W. (2019b). BERT for Joint Intent Classification and Slot Filling. *arXiv:1902.10909.*

Chen, T., & Guestrin, C. (2016). XGBoost: A Scalable Tree Boosting System. *KDD.*

Chen, T., Zhang, W., Lu, Q., Chen, K., Zheng, Z., & Yu, Y. (2012). SVDFeature: A Toolkit for Feature-based Collaborative Filtering. *JMLR*.

Cheng, H., Koc, L., Harmsen, J., Shaked, T., Chandra, T., Aradhye, H., Anderson, G., Corrado, G., Chai, W., Ispir, M., Anil, R., Haque, Z., Hong, L., Jain, V., Liu, X., & Shah, H. (2016). Wide & Deep Learning for Recommender Systems. *DLRS*.

Cho, J. H., & Hariharan, B. (2019). On the Efficacy of Knowledge Distillation. *ICCV*.

Chopra, S., Auli, M., & Rush, A. M. (2016). Abstractive Sentence Summarization with Attentive Recurrent Neural Networks. *NAACL*.

Clevert, D., Unterthiner, T., & Hochreiter, S. (2016). Fast and Accurate Deep Network Learning by Exponential Linear Units (ELUs). *ICLR*.

Collaborative Filtering Advantages & Disadvantages | Machine Learning. (2022, July 18). Google Developers. Retrieved May 5, 2023, from https://developers.google.com/machine-learning/recommendation/collaborative/summary

Covington, P., Adams, J., & Sargin, E. (2016). Deep Neural Networks for YouTube Recommendations. *Proceedings of the 10th ACM Conference on Recommender Systems*.

Craswell, N., & Taylor, M. (2008). An experimental comparison of click position-bias models. *WSDM*.

Create an app installs campaign. (n.d.). Twitter for Business. Retrieved May 5, 2023, from https://business.twitter.com/en/help/campaign-setup/create-an-app-installs-campaign.html

Cui, P., Hu, L., & Liu, Y. (2020). Enhancing Extractive Text Summarization with Topic-Aware Graph Neural Networks. *COLING*.

Dahal, P. (n.d.). *Deep Learning Demystified.* DeepNotes | Deep Learning Demystified. Retrieved May 6, 2023, from https://deepnotes.io/deep-clustering#performance-metrics

Das, S., & Chen, M. (2001). Yahoo! For Amazon: Sentiment Parsing from Small Talk on the Web. *EFA 2001 Barcelona Meetings*.

Data Split Example | Machine Learning. (2022, July 18). Google Developers. Retrieved May 4, 2023, from https://developers.google.com/machine-learning/data-prep/construct/sampling-splitting/example

Davidson, J., Liebald, B., Liu, J., Nandy, P., Vleet, T. V., Gargi, U., Gupta, S., He, Y., Lambert, M., Livingston, B., & Sampath, D. (2010). The YouTube video recommendation system. *RecSys*.

Davis, J., & Goadrich, M. (2006). The relationship between Precision-Recall and ROC curves. *ICML*.

Devlin, J., Chang, M., Lee, K., & Toutanova, K. (2019). BERT: Pre-training of Deep Bidirectional Transformers for Language Understanding. *NAACL*.

Dilipkumar, D., & Chen, J. (2019, June 25). *A SplitNet architecture for ad candidate ranking*. Twitter Blog. Retrieved May 5, 2023, from https://blog.twitter.com/engineering/en_us/topics/infrastructure/2019/splitn et-architecture-for-ad-candidate-ranking

Discounted cumulative gain. (n.d.). Wikipedia. Retrieved May 5, 2023, from https://en.wikipedia.org/wiki/Discounted_cumulative_gain

Eksombatchai, C., Jindal, P., Liu, J. Z., Liu, Y., Sharma, R., Sugnet, C., Ulrich, M., & Leskovec, J. (2018). Pixie: A System for Recommending 3+ Billion Items to 200+ Million Users in Real-Time. *WWW*.

Elkan, C., & Noto, K. (2008). Learning classifiers from only positive and unlabeled data. *KDD*.

El-Kishky, A., Markovich, T., Park, S., Verma, C., Kim, B., Eskander, R., Malkov, Y. A., Portman, F., Samaniego, S., Xiao, Y., & Haghighi, A. (2022). TwHIN: Embedding the Twitter Heterogeneous Information Network for Personalized Recommendation. *KDD*.

Errickson, J. (n.d.). *Multiple Imputation*. Department of Statistics. Retrieved May 4, 2023, from https://dept.stat.lsa.umich.edu/~jerrick/courses/ stat701/notes/mi.html#mice-in-r

Fan, M., Guo, J., Zhu, S., Miao, S., Sun, M., & Li, P. (2019). MOBIUS: Towards the Next Generation of Query-Ad Matching in Baidu's Sponsored Search. *KDD*.

Fayyad, U., & Irani, K. (1993). Multi-Interval Discretization of Continuous-Valued Attributes for Classification Learning. *IJCAI*.

Frequently Asked Questions — xgboost 1.7.5 documentation. (n.d.). XGBoost Documentation. Retrieved May 4, 2023, from https://xgboost. readthedocs.io/en/stable/faq.html

Gehring, J., Auli, M., Grangier, D., Yarats, D., & Dauphin, Y. N. (2017). Convolutional Sequence to Sequence Learning. *ICML*.

Goel, A., Gupta, P., Sirois, J., Wang, D., Sharma, A., & Gurumurthy, S. (2015). The Who-To-Follow System at Twitter: Strategy, Algorithms, and Revenue Impact. *Interfaces, 45*(1), 98-107.

Gong, X., Feng, Q., Zhang, Y., Qin, J., Ding, W., Li, B., Jiang, P., & Gai, K. (2022). Real-time Short Video Recommendation on Mobile Devices. *CIKM*.

Grbovic, M., & Cheng, H. (2018). Real-time Personalization using Embeddings for Search Ranking at Airbnb. *KDD*.

Grbovic, M., Radosavljevic, V., Djuric, N., Bhamidipati, N., Savla, J., Bhagwan, V., & Sharp, D. (2015). E-commerce in Your Inbox: Product Recommendations at Scale. *KDD*.

Grover, A., & Leskovec, J. (2016). node2vec: Scalable Feature Learning for Networks. *KDD*.

Gu, S., Sheng, X., Fan, Y., Zhou, G., & Zhu, X. (2021). Real Negatives Matter: Continuous Training with Real Negatives for Delayed Feedback Modeling. *KDD*.

Guestrin, C. (2007, April 4). *Unsupervised learning or Clustering – K-means Gaussian mixture models*. Carnegie Mellon University. Retrieved May 4, 2023, from http://www.cs.cmu.edu/%7Eguestrin/Class/10701-S07/Slides/clustering.pdf

Gulati, A., Qin, J., Chiu, C., Parmar, N., Zhang, Y., Yu, J., Han, W., Wang, S., Zhang, Z., Wu, Y., & Pang, R. (2020). Conformer: Convolution-augmented Transformer for Speech Recognition. *Interspeech*.

Guo, D., Ktena, S. I., Huszar, F., Myana, P. K., Shi, W., & Tejani, A. (2020). Deep Bayesian Bandits: Exploring in Online Personalized Recommendations. *RecSys*.

Guo, H., Tang, R., Ye, Y., Li, Z., & He, X. (2017a). DeepFM: A Factorization-Machine based Neural Network for CTR Prediction. *IJCAI*.

Guo, X., Liu, X., Zhu, E., & Yin, J. (2017b). Deep Clustering with Convolutional Autoencoders. *ICONIP*.

Gupta, A., Chugh, D., Anjum, & Katarya, R. (2021). Automated News Summarization Using Transformers. *ICSAC*.

Gupta, U., Wu, C., Wang, X., Naumov, M., Reagen, B., Brooks, D., Cottel, B., Hazelwood, K., Jia, B., Lee, H. S., Malevich, A., Mudigere, D., Smelyanskiy, M., Xiong, L., & Zhang, X. (2020). The Architectural Implications of Facebook's DNN-based Personalized Recommendation. *HPCA*.

Han, S., Pool, J., Tran, J., & Dally, W. J. (2015). Learning both Weights and Connections for Efficient Neural Networks. *NIPS*.

Han, Y., Huang, G., Song, S., Yang, L., Wang, H., & Wang, Y. (2021). Dynamic Neural Networks: A Survey. *arXiv:2102.04906*.

Hartmann, J., Heitmann, M., Siebert, C., & Schamp, C. (2023). More than a Feeling: Accuracy and Application of Sentiment Analysis. *International Journal of Research in Marketing, 40*(1), 75-87.

Hazan, E., Rakhlin, A., & Bartlett, P. (2007). Adaptive Online Gradient Descent. *NIPS*.

He, X., Liao, L., Zhang, H., Nie, L., Hu, X., & Chua, T. (2017). Neural Collaborative Filtering. *WWW*.

He, X., Pan, J., Jin, O., Xu, T., Liu, B., Xu, T., Shi, Y., Atallah, A., Bowers, S., & Candela, J. Q. (2014). Practical Lessons from Predicting Clicks on Ads at Facebook. *ADKDD*.

He, Z., Wang, Z., Wei, W., Feng, S., Mao, X., & Jiang, S. (2020). A Survey on Recent Advances in Sequence Labeling from Deep Learning Models. *arXiv:2011.06727*.

Hinton, G., Vinyals, O., & Dean, J. (2014). Distilling the Knowledge in a Neural Network. *NIPS*.

Howard, A. G., Zhu, M., Chen, B., Kalenichenko, D., Wang, W., Weyand, T., Andreetto, M., & Adam, H. (2017). MobileNets: Efficient Convolutional Neural Networks for Mobile Vision Applications. *arXiv:1704.04861*.

Hu, J., Shen, L., Albanie, S., Sun, G., & Wu, E. (2018). Squeeze-and-Excitation Networks. *CVPR*.

Huang, Z. (1997). Clustering Large Data Sets with Mixed Numeric and Categorical Values. *Proceedings of the First Pacific Asia Knowledge Discovery and Data Mining Conference*.

Ilic, A., & Kabiljo, M. (2015, June 2). *Recommending items to more than a billion people*. Engineering at Meta. Retrieved May 5, 2023, from https://engineering.fb.com/2015/06/02/core-data/recommending-items-to-more-than-a-billion-people/

Imbalanced Data | Machine Learning. (2022, July 18). Google Developers. Retrieved May 4, 2023, from https://developers.google.com/machine-learning/data-prep/construct/sampling-splitting/imbalanced-data

Introduction | Kubeflow. (2022, September 15). Kubeflow. Retrieved May 6, 2023, from https://www.kubeflow.org/docs/components/pipelines/v1/introduction/

Introduction | Machine Learning. (2022, July 18). Google Developers. Retrieved May 5, 2023, from https://developers.google.com/machine-learning/recommendation

Introduction to the Keras Tuner. (2022, December 15). TensorFlow. Retrieved May 6, 2023, from https://www.tensorflow.org/tutorials/ keras/keras_tuner

Introduction to Variables. (2022, December 15). TensorFlow. Retrieved May 4, 2023, from https://www.tensorflow.org/guide/variable

Iscen, A., Tolias, G., Avrithis, Y., & Chum, O. (2019). Label Propagation for Deep Semi-supervised Learning. *CVPR*.

Jagarlamudi, J., Daumé, H., & Udupa, R. (2012). Incorporating lexical priors into topic models. *EACL*.

Kalyan, K. S., Rajasekharan, A., & Sangeetha, S. (2021). AMMUS : A Survey of Transformer-based Pretrained Models in Natural Language Processing. *arXiv:2108.05542*.

Keras debugging tips. (2020, May 16). Keras. Retrieved May 4, 2023, from https://keras.io/examples/keras_recipes/debugging_tips/

Khandelwal, H., Ha-Thuc, V., Dutta, A., Lu, Y., Du, N., Li, Z., & Huang, Q. (2021). Jointly Optimize Capacity, Latency and Engagement in Large-scale Recommendation Systems. *RecSys*.

Kim, C. (n.d.). *MFCC Feature extraction for Sound Classification*. Kaggle. Retrieved May 7, 2023, from https://www.kaggle.com/code/seriousran/mfcc-feature-extraction-for-sound-classification

Kingma, D. P., Rezende, D. J., Mohamed, S., & Welling, M. (2014). Semi-Supervised Learning with Deep Generative Models. *NIPS*.

Klambauer, G., Unterthiner, T., Mayr, A., & Hochreiter, S. (2017). Self-Normalizing Neural Networks. *NIPS*.

Knight, K. (2009, September). *Bayesian Inference with Tears*. Retrieved May 7, 2023, from https://sites.socsci.uci.edu/~lpearl/courses/readings/Knight2009_BayesWithTears.pdf

Koren, Y. (2008). Factorization meets the neighborhood: a multifaceted collaborative filtering model. *KDD*.

Ktena, S. I., Tejani, A., Theis, L., Myana, P. K., Dilipkumar, D., Huszar, F., Yoo, S., & Shi, W. (2019). Addressing Delayed Feedback for Continuous Training with Neural Networks in CTR prediction. *RecSys*.

Kuhn, M., & Johnson, K. (2019). *Feature Engineering and Selection: A Practical Approach for Predictive Models*. CRC Press, Taylor & Francis Group.

Kyubyong/g2p: g2p: English Grapheme To Phoneme Conversion. (n.d.). github. Retrieved May 5, 2023, from https://github.com/Kyubyong/g2p

Lambert, N., Castricato, L., Werra, L. v., & Havrilla, A. (2022, December 9). *Illustrating Reinforcement Learning from Human Feedback (RLHF)*. Hugging Face. Retrieved May 7, 2023, from https://huggingface.co/blog/rlhf

Langer, M., He, Z., Rahayu, W., & Xue, Y. (2020). Distributed Training of Deep Learning Models: A Taxonomic Perspective. *IEEE Transactions on Parallel and Distributed Systems, 31*(12), 2802-2818.

Latent semantic analysis. (n.d.). Wikipedia. Retrieved May 5, 2023, from https://en.wikipedia.org/wiki/Latent_semantic_analysis

Lau, J. H., Newman, D., & Baldwin, T. (2014). Machine Reading Tea Leaves: Automatically Evaluating Topic Coherence and Topic Model Quality. *EACL.*

Least squares. (n.d.). Wikipedia. Retrieved May 4, 2023, from https://en.wikipedia.org/wiki/Least_squares

Lerer, A., Wu, L., Shen, J., Lacroix, T., Wehrstedt, L., Bose, A., & Peysakhovich, A. (2019). PyTorch-BigGraph: A Large-scale Graph Embedding System. *Proceedings of The Conference on Systems and Machine Learning.*

Lewis, M., Liu, Y., Goyal, N., Ghazvininejad, M., Mohamed, A., Levy, O., Stoyanov, V., & Zettlemoyer, L. (2020). BART: Denoising Sequence-to-Sequence Pre-training for Natural Language Generation, Translation, and Comprehension. *ACL.*

Li, K. (1994). Reservoir-sampling algorithms of time complexity O(n(1 + log(N/n))). *ACM Transactions on Mathematical Software, 20*(4), 481-493.

Li, L., Chu, W., Langford, J., & Schapire, R. E. (2010). A Contextual-Bandit Approach to Personalized News Article Recommendation. *WWW.*

Li, Y. (2020). Handling Position Bias for Unbiased Learning to Rank in Hotels Search. *arXiv:2002.12528.*

Lian, J., Zhou, X., Zhang, F., Chen, Z., Xie, X., & Sun, G. (2018). xDeepFM: Combining Explicit and Implicit Feature Interactions for Recommender Systems. *KDD.*

Lin, J., & Dyer, C. (2010). *Data-Intensive Text Processing with MapReduce* (1st ed.). Morgan and Claypool Publishers.

Listwise ranking. (2022, September 27). TensorFlow. Retrieved May 5, 2023, from https://www.tensorflow.org/recommenders/examples/listwise_ranking#training_the_models

Liu, P. J., & Zhao, Y. (2020, June 9). *PEGASUS: A State-of-the-Art Model for Abstractive Text Summarization.* Google AI Blog. Retrieved May 5, 2023, from https://ai.googleblog.com/2020/06/pegasus-state-of-art-model-for.html

Liu, S., Xiao, F., Ou, W., & Si, L. (2017). Cascade Ranking for Operational E-commerce Search. *KDD.*

Liu, S., Yang, H., Li, J., & Kolmanič, S. (2021). Chinese Named Entity Recognition Method in History and Culture Field Based on BERT. *International Journal of Computational Intelligence Systems.*

Liu, Y., Ott, M., Goyal, N., Du, J., Joshi, M., Chen, D., Levy, O., Lewis, M., Zettlemoyer, L., & Stoyanov, V. (2019). RoBERTa: A Robustly Optimized BERT Pretraining Approach. *arXiv:1907.11692.*

Liu, Z., Zou, L., Zou, X., Wang, C., Zhang, B., Tang, D., Zhu, B., Zhu, Y., Wu, P., Wang, K., & Cheng, Y. (2022). Monolith: Real Time Recommendation System With Collisionless Embedding Table. *arXiv:2209.07663*.

López, V., Fernández, A., García, S., Palade, V., & Herrera, F. (2013). An insight into classification with imbalanced data: Empirical results and current trends on using data intrinsic characteristics. *Information Sciences, 250,* 113-141.

Ma, J., Zhao, Z., Yi, X., Chen, J., Hong, L., & Chi, E. (2018). Modeling Task Relationships in Multi-task Learning with Multi-gate Mixture-of-Experts. *KDD*.

Ma, X., & Hovy, E. (2016). End-to-end Sequence Labeling via Bi-directional LSTM-CNNs-CRF. *ACL*.

Ma, Y., Chen, R., Li, W., Shang, F., Yu, W., Cho, M., & Yu, B. (2019). A Unified Approximation Framework for Compressing and Accelerating Deep Neural Networks. *ICTAI*.

Machine Learning for Snapchat Ad Ranking. (2022, February 11). Snap Engineering. Retrieved May 5, 2023, from https://eng.snap.com/machine-learning-snap-ad-ranking

MacKenzie, I., Meyer, C., & Noble, S. (2013, October 1). *How retailers can keep up with consumers.* McKinsey. Retrieved May 5, 2023, from https://www.mckinsey.com/industries/retail/our-insights/how-retailers-can-keep-up-with-consumers

Madireddy, S., Balaprakash, P., Carns, P., Latham, R., Ross, R., Snyder, S., & Wild, S. (2018). Modeling I/O Performance Variability Using Conditional Variational Autoencoders. *IEEE International Conference on Cluster Computing (CLUSTER)*.

Malkov, Y. A., & Yashunin, D. A. (2020). Efficient and robust approximate nearest neighbor search using Hierarchical Navigable Small World graphs. *IEEE Transactions on Pattern Analysis and Machine Intelligence, 42*(4), 824-836.

Mason, W., & Suri, S. (2012). Conducting behavioral research on Amazon's Mechanical Turk. *Behavior Research Methods, 44,* 1-23.

McAlone, N. (2016, June 14). *Netflix Recommendation Engine Worth $1 Billion Per Year.* Business Insider. Retrieved May 5, 2023, from https://www.businessinsider.com/netflix-recommendation-engine-worth-1-billion-per-year-2016-6

Mcauliffe, J., & Blei, D. (2007). Supervised Topic Models. *NIPS*.

McCaffrey, J. D. (2013, November 5). *Why You Should Use Cross-Entropy Error Instead Of Classification Error Or Mean Squared Error For Neural*

Network Classifier Training. Retrieved May 4, 2023, from
https://jamesmccaffrey.wordpress.com/2013/11/05/why-you-should-use-cro
ss-entropy-error-instead-of-classification-error-or-mean-squared-error-for-n
eural-network-classifier-training/

McMahan, H., Holt, G., Sculley, D., Young, M., Ebner, D., Grady, J., Nie, L.,
Phillips, T., Davydov, E., Golovin, D., Chikkerur, S., Liu, D., Wattenberg, M.,
Hrafnkelsson, A. M., Boulos, T., & Kubica, J. (2013). Ad Click Prediction: a
View from the Trenches. *KDD.*

Meddeb, A., & Romdhane, L. B. (2022). Using Topic Modeling and Word
Embedding for Topic Extraction in Twitter. *Procedia Computer Science,
207,* 790-799.

Miao, Y., Grefenstette, E., & Blunsom, P. (2017). Discovering Discrete Latent
Topics with Neural Variational Inference. *ICML.*

Miao, Y., Yu, L., & Blunsom, P. (2016). Neural Variational Inference for Text
Processing. *ICML.*

*Minimizing real-time prediction serving latency in machine learning | Cloud
Architecture Center.* (2023, May 3). Google Cloud. Retrieved May 6, 2023,
from https://cloud.google.com/architecture/minimizing-predictive-
serving-latency-in-machine-learning

Minka, T. (2003). A Comparison of Numerical Optimizers for Logistic
Regression. https://www.microsoft.com/en-us/research/publication/
comparison-numerical-optimizers-logistic-regression/

Mirza, M., & Osindero, S. (2014). Conditional Generative Adversarial Nets.
arXiv:1411.1784.

Model optimization. (2021, October 20). TensorFlow. Retrieved May 6, 2023,
from https://www.tensorflow.org/lite/performance/model_optimization#
quantization

Mohamed, A., Okhonko, D., & Zettlemoyer, L. (2019). Transformers with
convolutional context for ASR. *arXiv:1904.11660.*

Moses - Moses/Background. (2013, July 28). Statmt.org. Retrieved May 7, 2023,
from http://www2.statmt.org/moses/?n=Moses.Background

Müller, P. H. (2021, April 25). *Attribution in iOS 14.5 — what is allowed?*
Adjust. Retrieved May 6, 2023, from https://www.adjust.com/blog/
making-sense-of-ios-14-5-attribution-methods/

Nakkiran, P., Alvarez, R., Prabhavalkar, R., & Parada, C. (2015). Compressing
Deep Neural Networks using a Rank-Constrained Topology. *Interspeech.*

Nallapati, R., Zhou, B., Nogueira dos santos, C., Gulcehre, C., & Xiang, B.
(2016). Abstractive Text Summarization Using Sequence-to-Sequence
RNNs and Beyond. *CoNLL.*

Naumov, M., Mudigere, D., Shi, H. M., Huang, J., Sundaraman, N., Park, J., Wang, X., Gupta, U., Wu, C., Azzolini, A. G., Dzhulgakov, D., Mallevich, A., Cherniavskii, I., Lu, Y., Krishnamoorthi, R., Yu, A., Kondratenko, V., Pereira, S., Chen, X., … Smelyanskiy, M. (2019). Deep Learning Recommendation Model for Personalization and Recommendation Systems. *arXiv:1906.00091*.

NetSci 10-1 Small World Model. (2020, October 5). YouTube. Retrieved May 5, 2023, from https://www.youtube.com/watch?v=Pnh6Kg4nYbE

Neural machine translation with a Transformer and Keras | Text. (2023, April 8). TensorFlow. Retrieved May 5, 2023, from https://www.tensorflow.org/text/tutorials/transformer

Ng, A. (n.d.). *Machine Learning Specialization (DeepLearning.AI)*. Coursera. Retrieved May 4, 2023, from https://www.coursera.org/specializations/machine-learning-introduction

Niu, F., Recht, B., Re, C., & Wright, S. J. (2011). HOGWILD!: A Lock-Free Approach to Parallelizing Stochastic Gradient Descent. *NIPS*.

O'Brien, M., & Keane, M. T. (2006). Modeling Result-List Searching in the World Wide Web: The Role of Relevance Topologies and Trust Bias. *Proceedings of the Annual Meeting of the Cognitive Science Society, 28*.

Okura, S., Tagami, Y., Ono, S., & Tajima, A. (2017). Embedding-based News Recommendation for Millions of Users. *KDD*.

Oord, A. v., Dieleman, S., & Schrauwen, B. (2013). Deep content-based music recommendation. *NIPS*.

OpenAI. (2023). GPT-4 Technical Report. *arXiv:2303.08774*.

Ostermiller, S. (n.d.). *Efficiently Implementing Dilate and Erode Image Functions - Stephen Ostermiller*. Retrieved May 5, 2023, from https://blog.ostermiller.org/efficiently-implementing-dilate-and-erode-image-functions/

Overfit and underfit. (2022, December 15). TensorFlow. Retrieved May 4, 2023, from https://www.tensorflow.org/tutorials/keras/overfit_and_underfit

Pal, A., Eksombatchai, C., Zhou, Y., Zhao, B., Rosenberg, C., & Leskovec, J. (2020). PinnerSage: Multi-Modal User Embedding Framework for Recommendations at Pinterest. *KDD*.

Palczewska, A., Palczewski, J., Robinson, R. M., & Neagu, D. (2013). *Interpreting random forest classification models using a feature contribution method*. IEEE IRI.

Pasumarthi, R. K., Bruch, S., Wang, X., Li, C., Bendersky, M., Najork, M., Pfeifer, J., Golbandi, N., Anil, R., & Wolf, S. (2019). TF-Ranking: Scalable TensorFlow Library for Learning-to-Rank. *KDD*.

Patarasuk, P., & Yuan, X. (2009). Bandwidth optimal all-reduce algorithms for clusters of workstations. *Journal of Parallel and Distributed Computing, 69*(2), 117–124.

Pennington, J., Socher, R., & Manning, C. D. (2014). GloVe: Global Vectors for Word Representation. *EMNLP.*

Perform Automatic Model Tuning with SageMaker - Amazon SageMaker. (n.d.). AWS Documentation. Retrieved May 6, 2023, from https://docs.aws.amazon.com/sagemaker/latest/dg/automatic-model-tuning.html

Persson, A. (n.d.). *Machine-Learning-Collection/ML/algorithms.* github. Retrieved May 4, 2023, from https://github.com/aladdinpersson/Machine-Learning-Collection/tree/master/ML/algorithms

Prepare Data | Machine Learning. (2022, July 18). Google Developers. Retrieved May 5, 2023, from https://developers.google.com/machine-learning/clustering/prepare-data

Prokhorov, V., Shareghi, E., Li, Y., Pilehvar, M. T., & Collier, N. (2019). On the Importance of the Kullback-Leibler Divergence Term in Variational Autoencoders for Text Generation. *WNGT.*

Proximal Policy Optimization — Spinning Up documentation. (n.d.). OpenAI. Retrieved May 7, 2023, from https://spinningup.openai.com/en/latest/algorithms/ppo.html#background

Puri, C., Kooijman, G., Long, X., Hamelmann, P., Asvadi, S., Vanrumste, B., & Luca, S. (2021). Feature selection for unbiased imputation of missing values: A case study in healthcare. *Annu Int Conf IEEE Eng Med Biol Soc,* 1911-1915.

Raffel, C., Shazeer, N., Roberts, A., Lee, K., Narang, S., Matena, M., Zhou, Y., Li, W., & Liu, P. J. (2020). Exploring the Limits of Transfer Learning with a Unified Text-to-Text Transformer. *JMLR.*

Ramachandran, P., Zoph, B., & Le, Q. V. (2017). Swish: a Self-Gated Activation Function. *arXiv:1710.05941.*

Ramage, D., Hall, D., Nallapati, R., & Manning, C. D. (2009). Labeled LDA: A supervised topic model for credit attribution in multi-labeled corpora. *EMNLP.*

Ramsey, L. (2018, November 1). *Optimizing TensorFlow Models for Serving | by Lukman Ramsey | Google Cloud - Community.* Medium. Retrieved May 6, 2023, from https://medium.com/google-cloud/optimizing-tensorflow-models-for-serving-959080e9ddbf

Recommendation Systems Overview | Machine Learning. (2022, July 18). Google Developers. Retrieved May 5, 2023, from https://developers. google.com/machine-learning/recommendation/overview/types

Ren, Y., Tang, H., & Zhu, S. (2019). Unbiased Pairwise Learning to Rank in Recommender Systems. *WWW.*

Rendle, S. (2010). Factorization Machines. *IEEE International Conference on Data Mining.*

Rendle, S., Freudenthaler, C., Gantner, Z., & Schmidt-Thieme, L. (2009). BPR: Bayesian Personalized Ranking from Implicit Feedback. *UAI.*

Resilient ad serving at Twitter-scale. (2016, March 30). Twitter Blog. Retrieved May 6, 2023, from https://blog.twitter.com/engineering/en_us/a/ 2016/resilient-ad-serving-at-twitter-scale

Richardson, M., Dominowska, E., & Ragno, R. (2007). Predicting Clicks: Estimating the Click-Through Rate for New Ads. *WWW.*

Romano, J., Vinh, N. X., Bailey, J., & Verspoor, K. (2016). Adjusting for Chance Clustering Comparison Measures. *JMLR, 17*(134), 1-32.

Ruder, S. (2016, January 19). *An overview of gradient descent optimization algorithms.* ruder.io. Retrieved May 4, 2023, from https://www.ruder.io/ optimizing-gradient-descent/

Saravanou, A., Tomasi, F., Mehrotra, R., & Lalmas, M. (2021, October 29). *Multi-Task Learning of Graph-based Inductive Representations of Music Content - Spotify Research.* Spotify Research. Retrieved May 5, 2023, from https://research.atspotify.com/2021/10/multi-task-learning-of-graph-based-inductive-representations-of-music-content/

Sataluri, V., Wu, Y., Zheng, X., Qian, Y., Wichers, B., Dai, Q., Tang, G. M., Jiang, J., & Lin, J. (2020). SimClusters: Community-Based Representations for Heterogeneous Recommendations at Twitter. *KDD.*

Saveski, M., Pouget-Abadie, J., Saint-Jacques, G., Duan, W., Ghosh, S., Xu, Y., & Airoldi, E. (2017). Detecting Network Effects: Randomizing Over Randomized Experiments. *KDD.*

Saxena, S. (2019, June 26). *What's the Difference Between RMSE and RMSLE? | by Sharoon Saxena | Analytics Vidhya.* Medium. Retrieved May 4, 2023, from https://medium.com/analytics-vidhya/root-mean-square-log-error-rmse-vs-rmlse-935c6cc1802a

Sell, T., & Pienaar, W. (2019, January 19). *Introducing Feast: an open source feature store for machine learning.* Google Cloud. Retrieved May 6, 2023, from https://cloud.google.com/blog/products/ai-machine-learning/ introducing-feast-an-open-source-feature-store-for-machine-learning *sentiment-analysis-using-roberta.ipynb - Colaboratory.* (n.d.). Google Colab. Retrieved May 5, 2023, from https://colab.research.google.com/github/DhavalTaunk08/NLP_scripts/blob/master/sentiment_analysis_using_roberta.ipynb#section05

Shalaby, W., Oh, S., Afsharinejad, A., Kumar, S., & Cui, X. (2022). M2TRec: Metadata-aware Multi-task Transformer for Large-scale and Cold-start free Session-based Recommendations. *RecSys.*

Sharma, A., Jiang, J., Bommannavar, P., Larson, B., & Lin, J. (2016). GraphJet: real-time content recommendations at twitter. *Proceedings of the VLDB Endowment, 9*(13), 1281-1292.

Shi, C., Li, Y., Zhang, J., Sun, Y., & Yu, P. S. (2016). A survey of heterogeneous information network analysis. *IEEE Transactions on Knowledge and Data Engineering, 29*(1), 17-37.

Shukla, N., Kolbeinsson, A., Otwell, K., Marla, L., & Yellepeddi, K. (2019). Dynamic Pricing for Airline Ancillaries with Customer Context. *KDD.*

Siddiqui, J. R. (2022, February 6). *Why Is Cross Entropy Equal to KL-Divergence?* Towards Data Science. Retrieved May 4, 2023, from https://towardsdatascience.com/why-is-cross-entropy-equal-to-kl-divergence-d4d2ec413864

The Size and Quality of a Data Set | Machine Learning. (2022, July 18). Google Developers. Retrieved May 4, 2023, from https://developers.google.com/machine-learning/data-prep/construct/collect/data-size-quality

sklearn.svm.LinearSVR. (n.d.). Scikit-learn. Retrieved May 6, 2023, from https://scikit-learn.org/stable/modules/generated/sklearn.svm.LinearSVR.html

Smith, B., & Linden, G. (2017). Two Decades of Recommender Systems at Amazon.com. *IEEE Internet Computing, 21*(3), 12-18.

Sohn, K., Lee, H., & Yan, X. (2015). Learning Structured Output Representation using Deep Conditional Generative Models. *NIPS.*

Srivastava, N., Hinton, G., Krizhevsky, A., Sutskever, I., & Salakhutdinov, R. (2014). Dropout: A Simple Way to Prevent Neural Networks from Overfitting. *JMLR, 15*(56), 1929–1958.

Steadman, B. (2020, October 9). *SteadBytes |Reservoir Sampling.* Ben Steadman. Retrieved May 5, 2023, from https://steadbytes.com/blog/reservoir-sampling/

Stiennon, N., Ouyang, L., Wu, J., Ziegler, D. M., Lowe, R., Voss, C., Radford, A., Amodei, D., & Christiano, P. (2020). Learning to summarize from human feedback. *NIPS.*

String-searching algorithm. (n.d.). Wikipedia. Retrieved May 5, 2023, from
https://en.wikipedia.org/wiki/String-searching_algorithm

Sun, W., Yan, L., Ma, X., Ren, P., Yin, D., & Ren, Z. (2023). Is ChatGPT Good at
Search? Investigating Large Language Models as Re-Ranking Agent.
arXiv:2304.09542.

Sun, Z., Deng, Z., Nie, J., & Tang, J. (2019). RotatE: Knowledge Graph
Embedding by Relational Rotation in Complex Space. *ICLR.*

Sutskever, I., Vinyals, O., & Le, Q. V. (2014). Sequence to Sequence Learning
with Neural Networks. *NIPS.*

Szandała, T. (2021). Review and Comparison of Commonly Used Activation
Functions for Deep Neural Networks. *Bio-Inspired Neurocomputing,
Springer, 903,* 203-224.

Tan, H. H., & Lim, K. H. (2019). Review of second-order optimization
techniques in artificial neural networks backpropagation. *IOP Conf. Ser.:
Mater. Sci. Eng., 495.*

Tan, M., & Le, Q. V. (2019). EfficientNet: Rethinking Model Scaling for
Convolutional Neural Networks. *ICML.*

Tang, J., Qu, M., Wang, M., Zhang, M., Yan, J., & Mei, Q. (2015). LINE:
Large-scale Information Network Embedding. *WWW.*

Tang, J., & Wang, K. (2018). Ranking Distillation: Learning Compact Ranking
Models With High Performance for Recommender System. *KDD.*

Tanner, G. (2020, September 29). *Logistic Regression.* ML Explained. Retrieved
May 4, 2023, from https://ml-explained.com/blog/logistic-
regression-explained#gradient-descent

Teh, Y. W., Jordan, M. I., Beal, M. J., & Blei, B. M. (2006). Hierarchical Dirichlet
Processes. *Journal of the American Statistical Association, 101*(476),
1566-1581.

TensorFlow Data Validation | TFX. (2023, March 15). TensorFlow. Retrieved
May 4, 2023, from https://www.tensorflow.org/tfx/tutorials/
data_validation/tfdv_basic

Tensorflow Serving Configuration | TFX. (2021, March 30). TensorFlow.
Retrieved May 4, 2023, from https://www.tensorflow.org/tfx/serving/
serving_config

TFX tutorials | TensorFlow. (2021, December 8). TensorFlow. Retrieved May 4,
2023, from https://www.tensorflow.org/tfx/tutorials

the-algorithm/cr-mixer. (n.d.). github. Retrieved May 5, 2023, from
https://github.com/twitter/the-algorithm/tree/main/cr-mixer

the-algorithm/src/scala/com/twitter/simclusters_v2. (n.d.). github. Retrieved May 5, 2023, from https://github.com/twitter/the-algorithm/tree/main/src/scala/com/twitter/simclusters_v2

Train and serve a TensorFlow model with TensorFlow Serving | TFX. (2023, March 15). TensorFlow. Retrieved May 4, 2023, from https://www.tensorflow.org/tfx/tutorials/serving/rest_simple

Training using the built-in wide and deep algorithm | AI Platform Training. (2023, May 3). Google Cloud. Retrieved May 4, 2023, from https://cloud.google.com/ai-platform/training/docs/algorithms/wide-and-deep#analysis

Transforming Your Data: Check Your Understanding | Machine Learning. (2022, July 18). Google Developers. Retrieved May 5, 2023, from https://developers.google.com/machine-learning/data-prep/transform/check-your-understanding

Turney, P. (2002). Thumbs Up or Thumbs Down? Semantic Orientation Applied to Unsupervised Classification of Reviews. *ACL.*

Tyagi, A., Sharma, V., Gupta, R., Samson, L., Zhuang, N., Wang, Z., & Campbell, W. M. (2020). Fast Intent Classification for Spoken-Language-Understanding Systems. *ICASSP.*

Tzeng, E., Hoffman, J., Saenko, K., & Darrell, T. (2017). Adversarial Discriminative Domain Adaptation. *CVPR.*

Understanding bidding basics - Google Ads Help. (n.d.). Google Support. Retrieved May 5, 2023, from https://support.google.com/google-ads/answer/2459326?hl=en

Understanding TFX Pipelines. (2023, April 4). TensorFlow. Retrieved May 6, 2023, from https://www.tensorflow.org/tfx/guide/understanding_tfx_pipelines

Vajjala, S., & Balasubramaniam, R. (2022). What do we Really Know about State of the Art NER? *LREC.*

Vasile, F., Smirnova, E., & Conneau, A. (2016). Meta-Prod2Vec - Product Embeddings Using Side-Information for Recommendation. *RecSys.*

Vaswani, A., Shazeer, N., Parmar, N., Uszkoreit, J., Jones, L., Gomez, A., Kaiser, Ł., & Polosukhin, I. (2017). Attention Is All You Need. *NIPS.*

Vernade, C., Cappé, O., & Perchet, V. (2017). Stochastic Bandit Models for Delayed Conversions. *Conference on Uncertainty in Artificial Intelligence.*

Versloot, C. (2020, December 29). *machine-learning-articles/differences-between-autoregressive-autoencoding-and-sequence-to-sequence-models-in-machine-learning.md.* github. Retrieved May 7, 2023, from https://github.com/christianversloot/machine-learning-articles/blob/

main/differences-between-autoregressive-autoencoding-and-sequence-to-s
equence-models-in-machine-learning.md

Volkovs, M., Yu, G., & Poutanen, T. (2017). DropoutNet: Addressing Cold Start
in Recommender Systems. *NIPS.*

Wang, C., & Blei, D. (2011). Collaborative topic modeling for recommending
scientific articles. *KDD.*

Wang, D., Cui, P., & Zhu, W. (2016a). Structural Deep Network Embedding.
KDD.

Wang, H. (2020, June 8). *A new approach: Metric learning for SplitNet.* Twitter
Blog. Retrieved May 5, 2023, from https://blog.twitter.com/
engineering/en_us/topics/insights/2020/a-new-approach-metric-learning-for
-splitnet

Wang, H., Wang, N., & Yeung, D. (2015). Collaborative Deep Learning for
Recommender Systems. *KDD.*

Wang, R., Fu, B., & Wang, M. (2017). Deep & Cross Network for Ad Click
Predictions. *Proceedings of AdKDD and TargetAd.*

Wang, R., Shivanna, R., Cheng, D. Z., Jain, S., Lin, D., Hong, L., & Chi, E. H.
(2021). DCN V2: Improved Deep & Cross Network and Practical Lessons
for Web-scale Learning to Rank Systems. *WWW.*

Wang, T., Roberts, A., Hesslow, D., Scao, T. L., Chung, H. W., Beltagy, I., Launay,
J., & Raffel, C. (2022). What Language Model Architecture and Pretraining
Objective Work Best for Zero-Shot Generalization? *arXiv:2204.05832.*

Wang, W., Gan, Z., Xu, H., Zhang, R., Wang, G., Shen, D., Chen, C., & Carin, L.
(2019a). Topic-Guided Variational Autoencoders for Text Generation.
NAACL.

Wang, W., Jin, J., Hao, J., Chen, C., Yu, C., Zhang, W., Wang, J., Hao, X., Wang,
Y., Li, H., Xu, J., & Gai, K. (2019b). Learning Adaptive Display Exposure for
Real-Time Advertising. *CIKM.*

Wang, X., Bendersky, M., Metzler, D., & Najork, M. (2016b). Learning to Rank
with Selection Bias in Personal Search. *SIGIR.*

Wang, X., Golbandi, N., Bendersky, M., Metzler, D., & Najork, M. (2018).
Position Bias Estimation for Unbiased Learning to Rank in Personal
Search. *WSDM.*

Wang, Z., Zhao, L., Jiang, B., Zhou, G., Zhu, X., & Gai, K. (2020). COLD:
Towards the Next Generation of Pre-Ranking System. *DLP-KDD.*

Weight clustering | TensorFlow Model Optimization. (2022, August 3).
TensorFlow. Retrieved May 6, 2023, from https://www.tensorflow.org
/model_optimization/guide/clustering

What is Candidate Sampling. (n.d.). TensorFlow. Retrieved May 5, 2023, from https://www.tensorflow.org/extras/candidate_sampling.pdf

What is Functional Programming? | Scala 3 — Book. (n.d.). Scala Documentation. Retrieved May 5, 2023, from https://docs.scala-lang.org/scala3/book/fp-what-is-fp.html

Wong, J. P. (2022, January 20). *Model-based candidate generation for account recommendations.* Twitter Blog. Retrieved May 5, 2023, from https://blog.twitter.com/engineering/en_us/topics/insights/2022/model-based-candidate-generation-for-account-recommendations

Working with preprocessing layers. (2022, January 10). TensorFlow. Retrieved May 4, 2023, from https://www.tensorflow.org/guide/keras/preprocessing_layers

Wu, C., Wu, F., Qi, T., & Huang, Y. (2021). Empowering News Recommendation with Pre-trained Language Models. *SIGIR.*

Wu, L., Lin, H., Gao, Z., Tan, C., & Li, S. Z. (2023a). Self-supervised Learning on Graphs: Contrastive, Generative,or Predictive. *IEEE Transactions on Knowledge and Data Engineering, 35*(4), 4216-4235.

Wu, S., Irsoy, O., Dabravolski, V., Dredze, M., Gehrmann, S., Kambadur, P., Rosenberg, D., & Mann, G. (2023b). BloombergGPT: A Large Language Model for Finance. *arXiv:2303.17564.*

Wu, Y., Zhao, S., & Li, W. (2020). Phrase2Vec: Phrase embedding based on parsing. *Information Sciences, 517,* 100-127.

Wu, Z., Pan, S., Chen, F., Long, G., Zhang, C., & Yu, P. S. (2019). A Comprehensive Survey on Graph Neural Networks. *arXiv:1901.00596.*

Wubben, S., Bosch, A. v., & Krahmer, E. (2012). Sentence Simplification by Monolingual Machine Translation. *ACL.*

Xia, F., Liu, T., Wang, J., Zhang, W., & Li, H. (2008). Listwise approach to learning to rank: theory and algorithm. *ICML.*

Xia, Y., Fabbrizio, G. D., Vaibhav, S., & Datta, A. (2017). A content-based recommender system for e-commerce offers and coupons. *Proceedings of SIGIR eCom.*

Xie, J., Girshick, R., & Farhadi, A. (2016). Unsupervised Deep Embedding for Clustering Analysis. *ICML.*

Yang, Z., Ding, M., Zhou, C., Yang, H., Zhou, J., & Tang, J. (2020). Understanding Negative Sampling in Graph Representation Learning. *KDD.*

Ye, P., Qian, J., Chen, J., Wu, C., Zhou, Y., Mars, S. D., Yang, F., & Zhang, L. (2018). Customized Regression Model for Airbnb Dynamic Pricing. *KDD.*

Yi, X., Yang, J., Hong, L., Cheng, D. Z., Heldt, L., Kumthekar, A. A., Zhao, Z., Wei, L., & Chi, E. (2019). Sampling-Bias-Corrected Neural Modeling for Large Corpus Item Recommendations. *RecSys*.

Ying, R., He, R., Chen, K., Eksombatchai, P., Hamilton, W., & Leskovec, J. (2018). Graph Convolutional Neural Networks for Web-Scale Recommender Systems. *KDD*.

Yoshikawa, Y., & Imai, Y. (2018). A Nonparametric Delayed Feedback Model for Conversion Rate Prediction. *arXiv:1802.00255*.

Yu, F. X., Choromanski, K., Kumar, S., Jebara, T., & Chang, S. (2015). On Learning from Label Proportions. *arXiv:1402.5902*.

Yu, F. X., Liu, D., Kumar, S., Jebara, T., & Chang, S. (2013). $\propto$SVM for learning with label proportions. *ICML*.

Yuan, Z., Yuan, H., Tan, C., Wang, W., Huang, S., & Huang, F. (2023). RRHF: Rank Responses to Align Language Models with Human Feedback without tears. *arXiv:2304.05302*.

Yue, Y., Patel, R., & Roehrig, H. (2010). Beyond position bias: examining result attractiveness as a source of presentation bias in clickthrough data. *WWW*.

Zhang, J., Zhao, Y., Saleh, M., & Liu, P. J. (2020). PEGASUS: Pre-training with Extracted Gap-sentences for Abstractive Summarization. *ICML*.

Zhang, Q., Liao, X., Liu, Q., Xu, J., & Zheng, B. (2022). Leaving No One Behind: A Multi-Scenario Multi-Task Meta Learning Approach for Advertiser Modeling. *WSDM*.

Zhang, Q., Qiu, L., Wu, H., Wang, J., & Luo, H. (2019). Deep Learning Based Dynamic Pricing Model for Hotel Revenue Management. *ICDMW*.

Zhang, W., Chen, T., Wang, J., & Yu, Y. (2013). Optimizing top-n collaborative filtering via dynamic negative item sampling. *SIGIR*.

Zhang, X., Zhou, X., Lin, M., & Sun, J. (2018). ShuffleNet: An Extremely Efficient Convolutional Neural Network for Mobile Devices. *CVPR*.

Zhang, Z. (2016). Missing data imputation: focusing on single imputation. *Ann Transl Med*, *4*(1).

Zhao, H., Phung, D., Huynh, V., Jin, Y., Du, L., & Buntine, W. (2021). Topic Modelling Meets Deep Neural Networks: A Survey. *IJCAI*.

Zhao, X., Louca, R., Hu, D., & Hong, L. (2018). Learning Item-Interaction Embeddings for User Recommendations. *arXiv:1812.04407*.

Zhao, X., Zheng, X., Yang, X., Liu, X., & Tang, J. (2020). Jointly Learning to Recommend and Advertise. *KDD*.

Zhao, Z., Hong, L., Wei, L., Chen, J., Nath, A., Andrews, S., Kumthekar, A., Sathiamoorthy, M., Yi, X., & Chi, E. (2019). Recommending what video to watch next: a multitask ranking system. *RecSys*.

Zheng, H., Yang, Z., Liu, W., Liang, J., & Li, Y. (2015). Improving deep neural networks using softplus units. *IJCNN*.

Zheng, Y., Bian, J., Meng, G., Zhang, C., Wang, H., Zhang, Z., Li, S., Zhuang, T., Liu, Q., & Zeng, X. (2022). Multi-Objective Personalized Product Retrieval in Taobao Search. *arXiv:2210.04170*.

Zhou, L., & Brunskill, E. (2016). Latent Contextual Bandits and their Application to Personalized Recommendations for New Users. *IJCAI*.

Zhu, F., Xiao, W., Yu, Y., Wang, Z., Chen, Z., Lu, Q., Liu, Z., Wu, M., & Ni, S. (2022). Modeling Price Elasticity for Occupancy Prediction in Hotel Dynamic Pricing. *CIKM*.

Zhu, J., Shan, Y., Mao, J., Yu, D., Rahmanian, H., & Zhang, Y. (2017). Deep Embedding Forest: Forest-based Serving with Deep Embedding Features. *KDD*.

Zhuang, Y., Thiagarajan, A., & Sweeney, T. (2019, March 4). *Ranking Tweets with TensorFlow — The TensorFlow Blog*. The TensorFlow Blog. Retrieved May 5, 2023, from https://blog.tensorflow.org/2019/03/ranking-tweets-with-tensorflow.html

Zinkevich, M. (2023, January 5). *Rules of Machine Learning*. Google Developers. Retrieved May 4, 2023, from https://developers.google.com/machine-learning/guides/rules-of-ml

Žliobaitė, I. (2010). Learning under Concept Drift: an Overview. *arXiv:1010.4784*.

About the Author

Peng Shao has held ML leadership positions across a range of industries over the course of 15 years – including social media, ad-tech, fintech, and e-commerce. Having interviewed nearly a thousand candidates, he has developed a comprehensive understanding of the kinds of skills and experiences that make a strong ML candidate.

At Twitter, he served as a Staff ML Engineer, designing ML systems behind Twitter's recommendation algorithms, as well as ad prediction and ranking. Prior to that, he was co-founder of an AI startup called Roxy, which raised several million dollars in venture capital and was acquired in 2019.

Earlier in his career, he led ML teams at Amazon and FactSet. In these roles, he oversaw the development of a variety of ML systems including machine translation, tabular information extraction, named entity recognition, and topic modeling.

Peng specializes in high performance, low-latency ML ranking problems. As a ML practitioner, he adopts a holistic approach to ML design, encompassing data science, modeling, feature management, and infrastructure.

Made in the USA
Monee, IL
08 January 2025